Ethos, Pathos, and Logos:

The Best of The Advocates' Society Journal 1982–2004

Ethos, Pathos, and Logos:

The Best of The Advocates' Society Journal 1982–2004

Edited by David Stockwood, Q.C. and David E. Spiro

IRWIN
LAW

Ethos, Pathos, and Logos: The Best of *The Advocates' Society Journal* 1982–2004
© The Advocates' Society, 2005

Published in 2005 by

Irwin Law
347 Bay Street
Suite 501
Toronto, Ontario
M5H 2R7

www.irwinlaw.com

ISBN: 1-55221-099-5   ISBN: 978-155221-099-4

Library and Archives Canada Cataloguing in Publication

Ethos, pathos, and logos: the best of The Advocates' Society journal, 1982–2004 / edited by David Stockwood and David E. Spiro.

Includes bibliographical references.
ISBN 1-55221-099-5

1. Trial practice—Ontario. 2. Trial practice—Canada. I. Stockwood, David, 1941–
II. Spiro, David E. III. Advocates' Society

K1.D87 Suppl. 2005   347.713'052   C2004-907284-6

The publisher acknowledges the financial support of the Government of Canada through the Book Publishing Industry Development Program (BPIDP) for its publishing activities.

Printed and bound in Canada.

1 2 3 4 5   09 08 07 06 05

Table of Contents

Preface

For the past twenty-two years, *The Advocates' Society Journal* has played a unique role in legal education in Ontario. As a publication dedicated to informing advocates, it has brought together the ideas of our leading legal minds to provide experienced and insightful views on both advocacy and advocates. Indeed, the *Journal* has provided a veritable "how to" for the practice of advocacy before courts and tribunals.

The idea of the *Journal* originated in 1981 with the Publications Committee of The Advocates' Society, under the chair of Brian J.E. Brock, Q.C. The Society is indebted to those who have nurtured its development by contributing the ideas, the enthusiasm, and the editorial skills to make it a readable and informative publication. This volume, which brings together the "best articles on advocacy ... ever," is a reflection of their foresight, dedication, and hard work. In this regard we owe a debt of gratitude to Moishe Reiter, Q.C. (Editor, 1982–90), Anthony Keith, Q.C. (Publications Committee Chair/Managing Editor, 1982–90), Brian J.E. Brock, Q.C. (Editorial Board, 1982–89), Mark G. Appel, Q.C. (Advertising Editor, 1984–90), David Stockwood, Q.C. (Editor, 1991 to the present), Stuart Forbes, Q.C. (Managing Editor 1991–95), and Paul Le Vay (Managing Editor, 1995 to the present). In particular, David Stockwood has been the guiding force for many years, inspiring the foremost judges, advocates, and scholars of the day to contribute to the

Journal. The Advocates' Society thanks Mr. Stockwood, the members who have served in an editorial capacity, and all those who have contributed over the years to the success of this publication.

The concept of this "best of" volume originated with David E. Spiro, a member of the Society's Education Committee. David's inspiration for this task, which was embraced wholeheartedly by the Society, was to pay tribute to David Sgayias, Q.C., a member of our Board of Directors, whose untimely death in 2003 had an impact on all of his colleagues at the bar.

David Sgayias was an outstanding counsel, author, and legal scholar. As Chief General Counsel of the Federal Department of Justice, he was greatly admired and highly respected. He was the first Department of Justice lawyer to serve on the Board of The Advocates' Society, and his acceptance of the position was greeted with great enthusiasm. His reputation preceded him and we were not disappointed. We all came to appreciate his wisdom, insight, and compassion. David served the Society well, but, unfortunately, we had the privilege of serving with him for too short a time. He is missed. We were all better for his counsel.

The Board of The Advocates' Society wants to remember David and to honour him. We should remain vigilant to keep his legacy alive for future generations of lawyers. The tradition of advocacy reflected in this book will contribute to that goal.

Jeffrey S. Leon
President
The Advocates' Society
June 2004

Acknowledgments

We are indebted to Jeff Leon, immediate past President of The Advocates' Society, whose support for the publication of this volume was early and energetic. The book could not have been published without the close collaboration of Sonia Holiad, Director of Marketing & Communications at The Advocates' Society, who enthusiastically undertook a variety of time-sensitive tasks with her usual good humour and attention to detail. We are also grateful to Jeff Miller who, as publisher, generously committed the resources of Irwin Law to the project. Finally, we owe an enormous debt of gratitude to the members of the bench and Bar who shared their insights on advocacy with us over the years on the pages of *The Advocates' Society Journal*.

David Stockwood, Q.C.
David E. Spiro

I was fortunate to be the editor of *The Advocates' Society Journal* during the period when most of these articles appeared. However, it was David Spiro who had the idea of collecting "the greatest hits." It was a wonderful idea and this book is the result.

David Stockwood, Q.C.

David Sgayias, Q.C. — An Appreciation

In an era when public service is valued less than it ought to be, David Sgayias, Q.C. stood out as representing the great traditions both of the Bar and of the law officers of the Crown. This volume is a wonderful tribute to a thoughtful and eloquent advocate who was felled by a heart attack in August of last year. He was only fifty-two years old.

David was a gentle giant of a man, scrupulously fair in his work, discreetly droll in private, dispassionate, scholarly and courteously deferential to those he met, except when confronting what he took to be an unjustified attack on Her Majesty's interests, when his face would flush, his voice would drop an octave or two, and his oversize frame would gently rock with indignation.

We were friends for over twenty years, and worked on many trials and appeals together. David would generally provide the scholarship logic and organization, leaving it to me to try to "sex up" our presentation with a little purple prose. It was not until I joined the Supreme Court in 1998 that I realized the purple prose was entirely superfluous, if not actually detrimental to our cause. Judges held the same high opinion of David's compelling advocacy as did members of the Bar. When David died, Chief Justice Beverley McLachlin sent a letter of personal tribute to the Department of Justice acknowledging the great loss his death had occasioned to the Supreme Court Bar, a most unusual gesture. "All of us at the Court," she wrote, "regarded David as one of the very finest advocates in the Canadian legal community."

In another exceptional act, then Prime Minister Jean Chrétien, in a letter to David's family, wrote that he was "a distinguished public servant, who provided the Government of Canada with the highest calibre of legal advice and representation before the courts." The government had reason to be grateful. He had saved its bacon on more than a few occasions.

The Honourable Frank Iacobucci recalled that one of the first things he learned when he became Deputy Minister of Justice in 1985 was "Get me Sgayias." Indeed, ever since the early 1980s, the usual response in the federal government to a legal crisis exploding anywhere in the country was "What does David think?" Not many opinions of significance emerged from Justice without being looked at either by David or Graham Garton, Q.C., the two most erudite of the departmental workhorses.

David's office, like his mind, was uncluttered. He would sit Buddha-like when being briefed by panicked public servants, making the odd note, seldom making any reassuring noises, frequently sitting with his eyes half-shut. In his top drawer, he kept a copy of *Great Quotes from Great Leaders* and often a box of chocolates. Instead of assigning the research to students or younger lawyers, he invariably padded off to the Justice Law Library where he would wander from stack to stack collecting a large pile of authorities for study and contemplation. In that location, he was fair game for every passing lawyer, student, or *fonctionnaire* in search of scholarly or practical guidance, a mentor to them all. Within a few hours (despite interruptions) the opinion would be ready, short and precise, carefully researched, elegantly written, a work that would do credit to any law firm or court in the country, over an astonishing range of subjects from the trade and commerce power to the finer points of arresting a ship under the Federal Court Rules. Few could match David's curious enthusiasm for the Federal Court Rules.

I never heard him criticize a colleague, or unfairly disparage an opponent. He embodied professional civility. An actor at heart, his preferred stage was the courtroom, where he spent his happiest days. He was what used to be called a "Justice" man. The federal department had somehow, probably through the exercise of some black art, imprinted itself on his soul, and no one was ever able to lure him away to private practice, although many (including me) tried. We piled money under his nose in the hopes that at some point he would be sufficiently embarrassed to say "Enough" and accept the offer, but he never did. In part, he valued the sheer amount of court time a Departmental practice offered. More importantly, as we all came to realize, the Department of Justice, despite its frustrations, was more than a job. A lifelong bachelor, its members were his family. In asking him to change jobs, we were not really asking him to leave one place of employment for another. We were asking him to leave home. This was not something he could ever bring himself to do. After he died over 400 of his friends from the Department, the Ottawa Bar and his client departments, including then Justice Minister Martin Cauchon, attended a memorial celebration of his life at the National Arts Centre. Many spoke, including a cousin from his beloved Winnipeg, who recounted that when he told his three year old daughter that "the big man" would not be coming to their home next Christmas, the child replied, wide-eyed, "You mean Santa Claus is dead?" Well, in departmental terms, in a manner of speaking, yes.

His heart attack robbed the Bar of an advocate whose star was still rising and we are all the poorer for it.

Justice W. Ian Binnie
Supreme Court of Canada
October 2004

The Importance of Advocacy

The Honourable John D. Arnup, Q.C.[*]

[Editors' note: Notes of the address given by the Honourable John D. Arnup, Q.C. at The Advocates' Society End of Term Dinner, 18 June 1987, in accepting The Advocates' Society Medal.]

When Allan Houston telephoned me on the morning of May 14 and asked if I would be willing to accept The Advocates' Society Medal for Advocacy, I couldn't believe it. "Advocacy?" I said to myself, "I'm like Northern Dancer — I don't do it anymore."

When I had recovered from the initial shock, about ten seconds later, I said to myself: "You're still involved in advocacy. You're the chairman of the Board of Advisors of The Advocates' Society Institute, and you've been working on that project for over a year. It's your own decision not to appear as counsel in any tribunal or forum, judicial or otherwise."

So I said I would be honoured to receive it, and I am. Then Allan asked me if it was all right with me if Mac Austin made the speech leading up to the presentation. What could I say? I'd already accepted the invitation, which came with no strings attached. I couldn't very well say, "I like your offer, but I have some misgivings about one of its terms."

---

[*] The late John D. Arnup was a Judge of the Court of Appeal for Ontario from 1970 to 1985.

Besides, Austin is one of Her Majesty's judges, and all my life I've had great respect for the law and its judicial dispensers — most of them. I suppose I could have said, "With all respect to Caesar Wright and Bora Laskin, I taught Austin all the law he needed for the first sixteen years of his career." That wouldn't have been too smart, because it was what he learned in the next sixteen years that put him where he is today. (In other words, don't blame me!)

I am truly grateful to The Advocates' Society for honouring me in this way. I know how careful they have been in handing out this award, and I have watched with satisfaction and pride while men I admired, and who were my friends, received this medal. I am grateful also to Mr. Justice Austin for all the kind things he said about me. Most of them he has said before, in other places, and I do not want to disillusion him. After all, he's been a judge for six months and is disillusioned enough as it is.

Our president has great confidence in my ability to talk about advocacy. He suggested I should speak about advocacy, first, as I saw it from the bar; second, as I saw it from the bench; and third, where I feel it is going in the future — and to do it in twenty minutes! In the Court of Appeal the only thing you can start and finish in twenty minutes is a coffee break.

I took it that what he really wanted was for me to say a few things about advocacy from my perspective of over fifty years in the courts, and I am keen to do so, for two reasons: first, because this Society is on the threshold of one of the most promising endeavours in which it has ever engaged; and second, because in my opinion the courts of this province, at all levels, are faced with a crisis that threatens the very life of justice itself.

Better advocacy alone will not cure all our ailments, but it offers more hope than any other single factor that may be thrown into the equation.

I began giving lectures about advocacy on appeals more than thirty-eight years ago. Continuing legal education at that time consisted entirely of a day-and-a-half of lectures each spring, under the auspices of the Law Society. Only a few of you will recall that the idea of continuing legal education in Ontario arose out of the special lectures and classes organized for the lawyers and students returning from the armed forces at the end of World War II. Men like John Cartwright and Frank Hughes and other leaders of the Bar pooled their talents for the benefit of these almost disoriented veterans.

The Canadian Bar Association called for volunteers to go out to county towns, to give lectures, usually in pairs. I went out to such hotbeds of eager appellate learners as Chatham, Owen Sound, and Belleville. For a while, Terry Sheard and I went as a team, usually on a weekend.

A few years after the Bar Admission course started in 1957, a week of special lectures on advocacy was organized, and I lectured there for over fifteen years, along with people like John Robinette, Arthur Martin, Chief Justice Gale, and several others. I updated my lecture on appeals a couple of times by inviting comments from friends of mine on the Court of Appeal. Jim McLennan and Arthur Jessup in particular made useful suggestions. A lot of what I had to say stood the test of time very well, and a goodly portion of it is as true today as when I gave it to The Advocates' Society, back when Walter Williston was our president.

Some parts of it are obsolete. Part of this obsolescence I will explain when I come to what I call "the new advocacy." Other parts, especially, my recommended methods of preparation, are very expensive to follow in today's world of high salaries and high rents. There are also serious omissions, mostly related to today's technology. The computer and word processor are just beginning to find their way into the lawyer's private office. The experts tell us that the lawyer who doesn't learn how to use them, and learn fast, is going to be out of the game. The Law Society is about to reveal a new learning experience with computers, available to lawyers and students, that will save time and money. One of the world's largest companies is going to provide the hardware. Watch for details.

Certain basic rules of advocacy are as true today as they were fifty years ago. I list them, without elaboration.

1) Everything you do to make it easier for the judge is a plus. Everything you do that distracts the court from the task at hand is a minus.
2) Short sentences make crisp writing and cogent oral argument. A blue pencil is worth five pens.
3) Best points go first, and bad points go out with the garbage.
4) Orderly structure is appealing. Disorganized sloppiness leads judges to despair. Every good argument has a plan. It should end up in the judge's notebook.
5) Good delivery is not something you're born with. Enunciation and proper emphasis take practice. Your argument is not supposed to be directed toward your notebook. It's heard it all before.
6) When you've said it the best you know how, shut up and sit down.

"Advocacy as I saw it from the bench," the man said. I saw and heard some very good advocacy there. I saw a lot of the other stuff too. I've seen some people who in one appeal managed to break all six of my basic rules, and two or three more besides. There is, of course, a very big gap between the best and the worst. That's not new. I suspect it has been a fact of life for a long time.

I am daring enough to say, and to say with pleasure, that in my last five years on the court the spread between the best and worst was noticeably narrower among women than among men. A good sign, that, because the way things are going, women will soon constitute more than half of the newly-called lawyers.

Over twenty years ago some very great senior counsel, led by Tom Phelan and Isadore Levinter, got a dozen of us together and said: "We older fellows owe a great debt to our profession. We can repay it best by helping the young counsel who want to improve their skills."

Out of this grew The Advocates' Society. I am glad I am not the only founding director still around. What motivated us then is what has motivated a group of us, and then the entire board of directors, to try to put on an organized basis the teaching of the skills involved in all forms of good advocacy. I said I would help to get this program off the ground, and I have. It is a formidable task. It will need the co-operation of all of you, in one capacity or another. Keep listening for the call!

Now for the "new advocacy." Crowded daily dockets, long lists of pending cases, and the increasing complexity of all litigation demand a new approach to advocacy. I don't know what Mr. Justice Zuber is going to propose — I know what Ian Scott hopes he's going to propose — but whatever it is, it's going to take time to put it in place. Something has to happen now, or the whole process is going to grind to a halt.

This means counsel have to find ways to present a good argument, but in less time. The bar as a whole has to learn to do this, or else you're going to face measures you won't like. These may include a time limit on oral argument; written argument on motions (with a limit on the number of pages); directions from the Court of Appeal and the Divisional Court that they only want to hear oral argument on points two and four; *per curiam* opinions, such as the Americans use for two-thirds of their cases in state courts, containing only very abbreviated reasons; or, worst of all, a series of presiding judges who ride herd on counsel like cattle-prodders in an abattoir.

This means counsel must be more ruthless than ever before in throwing away marginal points. They must forgo elaboration beyond a complete but spare statement of propositions. They must do it quicker, or they won't be doing it at all. (I know that isn't grammatical, but it's quicker.)

And as for me, what do I care? I won't be there, on either side of the bench. Well, I do care, because I still have a deep passion for justice, an unshakable belief in fair play as its principal characteristic, and I believe in you, the advocates of the future. I expect you to nourish and enrich the principles and standards on which this Society, and this profession, were founded.

Don't let me down!

[This article first appeared in the October 1987 issue of *The Advocates' Society Journal*.]

The Many Faces of Advocacy

Justice John Sopinka*

[Editors' note: This article was presented as an address to The Advocates' Society 1989 Fall Convention in Toronto on 27 October 1989.]

When I was asked to speak on this occasion, my normal reaction was to ask a law clerk to draft my speech. In practice I was known as an inveterate delegator. In fact, this trait was the subject of considerable sport among my associates in the litigation department, both at Fasken's and Stikeman's. It backfired only once.

We happened to have a particularly independent law student who considered himself above some of the more menial tasks imposed on students. I had agreed to speak at a professional seminar, but somehow had failed to delegate the preparation of the draft. The speech was to be on a Tuesday at noon, with the Thanksgiving weekend intervening.

I had planned a weekend at the farm and was heading out on Friday afternoon when my secretary sweetly said, "Have you got the materials for your speech on Tuesday?"

"What speech?" I replied. Panic time. I called in the only student still there on Friday at 5:00 p.m. — it was he. "Geoffrey," I said, "I am giving a speech on Tuesday. Here is the invitation. I want you to draft the speech and have it for me on Tuesday morning."

---

*   Mr. Justice John Sopinka, Supreme Court of Canada.

"But, sir," he said, "I'm going away on the weekend. It's my wife's mother's birthday and they've planned a family reunion in Vancouver."

I was in a rush and snapped, "Never mind that. On my desk on Tuesday morning." And out I went.

When I came back on Tuesday morning, there it was, sitting on my desk, beautifully typed. I glanced over it — it looked very good. It was a very busy morning. The trial list had collapsed, and I spent most of the morning negotiating for an adjournment on the basis that I had this speech to give.

In the taxi on the way to the hotel, I read through all but the last page. It raised some really interesting questions that would, it said, be answered in the conclusion. I didn't get to read the conclusion but was confident that its quality would match the rest of the speech.

I was already being introduced when I entered the lecture hall. The speech was even better when delivered *viva voce*, and I could see that it kept the attention of the audience as they waited for the conclusion.

"In conclusion, as promised, here are my answers to the perplexing problems which I have raised ... ."

But instead of giving answers, the speech read, in bold type:

"Now improvise, you S.O.B."

It was not just the reminder of this story that led me to conclude that this was one I couldn't delegate. As I thought about the subject, about advocacy and what it is, and what makes a good or excellent advocate, I realized that it is not something that can be found in a book. Rather, it would have to be a distillation of the experiences of over a quarter-century at the bar, working with and against a variety of advocates — some good, some great, some not so good, and some bad.

In asking myself what distinguishes a great advocate, I concluded that even among the great advocates, the degree of skill will vary with respect to the various aspects of the art. Some depend on and excel at cross-examination to win; others, closing argument; others, tactics; and still others, a combination of all, without marked emphasis on or excellence in either. There are many faces to the art of advocacy.

The Basics: Dos and Don'ts

These are the rules that separate the bad from the average advocate. They proceed logically from the realization of a basic truth. A counsel, like a coach of a football team and the manager of a baseball team, only counts for so much. In football we used to say, "If you ain't got the horses, no amount of coaching will help." Conversely, with the right horses, all you have to do is open the gate. So, in litigation, if you don't have the case, no amount of advocacy will win it. There are exceptions, but they are miscarriages of justice. Conversely, if you open the gate and prove the basic facts, you can't lose. I would roughly assess the importance of counsel to the outcome of a case as follows:

> Trial: up to 50 percent.
> Appeal to the Court of Appeal: about 25 percent.
> Supreme Court of Canada: 10 to 20 percent.

Bearing this in mind, the first basic rule in litigation, as in medicine, is "Above all else, do no harm." In order to comply with this minimal standard, the following simple rules must be followed:

1)   Prove the essential ingredients of the claim or defence.
2)   Don't get the judge or jury mad at you because you are too adversarial, too argumentative, or too long.

The second point can be illustrated by the apocryphal story about an English trial outside of London that was winding down on a Friday afternoon. Both the trial judge and the senior barrister for the defendant were from the City of London and anxious to leave in order to beat the rush hour traffic. A youngish counsel for the plaintiff was replying at undue length, whereupon the seasoned barrister passed him a note that read, "Why don't you sit down? Can't you see the old bastard is with you?"

The judge noted the passing of the note and asked plaintiff's counsel, "Does that note have anything to do with this case?" Counsel, in a quivering voice, responded, "Yes, my lord." "May I see it?" asked his lordship. Hesitatingly and diffidently, counsel for the plaintiff passed the note up, and the judge read it. "Well," said the judge, "have you read it?" "Yes, my lord," said counsel for the plaintiff. "Well, read it again," said the judge.

3)   If you don't know exactly what you want from a cross-examination, or if your chances of getting it are less than 75 percent, don't cross-examine except when you must to comply with the rule in *Browne and Dunne*.

Bad answers on a cross-examination can assume an importance out of proportion to their content and destroy your own evidence as to an essential ingredient.

4)   If you can prove it otherwise, don't ask on cross-examination.
5)   Ask for the appropriate relief.

Tactics

I do not include in this discussion the subject of developing an overall strategy for a case, sometimes referred to as a game plan. This is a very elusive subject. The overall strategy in the vast majority of cases is to marshall the best evidence and skills toward proving one's own case or destroying the other side's case. One then applies all one's skills in all the facets of litigation toward that end. In twenty-eight years of practice, I can think of only one case that was won by sheer tactics in this sense. It was an annexation case before the Ontario Municipal Board.

I will concentrate on what might be called microtactics. When I started practising, there was much more emphasis on such tactics than there is today. Perhaps there was too much emphasis. If tactics are apparent, there is often a judicial tendency to ensure that they don't work. Judges don't like the idea that the result is skewered by the manouevres of counsel. That is not to say, however, that tactics do not play a part. The following are a few examples of both kinds: those that work, and those that sometimes work but often misfire or backfire.

1) Don't leave the examiner time to prepare

Even with our sophisticated rules of discovery, in a trial of any length there are witnesses whose evidence is to some extent new and unexpected. An adjournment to prepare immediately following the examination-in-chief would be necessary for a good cross-examination. That is usually unavailable through the usual route. More often than not, it is provided by the other side. The witness is examined until the morning break, the lunch adjournment, the evening adjournment, or the weekend. The tacticians never do that. They leave the witness so that there is time to cross-examine without a break. Of course the cross-examiner can filibuster, but it may annoy the trier of fact.

2) Give the other side something to worry about

This tactic was used by J.J. Robinette against me in the *Pope and O & Q Railway v. CP* case. In that case Jake Howard and Jim Garrow acted for one set of minority shareholders and I for another set. We sought to set aside certain transactions on the grounds that the conduct of the CP and the O & Q directors it had appointed were a fraud on the minority. As you know, that term does not mean fraud as it is used in its ordinary sense. We had both named the directors as defendants, but Jake dropped them at the opening of trial. I was under instructions not to, whereupon Robinette announced that he would be seeking solicitor-and-his-own client costs against my client for keeping them in. In a six-week trial, that is a lot of money.

His argument was that the allegation of fraud was unfounded. That bothered me, because I was quite certain we would not succeed against the directors. On the other hand, I was quite sure that the trial judge would not buy the argument that it was fraud in the traditional sense, but I wasn't certain. The trial judge rejected Robinette's argument. Sometime after the trial I asked John why he had persisted in the argument. I knew it wouldn't succeed," he said, "but it gave you something to worry about and I figured you might forget something else."

3) Baiting the judge doesn't always succeed

This tactic can backfire with serious consequences, not only to the case but to counsel. It consists of needling or otherwise annoying the judge in order to provoke him or her into an error. It is employed more frequently in jury trials, where it is used to win sympathy from a jury for what is perceived to be an overbearing judge. That was the case in *R. v. Shumiatcher*,[1] in which Morris Shumiatcher repeatedly objected to the trial judge's conduct in "pushing around" or "badgering" a witness. In finding Mr. Shumiatcher guilty of contempt, the trial judge said, "I think also that it should be recorded that the tactics failed. Evidently Mr. Shumiatcher could find no miscarriage of justice in the conduct of the trial!"

---

1   (1967), 64 D.L.R. (2d) 24.

The Tools

I will not present a detailed exposition of the opening statement, examination, and cross-examination of witnesses, and closing argument. The limited purpose of my remarks is to emphasize what distinguishes the good advocate from the mediocre in the deployment of these skills.

Opening Statement

The most telling characteristic of a bad counsel is the failure to begin with a prepared opening statement. A short and crisp opening statement lifts counsel from mediocrity to a higher level. I confine this rule to plaintiffs, because different considerations apply to defendants and in criminal cases. On the other hand, no one to my knowledge has built his or her reputation on the excellence of an opening statement alone. Its purpose is to draw a road map for the trier of fact. The main pitfall to avoid is overstating your case or giving too much detail. This leads to invidious comparisons with the case that is presented.

Examination and Cross-examination of Witnesses

Examination-in-chief

Although less glamorous than cross-examination, examination-in-chief is probably more important. The world's best cross-examination will be to no avail if the basic facts are not established either because they are not elicited from the witnesses called to testify or because the witnesses are not believed.

Many counsel who were not great cross-examiners achieved the highest rank by dint of their knack to get out the essential facts, coupled with an ability to make the most out of these facts in closing argument.

There are many facets to the technique of examining witnesses, but I single out the following two as the most important.

1) Learn to ask a question that elicits the desired answer without suggesting it. Leading questions are not only contrary to the rules of evidence, but bad advocacy. It is the witness, not counsel, that the court wants to hear. In this respect, a good examination-in-chief is like a good interview on radio or television. In both cases, the personality of the person

being examined is exposed through short, unobtrusive questions that keep the examiner in the background but keep the narrative moving.

2) Try to make it interesting by injecting some drama or excitement into the evidence. Often counsel about to examine a witness sympathize with Mickey Rooney's eighth wife, who is said to have exclaimed on their wedding night, "It's not that I don't know what to do, but how to make it interesting."

Don't squander the attention of the court on long, boring preliminaries when it is anxious to hear the crucial testimony. An illustration that comes to mind is the evidence of Susan Nelles at the Grange Inquiry.

The drama building up to her testimony was something I had never witnessed before. Although there had been a lengthy preliminary hearing and a constant public discussion of the issue and of Susan, she had not uttered a single word publicly in three years. She had not testified at the preliminary hearing, and she had not made any public statements. The public would now hear her story for the first time. A few days before her testimony, I decided to sneak into the back of the hearing room with her in order to give her an idea of the set-up and to make her feel more comfortable when she came to give her testimony. This appearance was the story of the day in Toronto newspapers and on radio and TV.

When the day came for her to testify, as we approached 180 Dundas Street, where the hearing was carried out, we could tell that there was no way that we would gain entrance by the conventional route. The police arranged for Susan and counsel to be admitted via a loading dock, and she reached the hearing room by using a freight elevator. The hearing room was a sea of cameras. As she was sworn, there was dead silence as the crowded hearing room and millions of television viewers waited for her first utterances. I did not wish to squander this dramatic moment with preliminaries, and I began with questions that went to the heart of the issue:

Q. Did you at any time administer digoxin or any other drug that was not prescribed to any child?

A. No, I didn't.

Q. Did you at any time consciously administer digoxin or any other drug to a child in excess of the amount prescribed?

A. No, I did not.

Ultimately her evidence was accepted by Justice Grange.

Cross-examination

It has been said that cross-examination is the greatest engine for the ascertainment of truth ever devised. In this regard, the threat of cross-examination is often more important than the cross-examination itself. The witness knows that what he or she says will be tested. Even if the threat is an idle one because counsel opposite cannot cross-examine effectively, the witness will not necessarily know that. Accordingly, the cross-examiner has one of the principal benefits of cross-examination without asking a question.

If cross-examination is not your forte, adopt a very conservative approach. Ask only safe questions, so that you obtain something positive from the cross-examination. Don't set up headwinds to be overcome by asking questions that hurt your case. Comply with the rules that require that adverse imputations with respect to the witness's evidence must be put to the witness, and retire with grace.

Conversely, those few that have mastered the art of cross-examination take a bolder approach. While not asking a question to which you don't know the answer is a standard piece of advice, its application will produce few winning cross-examinations. Instead, the questions leading up to the desired answer should be structured in such a way that the wrong answer lacks credibility. Impeachment is not difficult when the evidence of the witness is contradicted by other evidence and by previous inconsistent statements.

The real test of the cross-examiner is the witness whose evidence is consistent with the general trend of the evidence when there are no materials readily at hand with which to challenge the witness's testimony. Horace Rindress, in *R. v. McNamara* (the dredging trial), was such a witness. He was fired by the chief executives of one of the accused companies when he alerted them that the RCMP were investigating and sought an assurance that they would stick together. He then gathered up all his papers and spent a year in a tropical retreat preparing a brief for the RCMP. With such a witness, the cross-examination can only hope to build up an atmosphere based on a series of adverse nuances rather than outright contradictions. The latter are generally not obtainable from such a witness. An attempt to meet the witness head-on results in the reaffirmation of the witness's evidence-in-chief.

Closing Argument

Of all the aspects of advocacy, this is probably the most important. Notwithstanding that your witnesses may have been reticent and forgetful, and your cross-examinations less than scintillating, the case can still be won in final argument. Conversely, the many subtleties and nuances brought out in the evidence may be completely lost if not explained and tied together in closing argument. There is an additional ally — the law. The party who can weave the facts and the law into the most attractive quilt will usually win.

It need not be solely a *tour de force* of logic. It must not be forgotten that judges are not machines. They are susceptible to an appeal to the emotions. Chief Justice Robertson remarked that "every judge is a juror at heart." Indeed, my experience leads me to believe that judges are more jurors than are jurors. In *Hellenius v. Lees* I acted for a courageous plaintiff who was a quadriplegic as a result of an accident that occurred when his friend's car had a blowout and rolled onto the median on Highway 401. He showed tremendous courage at the trial, refusing to interrupt the proceedings when it was obvious that he was in considerable pain. When the jury came back and dismissed his action, Henderson J. came down from the bench in tears and shook the plaintiff's hand. There was no question in my mind which way the decision would have gone if tried by judge alone.

The golden rule of all advocacy applies here *a fortiori*. Prepare and present the argument with the judge in mind. Work out in advance what the structure is and how much time it will take. Many good arguments are spoiled by repetition. The degree of tolerance in this regard will vary from judge to judge, but every judge has a limit.

Make sure the judge is following you. Many counsel — even good counsel — overestimate the ability of the court to follow an argument. They have lived with the case for months, perhaps years. To the judge it is relatively new.

Having announced in opening the argument the points you intend to address, make it clear at all times which point you are on. Refer the court to key passages in the evidence and the cases. Speak at a moderate speed. I have found that in our court, many counsel have adapted to the time limits by speaking twice as fast. They do not allow time for the court to get out the Case on Appeal or the authorities, and often they do not read the passages at all. This is a mistake. The proper approach is to deal with the essential points, but at the same tempo and technique as if time were unlimited. The technique of asking the court to look at Case on Appeal at pages 10, 40, and 60 without turning it up may be to no avail. If the judges have not already read and digested those references, they will not do so before the conference that follows immediately after oral argument. That is usually when the die is cast. If these are important, have the court read them with you.

Conclusion

In the past, advocacy skills could only be acquired through the observation of great advocates. Some of us were lucky enough to be trained by them. With the growth of litigation, this is no longer possible. We are fortunate, therefore, that we have The Advocates' Society Institute, which is devoted to this task. Expert training will no longer depend on the luck of the draw in landing a job with a great counsel. This is a very important step forward, and one which I wholeheartedly support.

I must sound a word of caution. The art of the advocate is a highly individualized skill. While there is great value in learning the techniques and methods of skilled advocates, they must be adapted to your own style and personality. A courtroom demeanour that is alien to a lawyer's personality is bound to look artificial and even phony. While the teachings of others are important in eliminating bad habits and exposing you to a variety of approaches, it is necessary to ensure that others' ideas are adopted only when they enhance, not hinder, your ability to persuade.

[This article first appeared in the March 1990 issue of *The Advocates' Society Journal*.]

In Praise of Oral Advocacy

Justice W. Ian Binnie*

[Editors' note: This article is the edited text of the third Charles Dubin Lecture on Advocacy, presented on 23 October 2002.]

It is a great privilege to be asked to give this year's Dubin Lecture on Advocacy. I read with interest the contributions of my two predecessors, Edward Greenspan, Q.C., and Sir Sydney Kentridge, Q.C., whose lectures offered up a witch's brew of tendentious preaching, over-arching generalities, ethical lapses, comic relief, and moral ambivalence. I intend to continue in that tradition.

At the time I was called to the Bar, we didn't have to suffer through too many lectures on advocacy. We still had the apprenticeship system. The junior lawyers followed the senior lawyers around, and eventually we grew into mutant copies. So Walter Williston's juniors learned how to mumble, some of Barry Pepper's juniors acquired fake English accents, and George Finlayson's juniors developed what today would be called an "attitude problem." Even physical attributes were copied. Malcolm Robb had been shot up as a fighter pilot in the Second World War, which caused him to carry his head at an odd tilt. His juniors carried their heads at the same tilt — though none, to my knowledge, was a war

---

*   Mr. Justice W. Ian Binnie, Supreme Court of Canada.

hero. Charlie Dubin's juniors tended to be quite bright, but they all talked too much. I had the privilege of articling for Bert MacKinnon, who was a perfect gentleman.[1]

The Dubin organizing committee suggested that as I am the first of the Dubin lecturers to speak from the exile of the bench, I could useful-ly say something about appellate advocacy. If I knew then what I know now, would I do it differently?

Some lawyers say that oral advocacy, particularly in the Supreme Court, is less important than it was and less important than written advocacy, but I don't believe it. I am going to spend the next few min-utes trying to explain why I don't believe it. The big difference between a factum and an oral argument is that the factum gives you a crack at us but, from the judges' point of view, the oral argument gives us a crack at you. It is in the heat and apparent confusion of that exchange that appel-late victories are often determined. This is not because good lawyers can get the weak judges to make bad law, but because on occasion a key fact or important legal principle, differently appreciated, can push a close case one way or the other. Any competent advocate can win (or lose) a 9–0 unanimous judgment in the Supreme Court of Canada, but it sometimes takes serious skill to push the court over the line on a 5–4 split.

The relationship between the judge and the advocate can be mutu-ally destructive or it can be quite heartwarming. I have a nostalgic recol-lection of a winter morning in 1982, when I happened to be in the Supreme Court. Justice Ronald Martland was retiring, and there was what is quaintly called a "swearing-out ceremony." The Attorney Gener-al of Canada and the Attorneys General for some provinces and various dignitaries were there to say nice things about his decades on the bench. When it came time for Justice Martland to respond, which he did with wit and emotion, he turned to Mr. John Robinette, Q.C., who was there to represent the practising bar, and said words to the following effect:

> When I was appointed to this Court on 15 January 1958, I was greeted
> by John Robinette, Q.C., on behalf of the legal profession. Now that I

---

1   In this ongoing tradition, I wish to express my appreciation to my law clerk, Patricia McMahon, who was able to dig up the citations for my more obscure references including, incredibly, the citation of the "swimming pool ledge" case in note
13, *infra*.

am leaving, twenty-four years later, Mr. Robinette is here to say good-
bye, now as then the dean of the Supreme Court bar.

It was a poignant moment as the departing justice and the great advocate saluted each other across a lifetime of practice and almost a quarter
century of pitched battles at the top end of the legal system.

Other eminent counsel never achieved this rosy glow of judicial
acceptance. I refer to a recent character sketch of Justice Milt Harradence, who retired six years ago as a judge of the Alberta Court of
Appeal.[2] Justice Harradence was a leading member of the criminal
defence bar in western Canada. So great was his eminence that it was
said in the Calgary press that "if you're guilty, call Milty." His biographer
tells of the time he accompanied Milt Harradence to Ottawa on an application for leave to appeal a conviction which they both regarded as a fla-
grant miscarriage of justice:

> Milt had not had great success as an advocate before the Supreme
> Court in Ottawa. In fact, his experiences before that nest of remote
> and chilly autocrats who peopled its woolsack in the early '60s was
> discouraging to say the least. I accompanied him once as his junior,
> and it was a horrible experience. This was an application for leave in a
> criminal matter, meritorious I say, and the Court was singularly unre-
> ceptive. I marveled as my Learned Senior crawled uphill on broken
> glass to be summarily kissed off. Later, we walked the icy, windblown
> streets of the foreign capital, two alienated aliens, strangers in a weird
> land. "Let's get out of this Goddamn place," growled Milt. "Let's get
> back to Canada!"[3]

I have spent my professional lifetime trying to figure out what makes
the difference between getting "kissed off" by appellate judges and
being showered with their compliments on great state occasions.

There are a handful of advocates who could tell us. I do not pretend
to be among them. My Lord Dubin, who is rarely silent on any subject,
so far seems reticent to share with us the secrets of his professional success. He has left it to others to give lectures that he could more authori-
tatively provide himself. Perhaps it could still be said, as it used to be

2   C.D. Evans, *Milt Harradence: The Western Flair* (Calgary: Durance Vile Publications,
     2001).
3   *Ibid.* at 270.

said before he went to the bench, that it was easier to open an oyster without a knife than Charlie Dubin's mouth without a fee.

In general, however, when My Lord Dubin left the practice and went to the bench, his verbal floodgates opened. During a twenty-three-year reign of terror on the Ontario Court of Appeal,[4] he deployed the inquisitorial method with a skill not seen since Robespierre presided over *le tribunal révolutionnaire*. Every appeal was initiated with a firestorm of questions which rarely let up. At some point in the storm, with luck, some sort of coherence would begin to emerge and the reluctant participating lawyers — *les misérables* — got the impression that having narrowed his inquiry to the essential questions, the Chief Justice was *au grand galop* on a search for answers. The search, like the questions, branched out in all directions, but at some point you would be presented by Chief Justice Dubin — *le grand inquisiteur* — with a working hypothesis — what Chief Justice Dubin *thought* the case was all about, and therefore, for all practical purposes, what the case *was* all about.

At that stage, counsel who was on the wrong end of the momentum began to hear the tumbrels coming from *la place de la guillotine* as My Lord Dubin helpfully raised numerous other objections to reinforce the frailties of your position. If, on the other hand, momentum was running in your favour, you would be celebrated as a sort of *avocat du jour* with soft lobs of easy questions to even further strengthen what was developing into an impregnable position. Eventually a sort of *épiphanie* occurred in which the destiny of the case was made manifest to all those in the courtroom.

Thus described, an appeal before the Dubin court fell into five discrete sections, namely: identification of the questions, the search for answers, the working hypothesis, the testing period, and the epiphany. In reality, of course, these stages would often be run together, and occasionally the epiphany was made manifest as soon as you got to your feet.

It came to me belatedly, after sitting for some time as a judge, that the Dubin rules of engagement were nothing more than the flip side of the tactics of oral advocacy he employed as counsel, tactics he shared with John Robinette, Arthur Martin, John Arnup, Bert MacKinnon, and the other robed warriors who dominated the Ontario courts in the

---

4   The Honourable Charles Dubin was a member of the Court of Appeal from 1973 to 1990 and was Chief Justice of Ontario from 1990 to 1996.

1960s, '70s, and even into the '80s. I want to try to give this afternoon at least some impression of what I think they did, why they did what they did, why they were effective, and why it was, from the bench's point of view, skillful advocacy. I think their approach still works, so I propose to address each of these five stages in turn.

The Opening Question

What is the question raised by the appeal? It was said that when Gertrude Stein, a lifelong atheist, was on her death bed, she was attended on by a dear friend who had become a spiritualist. The friend evidently expected Gertrude to provide some sort of deathbed revelation. As Gertrude slipped in and out of death's door, the friend anxiously asked, "Gertrude, Gertrude, what is the answer?" And Gertrude, drifting back into life for one last time, opened one eye and said, "What is the question?" And having made her point, she rolled over and died.[5]

We quite often sit on the bench listening to counsel give elaborate answers but, if truth were to be told, we sometimes don't know what they think the question is.

Those of you who are familiar with Shakespeare's *King Lear* will remember that Lear's first speech in the play states the question around which all else revolves — "Tell me, my daughters, since now we will divest us, both of rule, interest of territory, cares of state, which of you shall we say doth love us most?"[6] —and the insanity of the rest of the play is all built around that opening framework.

Shakespeare knew enough to let his audience in on the question before he began to lay on the answers.

Inexperienced counsel go into a courtroom assuming that everybody is agreed on what the question is. In fact, much of the time, counsel are in silent, unacknowledged, semi-conscious disagreement over "what the case is about." These unarticulated differences of approach create much of the adversarial fog that sometimes envelops us. In the

---

5   See Robert Andrews, Mary Biggs, & Michael Seidel (eds.), *The Columbia World of Quotations* (New York: Columbia University Press, 1996). See also bartleby.com, 2001. According to *Columbia World*, the original source of the quotation is Donald Sutherland, *Gertrude Stein: A Biography of Her Work* (New Haven, CT: Yale University Press, 1951), c. 6.

6   William Shakespeare, *King Lear*, Act 1, Scene 1, ll. 49–52.

case of Charles Dubin, as a practitioner, steering a court to his preferred view of the right question was a major step towards victory. For My Lord Dubin, as a judge, formulating the defining question was his way to take control of the agenda. It set the stage for the inspired chaos of his court-room for the next few hours.

Let me offer a few other examples. In *Regina v. John Robin Sharpe*,[7] the recent child pornography case, the trial judge was persuaded that the essential question was freedom of expression.[8] The Crown, conceding a violation of freedom of expression, argued that the criminalization of possession of child pornography was vital for the protection of children. In reality, of course, the appeal required the courts to balance both inter-ests, but from an advocate's perspective, the eventual outcome was greatly influenced by which aspect emerged as dominant.

Now there is an evolution of the key question(s) as you move up through the court system, as there was in the *Sharpe* case, and it may well be that the question you successfully answered before the trial judge changes its complexion in the Court of Appeal and again in the Supreme Court of Canada. Some counsel exhibit considerable resent-ment at this evolution. We had a recent case in the Supreme Court[9] hav-ing to do with the British Columbia Liquor Licensing Board and an allegation that its members, having been appointed at the pleasure of the Crown, lacked institutional independence and impartiality. In the Court of Appeal, the Crown had acknowledged as applicable to adminis-trative boards the principles of judicial independence and impartiality applicable to the courts. When the Crown got to us, of course, this con-cession was withdrawn. The Crown was now saying "the question" has nothing to do with the independence of judges; it has to do with the independence of administrative boards. As licensing boards are part of the executive, they cannot be in any meaningful sense "independent" of it. The respondent's lawyer, sensing the appeal slipping from his grasp, made a rather bitter aside, which I quote from the hearing transcript: "In fairness to the Court of Appeal," he said, "who wrote a considered judgment in the way the case had been argued by the Crown, when I

---

7   [2001] 1 S.C.R. 45.

8   *R. v. Sharpe* (1999), 169 D.L.R. (4) 536 (B.C.S.C.).

9   *Ocean Port Hotel Ltd. v. British Columbia (General Manager, Liquor Control and Licensing Branch)*, [2001] 2 S.C.R. 781.

look at my friend's argument in this court, it makes the Court of Appeal look like they're not very bright. But," he added, remembering he had to go back to British Columbia, "that's not the case."[10]

I think the continuing formulation and reformulation of the key questions as a case moves through the courts shows the system working as it should, so long as neither side is ambushed or prejudiced in terms of the evidentiary record.[11] Refinement is the natural outcome of lawyers and judges continuing to drill down through the layers of bumpf deeper into the heart of a case. Most counsel do their best thinking, fuelled by fright and adrenalin, in the twenty-four hours before an appeal is heard, and in some cases, ten or fifteen minutes beforehand, or perhaps not until the hearing itself. Every episode of intense thinking about a case brings new insights. The objective of the system is to get to the right result. The objective of appellate counsel is to be seen to be co-operating in this exercise of refinement while steering the case in a winning direction. If the debate moves on and you can't divert it, you have to move with it. Otherwise, your participation ceases to be relevant to the outcome.

An example in which John Robinette was unsuccessful in steering the debate was the *Ontario Separate Schools Funding* case.[12] In an opinion provided before the litigation was commenced, he expressed the view that the fundamental question raised by separate schools for religious minorities was equality rights. He argued that allowing the government to pick and choose among minority religious groups, funding some and not others, violated section 15 of the *Canadian Charter of Rights and Freedoms*. Others said the fundamental question was whether provincial governments were prepared to live up to the pact of Confederation in which minority rights of Catholic denominational schools had been expressly guaranteed. Historical entitlement, they said, should not be trumped by the *Charter*'s late-flowering focus on equality. Again, a plausible argument could be made either way, and the Robinette side ultimately lost because it was unable to persuade the Supreme Court that the question at the heart of the case was about equality. In other words, it lost control of the agenda.

---

10   Transcript of oral proceedings, 22 March 2001, at 74.
11   See *Performance Industries Ltd. v. Sylvan Lake Golf & Tennis Club Ltd.* (2002 S.C.C. 19), at para. 33.
12   *Re Bill 30 (Ontario Separate School Funding)*, [1987] 1 S.C.R. 1148.

In a better-known example, lawyers for O.J. Simpson were apparently able to persuade the jury in Los Angeles that the real issue in the
prosecution was not the conduct of O.J. Simpson himself but racism in
the Los Angeles Police Department.

The late Edson Haines was an expert at getting the court to define
the question in a way favourable to his position. I once heard him talk
about an insurance claim brought by a young boy who had broken his
neck on a concrete ledge in a swimming pool.[13] The defence not only
developed the theory that the ledge was installed to protect waders at the
shallow end of the pool, but introduced the term "safety ledge" for the
concrete protrusion that broke the plaintiff's neck. Even the plaintiff's
lawyer began referring to the protrusion as a "safety ledge." Once the
question had resolved into whether or not it was negligent to install a
safety ledge, the insurance company was home free.

Sometimes the court's imagination can be captured with a clever
question in opening. In the *Port Arthur Shipbuilding* case,[14] dealing with
the judicial review of a labour arbitrator, Mr. Robinette was confronted
with an earlier Supreme Court of Canada decision somewhat against
him called *Howe Sound Company v. International Union of Mine, Mill and
Smelter Workers (Canada), Local 663.*[15] The *Howe Sound* decision appeared
to suggest that at least in British Columbia judicial review by way of certiorari was not available against a private labour arbitrator. Robinette's
job was either to distinguish the *Howe Sound* decision or to get it overruled. He opened his appeal with the words, "How sound, My Lords,
how sound is *Howe Sound?*" With such a beguiling opening line, he
couldn't lose, and he didn't.

In all of these examples, the ultimate success of the advocate
depended largely on persuading the court to accept the formulation of
the question that favoured the client. Once defined, the question as you
have framed it should determine the content of everything else you say.

I myself won one of my few successes before My Lord Dubin in
Sheppard Estate v. McAllister.[16] The rather humdrum issue was whether

---

13   *Kester v. City of Hamilton* (1937), O.R. 420 (C.A.), cited by Edson Haines for the
     defence in, amongst other cases, *Street (Next Friend of) v. Colavecchio (c.o.b. Roll-a-
     Dance)*, [1952] O.J. No. 4.
14   *Port Arthur Shipbuilding Company v. Arthurs, et al.*, [1969] S.C.R. 85.
15   [1962] S.C.R. 318.
16   (1987), 60 O.R. (2d) 309.

collateral benefits under a private insurance policy should be deducted from the assessment of tort damages. As soon as My Lord Dubin was persuaded that the real issue in the case was whether or not his previous seminal decision — his renowned *locus classicus* — his *nec plus ultra* — in *Boarelli v. Flannigan*[17] was correctly decided, he closed his bench book. My client's success was swift and unqualified.[18] On other less fortunate occasions, I have shared Eddie Greenspan's experience of not being able to get him even to *open* his bench book in the first place.

The Search for a Solution

We move to the second phase. Once My Lord Dubin had satisfied himself which of his several hundred questions captured the essence of his view of the appeal, the search was on for a solution. The inquiry branched out to try to pick up any stray bits of law and evidence that could conceivably assist in providing an answer.

The litigation lawyer's natural inclination at this stage is to give away as little as possible in argument in the hopes of preserving the maximum advantage for the client. This is a mistake. It is not how appellate courts work. The argument of an appeal is not like a pre-trial settlement conference. Winning counsel think themselves into the chairs of the judges and come up with workable solutions, not hardball negotiating positions.

In the course of the last thirty years of constitutional litigation, the Saskatchewan Attorney General's Department has been particularly astute in this regard.

In the *Patriation Reference* of 1982,[19] for example, the legal issue was whether the federal government could unilaterally go to England to obtain United Kingdom legislation ending Canada's constitutional dependence. Most of the provinces argued that Confederation consisted of a pact of all the provinces, a sort of contract of adhesion, and each

---

17 [1973] 3 O.R. 69.
18 I note that a few years later *Boarelli* was frowned on by the Supreme Court of Canada in *Ratych v. Bloomer*, [1990] 1 S.C.R. 940, and then given a bit of a reprieve in 1993 in *Cunningham v. Wheeler*, [1994] 2 S.C.R. 359; but by that time, it was somebody else's problem.
19 *Re Resolution to Amend the Constitution*, [1981] 1 S.C.R. 753.

member of the pact must consent before the federal government could go to Westminster to ask for any change. The argument had a certain simplistic attraction but would have produced a constitutional straitjacket. Unanimity on serious issues, as we know, is not a defining feature of federal/provincial conferences. The federal government said: "Consent would be nice, but it's optional, and it's of no significance legally. We can go to Westminster if, as and when we want to go." It was famously the Trudeau view that the federal government, and it alone, could speak for Canada. Provincial agreement, or the lack of it, was a matter of political expedience, not constitutional obligation. Each side marshalled precedents in its favour. Saskatchewan, rightly sensing that the Supreme Court was not comfortable with either extreme, came up with the theory that the federal government did not need *unanimous* provincial consent but it did require *substantial* provincial consent. (Pierre Trudeau argued years later in his lecture opening the Laskin Law Library, to the indignation of Chief Justice Dickson who was in the audience, that the historical basis for this proposition was rather thin.[20]) From an *advocacy* point of view, Saskatchewan's position was brilliant. I happened to be present in the court, sitting many rows behind and on the other side of the courtroom from My Lord McMurtry, when Saskatchewan made its argument. The judges were all ears. Instead of playing constitutional hardball, Kenneth Lysyk, then Deputy Attorney General of Saskatchewan, had found some middle ground. It was a practical proposal that laid a considerable burden on the federal government to work with the provinces without imposing a permanent constitutional freeze. Moreover, the test of *substantial* consent had the additional attraction that it defied any attempt at precise definition. The Saskatchewan solution was eventually endorsed in the court's judgment.[21]

My point today is that Saskatchewan may well have preferred the rule of unanimity and the theory of the all-provinces-are-equal Confederation pact. But pragmatism trumped dogmatism. Its counsel realized that the preferred solution was not achievable. And so Saskatchewan was able to move within the realm of the possible to salvage as much provincial autonomy as could be done.

---

20   See the criticism of Pierre Elliott Trudeau, Convocation Speech on receiving the degree of Doctor of Laws *honoris causa*, Convocation Hall, University of Toronto, Thursday, 21 March 1991, (1991) U.T.L.J. 295.

21   *Patriation Reference*, [1981] 1 S.C.R. 753, at 904–5.

Saskatchewan came up with a similarly creative argument in the *Quebec Secession Reference*[22] of 1998. In that case, as you may recall, the issue before the court was whether a clear vote of Quebecers on a clear question to secede from Canada would lawfully entitle the province to exit Confederation. The Constitution of course does not explicitly mention either unilateral secession or a referendum procedure. The federal government therefore argued that a successful referendum vote in Quebec would have no constitutional significance. The *amicus curiae* representing his view of the interests of Quebec brushed aside the Constitution as merely a minor local difficulty, and argued that the principle controlling the answer to the question was the international law concept of the self-determination of peoples. Saskatchewan, apparently uneasy both with what is considered to be the somewhat black letter approach of the federal government and with the suggestion of the *amicus curiae* that the Constitution was more or less irrelevant, advanced a theory of pan-Canadian reciprocity, building to some extent on its winning argument in the *Patriation Reference* of 1981. Saskatchewan argued that Canada could no more ignore the views of a clear majority of Quebecers to a clear referendum question than Quebec, in trying to achieve its political objectives, could ignore the views and interests of the rest of Canada. I want to give you a portion of the transcript of the oral submission of the Deputy Attorney General of Saskatchewan, John D. Whyte, Q.C.:

> A nation is built when the communities that comprise it make commitments to it, when they forego choices and opportunities on behalf of a nation, when they discover within the nation new opportunities, when the communities that comprise it make compromises, when they offer each other guarantees, when they make transfers and perhaps most pointedly, when they receive from others the benefits of national solidarity .... [A] thousand (1,000) acts of accommodation [create] the fabric of a nation, the net result is a structure of strong and important interests *and its dismantling requires the participation of others whose histories include the building* of this political identity.[23] [Emphasis added.]

Some would say this is political science, not law, but it was first-rate advocacy. Counsel, trying to put himself in the chairs of the judges, saw

---

22   *Reference re Secession of Quebec*, [1998] 2 S.C.R. 217.

23   Transcript of oral argument, Tuesday, 17 February 1998, at 21–22.

that the logical counter to unilateralism was a principle of mutuality. He sought to demonstrate that mutuality is not only Canadians' *preferred* way of doing things, but historically it has been seen by our constitutional actors as *obligatory* to at least make an effort to reach a *substantial* consensus. Accordingly, he argued, there was a legal obligation, a sort of constitutional convention, that required negotiations. At that point he left it to the court to find a way to express the idea of mutuality in more orthodox constitutional language.

I now offer an example of *failing* to put oneself in the judges' seat from international litigation. In 1984 I was a member of Canada's legal team before the International Court of Justice at The Hague in the *Gulf of Maine Maritime Boundary Dispute*. The court was asked by the parties to draw a maritime boundary between Canada and the United States out to the 200-mile limit. International law says the boundary must be drawn "in conformity with equitable principles having regard to all relevant circumstances in order to achieve an equitable result."[24] The rule is almost meaningless because international law says little about what those equitable principles are. Canada argued that equity was equality, and the boundary should therefore be drawn equidistant from the base points on the respective coasts of the two countries. Because of the southward extension of Nova Scotia into the Atlantic Ocean, the equidistance method pushed the boundary deep into the fishing grounds of Georges Bank, about 100 miles off the coast, to which the United States as well as Canada had strong historical links.

The United States argued that true equality was not equidistance but proportionality. Its geographers counted the miles of coastline of each country fronting on the Gulf of Maine and argued that the length of the U.S. "relevant" coasts greatly exceeded Canada's and that there should be a proportional allocation of the maritime area. This would give equal effect to every mile of coastline. The land, international law says, dominates the sea. (The United States also argued rather weakly that the body of water was *called* the Gulf of Maine, to which we responded that on that basis, they should give the Gulf of Mexico back to the Mexicans.) The American line cut north of Georges Bank and would have crippled the fishing effort off southwestern Nova Scotia.

---

24   *Case concerning Delimitation of the Maritime Boundary in the Gulf of Maine Area*, dated 12 October 1984, ICJ 1984, at para. 99.

My part of the argument related to the economic consequences of the various proposed boundaries. I endeavoured to introduce a little levity into the argument (always a risky strategy) by suggesting to the court that the American idea of equality was similar to the recipe of my Scottish forbears for horse and rabbit pie. Their recipe was also based on equality. One horse and one rabbit. (Unfortunately, the French judge on the court preferred horse meat to rabbit and probably thought this was an ideal recipe.)

Canada had on its legal team Professor Prosper Weil of the Université de Paris, a brilliant but temperamental international lawyer. (It was said that dealing with Prosper Weil was like dealing with Maria Callas — it was hell putting up with all those tantrums and temper, but when she got up to sing, or when he rose to his feet in the courtroom, the effect was spectacular.) Professor Weil delivered a brilliant elucidation of what he called *le principe de non principe* — the principle of no principle — in which he argued that the International Court should not allow itself to be seen to be more or less making up "the law" as it went along. Parties are entitled to a measure of predictability, he said, and this could only be achieved by a principled approach. Although Professor Weil's intention was to show the intellectual bankruptcy of an unprincipled approach, his *principe de non principe* seemed to be just what the court was looking for. We had misread their smoke signals.

We had not sufficiently put ourselves in the shoes of the court. A domestic court may search for certainty and predictability, but an international court needs to attract business. If states can determine in advance what the court's boundary delimitation would be, the government likely to end up on the short end of the judgment would simply refuse to accept the court's jurisdiction. The court would thereby undermine its ability to fulfill its institutional role of resolving international disputes. Thus, in its final judgment in the *Gulf of Maine* case, the International Court of Justice stated as follows:

> Each Party's reasoning is in fact based on a false premise. The error lies precisely in searching general international law for, as it were, a set of rules which are not there. This observation applies particularly to certain "principles" advanced by the Parties as constituting well established rules ....[25]

---

25   *Ibid.* at para. 110.

Put yourself in the position of the judges in The Hague. States usually take their boundary disputes to international tribunals because any boundary is sometimes better than no boundary and governments shrink from the responsibility of signing an agreement that abandons what is potentially part of the realm. Some governments think they look better if the result can be presented as the work of a distant and uncontrollable tribunal — the so-called remote and chilly autocrats — but even foolish governments would be unlikely to go before a tribunal where the odds of an acceptable result were seen in advance to be stacked against them. In this context, uncertainty and unpredictability were viewed by the International Court judges as marketing virtues. In my view, the boundary drawn by the court, which gave us the rich fishing grounds on the north slope of Georges Bank, was favourable to Canada, but the International Court's explicit adoption of *le principe de non principe* in its judgment drove Leonard Legault, Q.C., Canada's agent on the case, to observe that if Canada ever has another boundary dispute with the United States, we should go to war instead of litigation, because the outcome would be faster, cheaper, and the outcome more predictable.

There is an interesting postscript that illustrates another aspect of oral advocacy. Some years later, Canada was again before an international tribunal, this time against France in a dispute about the maritime boundaries of the French islands of St. Pierre and Miquelon, which lie off the south coast of Newfoundland. Again, my brief was to argue the potential economic consequences in general and the impact on the Atlantic fisheries in particular. Professor Prosper Weil participated, but this time as the *ad hoc* French judge. Again he urged his colleagues and the parties to adopt the equidistance method which, by dividing the distance between little St. Pierre and Miquelon and the surrounding Canadian coast of Nova Scotia and Newfoundland, happily gave the tiny French islands half the outer Gulf of St. Lawrence — thousands of square kilometres of what had been, historically, rich fishing grounds. When Prosper Weil confronted Canada with its earlier advocacy for equidistance in the *Gulf of Maine* case, Professor Derek Bowett, one of the other lawyers appearing for Canada, declined to be drawn into a profitless discussion and simply replied, "In my country we have a saying that you don't win cases by arguing with the judges." He then moved on. It was the right tactic. There was no way that Professor Bowett was going to persuade Prosper Weil, France's *ad hoc* judge, to accept Canada's point of view. Recognizing that the outcome of the case rested with the other judges, the only sensible response was to finesse Prosper Weil's question with a mildly amusing aphorism and move on.

(If on an appeal in the Supreme Court you're confronted with a rogue judge who seems more interested in argument than enlightenment, try Professor Bowett's approach. See what happens.)

In the *St. Pierre et Miquelon* case, Professor Weil was eventually isolated from his colleagues. What emerged in the decision was a little enclave around St. Pierre and Miquelon of about twelve miles, and then a thin strip of ocean running from the enclave out to the open sea which Prosper Weil described as *un pauvre petit misérable champignon*.

The task of the advocate is to go behind appearances and find out what is actually bothering the court as distinguished from what merely seems to be bothering it, or what, in counsel's view, *ought* to be bothering it. In the *Gulf of Maine* case, we found out by accident; in the great constitutional cases, Saskatchewan got it right by design. The advocate's task in the search phase of oral argument is to act as a sort of midwife to the court's embryonic grip on what it wants to do.

The Working Hypothesis

At the third stage comes the eventual unveiling, in the course of oral argument, of the court's working hypothesis that will, if unchanged, be dispositive of the appeal. I think this is a little understood phenomenon. Every lawyer appreciates in the course of an appeal that momentum is moving either in your direction or against you, but where the momentum begins and how to control it is a neglected topic. In his opening tribute this afternoon to My Lord Dubin, Justice John Laskin referred to an instance where Charles Dubin managed to lose both sides of the same issue in successive cases. Such things happen. Momentum is the product of different forces on different days. In fact, I was involved in back-to-back losses on opposite sides of the same issue on the same morning. I was junioring to the late Brian Kelsey in Courtroom No. 1 at Osgoode Hall many years ago. Our first case was a slam-dunk winner, but Mr. Justice John ("Black Jack") Aylesworth saw it otherwise, and nothing my learned senior could say could stop the court's headlong rush towards a miscarriage of justice. (It was not for nothing that the Ontario Court of Appeal was known in those days as "murderers' row.") In the innocence of youth, I was quite shocked by the crudeness of their behaviour, but Kelsey, who was a very good advocate, turned around and whispered reassuringly, "Relax, next time we'll get the benefit of their stupidity." He then got to his feet with great confidence to argue the second appeal, this time relying on the very proposition that had cost him the first appeal, and lost again. The tide had somehow turned in the space of a few minutes for reasons perhaps only astrologers could understand.

I am not sure, but I believe that was the appeal in which our learned opponent, although having the court clearly on his side, kept addressing My Lord Aylesworth as "Your Honour." And Justice Aylesworth said, "Well, in this court it's customary to refer to me as 'Your Lordship.'" The fellow was quite embarrassed but a little while later forgot himself and again referred to the judge as "Your Honour" and again was corrected. This went on all morning. I am glad to report that when the appeal was finally disposed of against us, it was done on the basis of costs on a County Court scale.

I have digressed from the point I was making about the working hypothesis. My Lord Dubin used to say, when he spoke of advocacy, that in his experience in the Supreme Court there would come a time when Justice Martland, having thought about the arguments and wiggled his brow, and thumbed through his papers, and whispered to his colleagues, would clear his throat and come up with what My Lord Dubin called "the Martland question." He called it a question, but it was really the statement of a working hypothesis. Invariably it captured the essence of the appeal. If you were able to give a satisfactory answer, you would succeed. If not, you were doomed. My Lord Dubin was not only an admirer of "the Martland question" but one of its most illustrious practitioners.

I make no pretensions to an ability to emulate either of these learned justices in the formulation of Martland-type questions, but it is certainly my experience that in the course of the hearing of an appeal there comes a point, perhaps at first subconsciously, when the judge begins to see a way of resolving the important inconsistencies in the record and any contradictions in the case law to produce a just result. You sense at least the beginning of "a good fit." At that point, the open mind of the judge begins to narrow and the appeal, I think, takes on a different complexion. That is the point at which momentum begins to build. The rules of engagement change. From the moment the working hypothesis is articulated, the judge's focus is on whether, on further questioning, it can be sustained or knocked down. Either way, it likely becomes dispositive.

This stage, I think, is the ultimate justification for oral argument. In the earlier process of written argument, you make an effort to steer the coming debate in a direction favourable to your client and marshal the facts and the law in support, but your view of what the court will think is, at that stage, no more than a prediction and not infrequently is off the mark. The full measure of your predicament is revealed only in the course of oral argument, when through its questioning the court discloses its preliminary thinking, and you can put yourself in the position of the judges who are trying to decide the case and say, "Aha, that's where they are coming from and therefore, if I'm going to win this thing, either I will have to kill their hypothesis with some brilliant intervention or I will have to push them sideways onto a different question altogether." If you achieve neither, you will probably hear the sound of the little carts returning from the *place de la guillotine* to get you.

This requires a high level of concentration during the hearing of an appeal. The modern practice, I regret to say, is for senior counsel to bring along younger lawyers to take notes that nobody ever reads. When I went to the court with Bert MacKinnon and began to take notes, I was ordered to put my pen down. He said, "Look at the judges. That's what you're here for." So I was taught from a very early stage that, if I really wanted to lose the appeal, I would spend my time scribbling reminders to myself or having my head buried in the books putting some finishing touches on a written speech. If you don't watch and listen to the judges, you won't realize that your written speech has been overtaken by events. Too many counsel are locked into the trajectory they had planned beforehand, like an intercontinental missile which, once launched, can be neither controlled nor recalled. Like the missile, their trip often comes to a catastrophic conclusion.

It is this intercontinental missile approach that I think regrettably dominates even in the Supreme Court.

Testing the Hypothesis

If the momentum of the court is running in your favour, of course you try to keep pushing the court, and pushing hard, in the same direction with any argument reasonably at your disposal. I have always been very taken with a fishing metaphor suggested by a great American lawyer called John W. Davis. In a famous lecture delivered to the New York City bar almost half a century ago, Mr. Davis compared the lawyer to a fly-fisherman, and the judge, rather unflatteringly, to a prize trout:

> [I]n the argument of an appeal the advocate is angling, consciously and deliberately angling, for the judicial mind. Whatever tends to attract judicial favour to the advocate's claim is useful. Whatever repels it is useless or worse. The whole art of the advocate consists in choosing the one and avoiding the other.[26]

Of course, the problem with applying this metaphor to the appellate level is that it presupposes all members of the court are attracted or repelled by the same things. This is not always so. In the great case of *Operation Dismantle*,[27] to take an example, it was obvious during the hearing that the Supreme Court judges were determined to affirm their jurisdiction to review the wisdom of the federal government's decision to permit the testing of cruise missiles over Canada. The judges seemed undeterred by my able submission that the judges had neither the background expertise nor information to set Canada's priorities in terms of national security.[28] My opponent, the late Gordon Henderson, Q.C., was encouraging the rising tide of judicial activism, but he was having great difficulty in discovering just why the court felt as it did. The questions from the bench showed a number of the judges were in agreement on the result but in obvious disagreement with each other on how to get there. Henderson did not wish, by agreeing with one group, to alienate the others. He looked like a pilot trying to land a crippled Jumbo 747 under the guidance of a bunch of feuding air traffic controllers. In those circumstances, the fly-fishing metaphor doesn't apply. The best approach, which Gordon adopted, was to say as little as decently possible.

John Robinette was the master of reinforcing what he sensed to be the direction of a court when he agreed with it. Of course, he was mas-

---

26   Davis, *The Argument of an Appeal* (1940), 26 A.B.A.J. 8, 895.

27   *Operation Dismantle Inc. v. The Queen*, [1985] 1 S.C.R. 441.

28   The question, Madam Justice Wilson was later to say in her judgment, is: "I think we should focus our attention on whether the courts *should* or *must* rather than on whether they *can* deal with such matters" (at 467 [emphasis in original]). From my perspective, that was not the correct question.

ter of most aspects of appellate advocacy. I did not work with him until late in his career, and then rather briefly, but I had several appeals against him in earlier years. My impression of the great advocate is rather different from the rather sanitized, sanctified view of John Robinette that has (rightly) put him on a pedestal, according to My Lord Dubin, as our finest counsel. The source of my admiration for Mr. Robinette is quite different. I see him as the ultimate player, a kind of knuckle-dusting advocate who spent fifty years in the courts propelled by a fiercely competitive nature and a love of robing room gossip, who started in 1929 when the *Colonial Laws Validity Act* was still on our books,[29] and in 1938 argued the *Adoption Reference*, still one of the leading cases on the jurisdiction of the superior courts, when he was thirty-two years old, and finished his career more than forty-five years later arguing *Charter* cases. To me, he was Gordie Howe in a pinstripe suit. His big elbows dominated the Supreme Court every time he got there. I was told early on by my mentor, Bert MacKinnon, to watch Robinette because, of all counsel I was likely to see, he was the one whose footwork was least visible. And so it was. His submissions came out as a seamless, self-explanatory, obviously correct exposition of the facts and the law. He was always a pleasure to listen to.

Others have written about Mr. Robinette's powers of exposition and the great simplicity with which he could make highly complex arguments, and all of this is true, but I want to talk about Mr. Robinette's left jab. I referred earlier to the *Patriation Reference*, where Saskatchewan came up with this theory of substantial consent. Mr. Robinette's primary brief for the federal government was to attack the legal effect of constitutional conventions. He famously insisted that a Parliamentary resolution to the United Kingdom demanding patriation of the Constitution would have no more effect in law than would a resolution wishing the Queen a Happy Birthday. However, his antennae had quickly picked up on the court's interest in the Saskatchewan theory of substantial consent, and he grasped the potential of that theory to divide and rule his opponents in the provinces. At one point in his argument he paused theatrically, looked sorrowfully at the ranks of provincial counsel (other

---

29   *Colonial Laws Validity Act*, 1865, c. 63, did not apply to any law passed after 12 November 1931 by a Dominion or by Provinces of Canada; 1931, c. 4, ss. 2(1), 7(2), 10.

than My Lord McMurtry, who had persuaded Ontario to take a different view), and said words to the effect that while it was no part of his brief to argue the point, he simply could not refrain from observing that Saskatchewan's position knocked the Confederation pact theory of the other provinces into a "cocked hat." He was correct, of course. Substantial consent was totally inconsistent with a rule of unanimity. Having set the opposing provinces against one another, he majestically returned to his brief about constitutional convention. The judges seemed deeply impressed by the apparent spontaneity of his gesture, the fact that the dean of the Supreme Court bar simply could not bite his lip in the face of such a momentous concession by a province, even though it was no part of his brief. His aside also found its way into the final judgment.[30]

The dramatic aside is in fact a much underrated device. Its apparent spontaneity adds greatly to its impact. Anyone can do it.

Mr. Chairman, it really has nothing to do with the third Charles Dubin Lecture on Advocacy, but I just cannot help myself from referring to a wonderful old book about Irish barristers called the *Old Munster Circuit*.[31] The author recalls a trial in a rural court house in Cork. As the learned barrister makes his submission, a donkey begins to bray in the field next door. The kindly judge looks down and says, "Please, please, one at a time." The donkey brays again. The barrister, cupping his hand over his ear, replies, "I'm sorry, m'lud, could you say that again. I couldn't hear because of the echo."

I predict you will remember this dramatic aside long after the rest of this lecture is gone and forgotten.

My first sighting of the great John Robinette in the Supreme Court of Canada was in 1968. The case involved a parking garage in downtown Toronto that had collapsed in the course of construction.[32] Bert MacKinnon led for the respondent. I was his bag carrier. John Robinette acted for the appellant. His habit was to go to Ottawa at the beginning of the session and stay at the old Skyline Hotel (now the Crowne Plaza) more or less for the duration of the sittings, frequently arguing several appeals in succession.

---

30   *Patriation Reference, supra* note 21, at 905–6.

31   Maurice Healy, *Old Munster Circuit: A Book of Memories and Traditions* (London: Michael Joseph, 1929).

32   *One Hundred Simcoe St. v. Dominion Insurance Corporation*, [1969] S.C.R. v.

Mr. Robinette also argued the case ahead of us. He took out his binder, got to his feet, surveyed the bench like an orchestra conductor, metaphorically rapped the podium for attention, and began. Shortly into his submissions, which were brief, he was interrupted by the squeaky voice of Louis Philippe Pigeon J., followed by some oom pah pah from Abbott J. They were almost immediately joined by Spence J. and Hall J. descanting in and around the principal themes, adding a few bells and whistles. Judson J. remained silent, but Pigeon J. made up for it by throwing his pencil at a critical moment. After an hour or so of cacophonous argument, Chief Justice Cartwright motioned his Team Canada into silence, leaned forward, and in three or four questions highlighted the weaknesses of the appeal that Robinette had so skillfully downplayed. Robinette, with pleasing affability, faced up to the negative implications of the Chief Justice's questions. I was deeply impressed by Mr. Robinette's imperturbability — his ability to absorb punishment without any outward sign of distress. Any fool can look good as a winner, but it takes a real champion to be seen to be "kissed off " without twitching a muscle. Of course, he had achieved the ultimate status of counsel of last resort, and solicitors all across the country were anxious to unload their losers into his capable hands, looking for a miracle. More often than not, that's what he delivered for them.

Mr. Robinette's methods of positive reinforcement were not always authorized by the Marquess of Queensberry. I recall arguing a case against him in the Ontario Court of Appeal in the late 1970s.[33] It involved the constitutional applicability of municipal land use controls to the lands of the federally regulated Hamilton Harbour Commissioners. As I made what I thought were powerful points, I became conscious of the fact the judges were not looking at me but at Mr. Robinette, who was sitting majestically ahead of me in the Q.C. row, like a visiting emperor. When a judge asked a question hostile to my position, Robinette would nod his great head approvingly at this unexpected flash of brilliance from the bench. Any response on my part would be greeted by Robinette with an expression of pained disbelief. If I, of course, had carried on that way while he was speaking, at least one of the judges would have had a stroke. In terms of the John Davis fishing analogy, the tactic

---

33   *City of Hamilton v. Hamilton Harbour Commission and the Attorney General of Canada* (1979), 21 O.R. (2d) 459.

in Robinette's hands attracted judicial favour. In my hands, it would have repelled — or worse. Times change. Courts are no longer tolerant of such distractions, even from icons. But Robinette, though an icon, was a child of his times. He was not there to win Canadian Bar Association awards, or even The Advocates' Society Medal for Civility. He was there to win the case for his client.

I offer a final example of positive reinforcement. Bert MacKinnon was defending the position of a widow who was spending her late husband's money and travelling the world with a young, high-testosterone male adventurer. The testator had provided that if his wife should remarry, her financial support should be cut off and the money revert to the children of a prior marriage. So the widow simply refused to marry. The children came to court arguing that their profligate stepmother was living in a common-law marriage and that payments from the estate should therefore cease. While expressing some disapproval of the widow's conduct, the court was inclining to the view that, as a technical matter, there had been no marriage within the scope of the *dum casta* clause. They were totally unprepared when MacKinnon, a fervent Baptist with somewhat rigid moral standards, launched an explosive attack on the cold and heartless testator who had cruelly condemned his saintly widow to live in sin. MacKinnon obtained for his client not only the benefit of a technical rule of wills interpretation but, unbelievably, the moral high ground. Today, he might be accused of being an opportunistic feminist. In those days, we considered it great advocacy.

Now, what about the situation where momentum is running against you? My opinion is that there are only two ways to kill the momentum. As I mentioned earlier, either you have to persuade the judges that they've landed on the wrong question, or you've got to kill the working hypothesis. If the working hypothesis consists of a number of elements, and you can kill one of those elements, it is possible the whole thing will collapse. But you have to go one or other of those two routes.

It is usually of little use, at that stage, to start quoting case law that you consider to be in your favour. ("Listen, my lords and ladies, to what Mr. Justice Judson had to say in *Smithers v. the Prince Edward Island Potato Marketing Board* ... .") I remember arguing one appeal before the Supreme Court of Canada in which momentum began to roll against the interest of my client. The other side's argument was completely answered by a prior decision of the Supreme Court, and I made an elaborate display of having the judges take out the book of authorities and crawl through the case with me. At the conclusion of the exercise, Justice Major closed his book and said, "I think the court was having an off day." My problem was not that the citation of the case was irrelevant — because it was in fact directly on point — but that it failed to address the court's working hypothesis, which at that point was floating free of such mundane considerations as decades-old case law.

Nor is it advantageous, when you find yourself on the wrong end of the momentum, to allow your frustration to show. Years ago, I appeared for the Attorney General of Canada in the Supreme Court in a case from Newfoundland[34] involving the question of whether seals could be hunted on Sunday. Two sealing captains were charged with unlawful "killing of seals." One of them was represented by the patriarch of the Newfoundland bar, Phil Lewis.[35] Mr. Lewis, who by then looked about ninety years old, turned up in court with his "junior," who must have been close to seventy-five. I noticed that Mr. Lewis had a bloody gash in the back of his head and mentioned it to a colleague, Ed Roberts, Q.C., an irascible character who is now, implausibly, the Lieutenant Governor of Newfoundland. He suggested that perhaps Mr. Lewis had been hit by his clients with a sealing club to provide encouragement. The Newfoundland legislation that prohibited sealing on Sunday was pre-Confederation. If the prohibition could be characterized as fisheries legislation, it was federal, and post-Confederation fisheries regulations had impliedly repealed the prohibition. If, on the other hand, the pre-Confederation ban against sealing on Sunday could be seen as labour legislation, it was squarely within Newfoundland's exclusive jurisdiction to change, and Newfoundland had never changed it. Chief Justice Laskin, presiding, was showing fairly strong momentum towards the federal characterization. "Surely," he asked Lewis, "the legislation regulates all aspects of the fishery, and the prohibition against sealing on Sunday as much as any other is federal fisheries." Lewis responded, "Oh no, Mr. Chief Justice, by God, it was not!" Chief Justice Laskin, taken aback by Lewis's vehemence, asked why he was so sure. "Because, by God," Mr. Lewis roared, "I was in the legislature in 1931 when it was last before the House of

---

34   *Moore v. Attorney General of Newfoundland*, [1982] 1 S.C.R. 115.
35   The other accused was represented by Tom Heintzman, Q.C.

Assembly." Lewis's outburst was great theatre, and it was responsive to Chief Justice Laskin's "working hypothesis." But in the eye of Milt Harradence's "chilly autocrats," it proved to be ineffectual.

We saw a similarly misguided intervention in the recent *Firearms Reference*.[36] Momentum was running against the provincial challenge. A young lawyer from Alberta delivered an incendiary address that had little to do with the ongoing legal argument. At the adjournment, he apparently left the courtroom and threw himself in front of the nation's television cameras. He was reported in the papers the next day as having said that if you can't make law, make the news.

Let me now give you some examples where the court's momentum was skillfully reversed using the strategy I have suggested. In *R. v. Sheppard*,[37] a recent decision of our court, we affirmed the obligation of trial judges in criminal cases to give sufficient reasons to permit an appellate court to adjudge the correctness of the lower-court decision. The Crown was making considerable headway with its *in terrorem* argument that in the busy provincial courts, where a judge might hear dozens of cases a day, the delivery of considered reasons was a luxury for which Provincial Court judges had neither the time nor the resources. The Crown's appeal to judicial sympathy was attracting a considerable level of judicial support. Defence counsel rose to his feet and met the issue head on. He declared the issue of judicial resources to be a red herring. He said he had managed to sum up the defence in about two pages of transcript and the Crown attorney had taken a fraction of that, and surely no less should be expected of the judge himself. Here is how the Newfoundland advocate, Mr. Richard S. Rogers, put the matter:

> In this case, it took myself and the Crown probably no more than two minutes — two to three minutes each, to give our summation of what we had just seen in this trial. Would it have been that difficult for Provincial Court Judge Barnable to do so likewise? I don't think so.[38]
>
> ...
>
> What harm or damage truly would be caused by invoking a responsibility upon a judge to give reasons? I really find no difficulty with

<hr>

36   *Reference re Firearms Act* (Can.), [2000] 1 S.C.R. 783.
37   *R. v. Sheppard*, 2002 SCC 26, released 21 March 2002.
38   Transcript of oral proceedings, 21 June 2001, at 35.

that. If I was a judge, I would find no difficulty giving reasons. I have to say that. As a defence lawyer, when I stand up, I have no difficulty giving a summation. If I did not give a summation in a case, I would be truly pressed by my client for an explanation: why did you not do a summation, Mr. Rogers? And likewise, I think that it's incumbent upon a judge to give an explanation.[39]

Instead of dancing about the fringes of the debate with secondary points, Mr. Rogers had launched his attack on the foundation of the Crown's argument and confronted the emerging working hypothesis of some members of the court. He reframed the question. He reworked the hypothesis. The Crown's point was how much justice could we afford. Defence counsel reversed the momentum by arguing that in most cases, there should be no significant cost at all. The question, correctly framed, was not lack of judicial resources but whether lack of reasons should be allowed effectively to preclude meaningful appellate review.

I refer again to the importance of oral argument. Positive reinforcement by an advocate in full flight has an impact out of all proportion to the impact of exactly the same information in writing. The human voice has a unique power to drive home the point. In the Supreme Court, moments after you stop speaking, the judges withdraw to the conference room to thrash through the issues. The freshest input into their deliberations is what you have just said in oral argument.

The working hypothesis can be attacked by any means at your disposal. Change the pace of the hearing. Take the judges through the critical evidence line by line. Pressed for time, it is tempting to just refer the court to the testimony or authority to be read "at your leisure." Such an off-hand comment is not enough. (It may also demonstrate an overly innocent view of what judges do "at their leisure.") A vague reference doesn't do anything to restrain the momentum of judges who are about to plunge into their conference a few minutes later.

In the Supreme Court argument on the 1999 *Donald Marshall* case, to give another example, the issue was whether a 1761 treaty entered into by the Micmac Indians with the British did or did not include a limited commercial fishing right. Although the surrounding negotiations clear-

---

39   *Ibid.* at 39.

ly suggested that it did, the treaty provisions themselves, drawn up by the British, were not explicit on the point. The treaty did explicitly confer a trading right, but the question was did the treaty *implicitly* confirm the prior negotiations to include a right to gather fish to have something to trade with? The working hypothesis of some members of the court was that if the treaty didn't spell out the fishing right, it wasn't there. The working hypothesis, however, overlooked key portions of the evidence, in particular, the admission of the Crown's chief expert that as a historian familiar with all the negotiations, a limited commercial fishing right was indeed implicit in the treaty. Such key evidence might count for nothing unless it is laid on the court with the power of a two-by-four at the critical juncture. Here is what the Crown witness had said:

> The Expert: Ah, right. I think the implication here is that there is a *right to trade* under a certain form of regulation —
>
> Counsel: Yes.
>
> The Expert: — that's laid down. And if you're [i.e., the defence is] saying *right to fish*, I've assumed that in recognizing the Micmac by treaty, the British were recognizing them as the people they were. They understood how they lived and that that meant that these people had a right to live in Nova Scotia in their traditional ways. And, to me, that *implies* that the British were accepting that the Micmac would continue to be a hunting and gathering people, that they would fish, that they would hunt to support themselves. I don't see any problem with that.
>
> It seems to me that *that's implicit* in the thing [i.e., the treaty]. Even though it doesn't say it, and I know that there seems to, in the twentieth century, be some reluctance to see the value of the 1760 and 1761 treaties because they're not so explicit on these matters, but I personally don't see the hang-up. Because it strikes me that there is a recognition that the Micmac are a people and they have the right to exist. And that has — carries certain implications with it.[40]

Such testimony, preferably read aloud line by line with dramatic emphasis, constitutes good reply because it targets the "working hypothesis" advocated by the Crown. It confronts the source of the momentum.

---

40   *R. v. Marshall*, [1999] 3 S.C.R. 456, at 488–89 (emphasis in original).

The questions and the expert's answers were ultimately reproduced in the majority judgment of the court.

Sometimes humour can be used to knock the momentum out of a court or tribunal. I recall that in the Sinclair Stevens Inquiry, where the late John Sopinka was acting for Stevens, a question arose with respect to the admissibility of certain evidence. Chief Justice William Parker, the commissioner, made it clear that he proposed to admit the evidence. Sopinka, always quick on his feet, said: "Well, if Your Lordship lets in this testimony, I'm going to have to add a new chapter to my book on evidence." The commissioner was sufficiently taken aback by this outrageous suggestion to reserve his ruling. I forget the eventual outcome, but I suspect that, after sleeping on the issue overnight, the commissioner gave Stevens the benefit of the doubt.

More recently, a defence counsel from British Columbia was attempting to hold an acquittal against the momentum created by the Crown's onslaught and began her respondent's submission as follows:

> My friend seems to agree that everyone is entitled to a reasonable doubt but he is wrong to suggest that in this case it should be given to the police.

It was an effective counter-thrust because it brushed aside secondary issues and ridiculed the Crown's working hypothesis. If believed, it would effectively destroy the Crown's case. If rejected, it would still probably win some favour with the judges for having brought a little sunshine into their day.

The Epiphany

I come now to the final stage of counsel's job, what I have called the epiphany, when all is made manifest. Your parting shot should bring the whole case into focus. Building on the written submissions and hours (or days) of oral argument, the judges look to you, in the name of the gods of advocacy, to state your winning point. The key to all aspects of oral advocacy is focus, but nowhere is focus more important than in your concluding submissions.

It is unfortunately no longer fashionable to offer a peroration. Perhaps no one since Joe Sedgwick, Q.C., has rolled out his Shakespeare in the dying moments of a criminal appeal. This is a pity, particularly if the appeal deals with human rights or civil liberties as opposed to collapsed parking garages.

My Lord Dubin, acting for the defence, orchestrated many epiphanies. In the great case of *R. v. Horsburgh*,[41] an ordained minister in southwestern Ontario had been convicted of contributing to acts of juvenile delinquency, namely sexual intercourse among teenagers attending some very popular social activities at his church. The case created an outcry in the press, and there was little sympathy for the defence. The case was lost at trial; it was lost again at the Court of Appeal; it was finally won in the Supreme Court of Canada because Mr. Dubin was able to get the judges to see beyond a narrow technical point about the need for corroboration under the *Juvenile Delinquents Act*. He elevated the stakes to the survival of the rule of law itself. He incited Justice Martland to thunder that even a vilified clergyman arraigned on sensational sex charges was "entitled to receive the same protection, in relation to the evidence of accomplices, as he would be entitled to receive in relation to any other charge."[42] The case had all the hallmarks of a Charles Dubin appeal. Not only was the court persuaded to ask the right question (lack of corroboration), but the defence of an allegedly wayward clergyman had been transformed into righteous indignation against the misplaced morality of an outraged community.

Mr. Dubin did it again on the less glamorous issue of corporate governance in *Canadian Aero Service Ltd. v. O'Malley*.[43] Some senior employees had taken for themselves a commercial opportunity they were supposed to be negotiating for their employer. Charles Dubin appeared for the wronged corporation. He lost at trial. He lost again at the Ontario Court of Appeal. It wasn't until he emerged into the sunlit uplands of the Supreme Court of Canada that reason finally prevailed.

Justice Bora Laskin's call in that case for corporate ethics rings as true today in the age of Enron and Worldcom as it did when first written almost thirty years ago. The courts, wrote Justice Laskin, must evolve the doctrines of equity as

> ... a necessary supplement, in the public interest, [to] statutory regulation and accountability which themselves are, at one and the same

---

41   [1967] S.C.R. 746.

42   *Ibid.*, at 758.

43   [1974] S.C.R. 592.

time, an acknowledgment of the importance of the corporation in the life of the community and of the need to compel obedience by it and by its promoters, directors and managers to norms of exemplary behaviour.[44]

Again, in Mr. Dubin's hands, the case was no longer about a lost job opportunity for aerial photography in Brazil; it was no longer a matter of interpreting dry provisions of the *Business Corporations Act*; it had become nothing less than the last chance to salvage the very pillars of corporate governance in Canada.

It is, I think, the highest role and function of the advocate to lift the court out of the humdrum detail of the law, to focus the appeal on some higher objective. One of the finest examples I know is the closing address of Robert Jackson,[45] a judge of the United States Supreme Court, who took a leave of absence to prosecute at the Nuremburg War Crimes Tribunal. The defence of the various accused had made some headway with blaming superior orders and had exposed uncertainty in the lines of Nazi authority and responsibility. There was such confusion about who had given what orders at what time and to what effect that perhaps no one was responsible for anything. To address this dodging of personal responsibility, Justice Jackson reviewed the facts in great detail and concluded as follows:

> It is against such a background that these defendants now ask this Tribunal to say that they are not guilty of planning, executing or conspiring to commit this long list of crimes and wrongs. They stand before the record of this trial, as bloodstained Gloucester stood by the body of his slain King.
>
> He begged of the widow as they beg of you, "Say I slew them not."
> And the Queen replied, "Then say they were not slain. But dead they are."
>
> If you were to say of these men that they are not guilty, it would be as true that there has been no war, there are no slain, there has been no crime.[46]

---

44   *Ibid.* at 610.

45   Robert Jackson was a U.S. Supreme Court Justice from 1941 until his death in 1954. He served as prosecutor at the Nuremburg War Crimes Tribunal while he was a Supreme Court Justice.

46   <www.law.umkc.edu/faculty/projects/ftrials/nuremberg/nuremberg.htm>.

There are those who dispute the accuracy of his Shakespeare,[47] but there is no denying that the poetry and power of his peroration lifted the whole argument above the level of facts and precedents to a high imperative of moral responsibility. The arguments of Jackson and his colleagues at Nuremburg changed the course of legal history and are the basis of such institutions as the International War Crimes Tribunal at The Hague, and the emerging International Criminal Court. Similar arguments have lifted the Supreme Court of Canada over the years, on everything from the presumption of innocence to the horrors of interjurisdictional legislative delegation. The ability to distill the ultimate meaning of a case, to draw out the important lessons, to show that your cause is greater than its immediate facts, and, if possible, to occupy the moral high ground; all of this, in my view, is what oral advocacy at its highest level is all about.

Conclusion

I conclude on a personal note. Oral advocacy is a sort of cerebral war game. It is also entertainment. Moreover, of all the cerebrally entertaining adult war games, it is one of the best paid.

However, as we know, there is a dark side. The highs are emotionally very high and the lows are sometimes devastating. Young advocates

---

47   William Shakespeare, *Richard III*, Act 1, Scene 2, ll. 88–92. The original reads as follows:

GLOUCESTER: Say that I slew them not?

ANNE: Why, then they are not dead:
But dead they are, and, devilish slave, by thee.

GLOUCESTER: I did not kill your husband.

ANNE: Why, then he is alive.

Quibblers will notice that Jackson erred in his attribution. Lady Anne was not yet queen. Her late husband was the Lancastrian heir, Prince Edward. She later became queen when she married Richard III (then the Yorkist, Gloucester). The quibble only increases my admiration for Jackson's speech. The lines from a half-remembered high school literature class probably floated through his brain as he sat in a Nuremburg hotel room with no accessible works of reference (except perhaps a Gideon Bible).

sometimes despair of managing the highs and the lows. They can't sleep. They say there's not much point in learning the skills of a great advocate by the age of thirty-four if, like Mozart, you're dead at thirty-five.

Some colleagues do die young, unfortunately. But we have, as Exhibit "A" for the defence, My Lord Dubin, still cherubic at eighty-one. John Robinette was about the same age when he argued the *Ontario Separate School Fund Case* in the Supreme Court. Brendan O'Brien, at ninety-two, is still going strong.

How do they do it? How do you not only avoid dying young but go on like My Lord Dubin to become *Charles Le Grand?* How do you prosper for four score years and more and have a series of exceptional advocacy lectures named in your honour? Their secret, I think, is the advice given by Governor Anne Richards of Texas in a speech at the height of the Clinton impeachment crisis, when she turned up at a dinner with the anguished President and bellowed at him — "MOVE ON! GET OVER IT!"

Good advice to advocates. Don't brood. Get on with it!

You can't carry the burden of your present caseload plus the accumulated weight of all of your previous courtroom disasters. Remember that we all experience stomach-churning despair. It is the glue that binds members of the Bar together.

My personal recipe was to allow myself one night (or maybe two in the case of a real catastrophe) to curse the darkness, to lie on the floor listing well-founded grievances against both the judges and my victorious opponent, perhaps seeking diversion in getting myself thrashed in a game or two of squash (part of the McCarthy Tétrault ethos), then to savour a sauna or a double Scotch while ruminating on all the points I had intended to make and forgot.

I would fondly repeat to myself Brian Kelsey's dictum: "Relax, sometimes you get the benefit of their stupidity."

Eventually I might think of Charles Dubin being kissed off by the trial division in *Horsburgh* and *O'Malley*, kissed off by the Court of Appeal in both those cases, but gathering his energy to fight again another day. A consoling feature of litigation is that you can lose every battle but the last.

Even with respect to that final battle in the Supreme Court, I might think of the great Robinette and the case of the collapsed parking garage. When his appeal was dismissed from the bench, he closed his book, put it to one side — that was the end of it. Not a twitch flickered across that leonine brow. He was the product of a lifetime of moving on.

Go thou and do likewise.

[This article first appeared in the Spring 2003 issue of *The Advocates' Society Journal*.]

The Argument of a Case at Trial

Justice William J. Anderson[*]

Speaking broadly, and speaking relatively, cases at trial are not well argued. I say broadly because there are certainly exceptions; I can recall a number in the last ten years. I say relatively because effective argument on motions, applications, and appeals is not nearly as rare. This criticism is not based alone on experience on the bench but includes a preceding period of thirty years at the Bar, during which I must confess to having been responsible for a good many arguments of the rambling, ineffectual, and inconclusive kind that I now find so eminently distressing, and susceptible of apt description only in language unsuited to a learned periodical.

Before turning to a cure, some analysis of the origins and nature of the disease is in order. On a motion, application, or appeal, the argument is the main course. It is only one part of a trial, coming at the end and preceded by other elements that take their toll of the time and energies of counsel and may seem more pressing and important. The date of commencement of a trial is frequently uncertain and often comes suddenly and at an inconvenient time. Witnesses must be corralled and cosseted, and their putative knowledge of the events given a final review and testing. Pleadings develop last minute gaps and frailties. All this before the first question is put to the first witness.

---

*   Mr. Justice William J. Anderson, the Supreme Court of Ontario.

Then there is the day-to-day pressure of getting in the evidence, with all the problems of examination-in-chief and cross-examination, dealing with the ill-founded objections and improper questions emanating from opposing counsel, and occasional intervention from the bench. Then, at a point as dismally difficult to predict as its opening, it all ends, and it is time for argument. So what's one to do about it? And believe me, something should be done. It is an aspect of great importance to your success at the trial level. Trial judges harbour a suspicion, which is not without foundation, that cases are often better argued on the appeal than they were at trial. It should always be borne in mind that appeal will not in every case make good a loss at trial. There is much to be said for winning on the first round, and in doing so a good argument is valuable.

First, start early to prepare your submissions. There is no reason why an outline cannot be made before the trial even opens. Such an outline can be of value to the organization and coherent presentation of the evidence. Prepare a chronology of material events, required in virtually every case, in greater or less detail as the nature of the case may require; of which and its uses, more anon. Analyse what are the salient issues of fact and law in the case. Examine and re-examine the pleadings to see whether they adequately reflect the issues. A case changes emphasis as it progresses, and surgery from time to time will be necessary to adapt your outline to these changes. But it should leave you at the end with a number of pegs, in a logical arrangement, upon which to hang your final submissions.

Even the best of advance efforts may leave you, at the critical moment, less adequately prepared than you would wish. If so, do not hesitate to say so, and to ask some time to prepare. Speaking only for myself (a time-honoured judicial caveat and disclaimer), I seldom refuse such a request, if reasonable at all. I am moved not by solicitude for counsel, though I try not to add to their burdens, but by pure self-interest. I want all the help I can get. There is an incredibly widespread failure on the part of counsel to appreciate the extent to which the bench is dependent on the Bar, and a fuming sense of irritation, dissatisfaction, and frustration of a judge who is left to resolve a case on ill-considered, half-baked, and inconclusive arguments. There is an inclination to say, *sotto voce*: "A plague on both your houses." Most trials are fact-finding exercises, and facts should have priority in your considerations. This is a generalization with attendant inevitable inaccuracy; but I stick to it though I recognize that some cases also involve questions of law. In any event, a case lost at trial for frailty in treatment of the law can be resurrected elsewhere; a case lost on the facts is usually history. So, tell the judge in words of one syllable what findings of fact you seek, and the evidence upon which, in your submission, such findings may be made. Failure to do so is, to me, a constant source of rancorous surprise.

Whether that phase of the argument precedes or follows your outline of the law will depend on the nature of the case, but whether it precedes or follows, do not, for the love of heaven and of your own success and prosperity, omit to do it. Some counsel are apparently under the impression that explicit submissions as to findings of fact trespass, in some way, on the territory of the judge. Not so. All argument is made to tell the judge how the case should be decided and, if conventionally offered in the language of deference, will give no offence, whether directed to fact or law.

At the opening of your argument, and perhaps again at closing, tell the judge, in the simplest, plainest, narrowest terms you can, what your case is really about. This should be a set piece, written out after careful thought; of the set piece, more later. The need to do this is widely understood, but the practice ill accords with the understanding. I hope and trust that it is only the querulous suspicion of advancing age that leads me not infrequently to the conclusion that the reason counsel don't tell what it is all about is because they don't know. Most cases, when surplusage is pared away, resolve themselves into a relatively small number of issues that are frequently not very complicated. Endeavour with all your intelligence and energy to know what they are, and put them to the judge accordingly.

If you have analysed your case as suggested above, your argument will easily and almost inevitably deal in understandable terms with each of the salient points. The great counsel are ones who trust their judgment as to what those salient points are, and press the argument accordingly. Remember that, whatever illusions may exist to the contrary, judges are busy people, and it is a sad fact that only a finite amount of time and effort can be devoted to your case. Make sure that the time and effort are applied where it counts and not frittered away in separating the fly-specks from the pepper.

In dealing with the facts, start with those that are admitted or not really in issue, and progress from there to those that are in dispute and to the bases upon which, in your submissions, a finding in your favour should be made. Most judges start with the undisputed facts and test the probabilities of conflicting evidence in the light of those facts. Vague generalizations about credibility are seldom helpful; in that area the judge indeed walks alone.

If there are real conflicts or improbabilities, substantial grounds for assailing the reliability of a witness, by all means raise them; but if in doubt, don't. Making findings of fact on conflicting evidence is one of the most difficult and least congenial responsibilities of a trial judge, but in its discharge counsel can render only limited assistance. Efforts to besmirch all the adverse testimony bespeak the amateur or the incompetent at the Bar. Try to be positive and accurate in your submissions as to what the evidence was. Sometimes critical testimony has the most force in the *ipsissima verba* of the witness. Court reporters are usually willing and able to transcribe a passage very quickly.

Do not omit, at some point in your argument, a clear statement of the result you seek. For a plaintiff it should be susceptible of accomplishment by reference to the statement of claim. If it is not, you may need an amendment and should seek it at the earliest possible moment. If it pertains only to the prayer for relief it will usually be granted, unless it is so substantial as to skew the whole action.

In any but the simplest case I advise counsel at the beginning that I want from them, as soon as possible but in any event no later than the commencement of argument, two documents already alluded to in these paragraphs: a chronology and a memorandum of fact and law. For the first I have a form that I ask be followed, showing, in columnar form:

Date	Event	Document or Exhibit (if applicable)

I suggest that counsel seek to agree on a common submission; otherwise, that each submit one and I will reconcile differences. I find such a chronology an indispensable aid in delivering reasons for judgment, and I am in no way diffident about asking for it. Counsel who is properly prepared will already have one that can readily be put in my form, and counsel who is not will benefit greatly from the exercise of preparing one.

The memorandum of fact and law is intended to be brief and simple — little more than a copy of the set piece that I have suggested counsel should have for purposes of argument. If it comes in more extended and elaborate form, I will not protest. The reason I wish to have this is because I find it helpful to have the basic submissions of counsel in their own words, rather than be dependent on my notes. Most judges develop a reasonable degree of competence in note-taking, but reliability is never free from doubt.

It is of great assistance if counsel can agree on a common volume containing all the cases to which each will make reference. It avoids having different citations for the same case and facilitates reference for all concerned. I, at any rate, colour code my volume as passages are referred to by counsel, and sometimes make notes on it as well, and it is preferable that all be in the same report.

A word about documents, although it does not relate strictly to argument. These are generally pretty well handled now by all but the incorrigibly inept, but quite frequently the books of documents are not produced in a sufficient number of copies. There should be one for each counsel, one to form part of the record (which can also serve witnesses while testifying), and one for the judge to use as a working document. This I find to be of great value, both during the trial and while preparing to give judgment. In a complicated case, an extra document book and case book for the use of the court reporter will make you a friend in a quarter where friendship is valuable.

Years ago I was much assisted by an experienced counsel with whom I had the good fortune to appear in many cases. He said, apropos of the preparation of a factum, "Always remember, Bill, what you are trying to do is to write the judgment." That advice, slightly changed in emphasis, will serve to conclude these suggestions of mine. If parts of your argument find reflection in the judgment you will probably not have a byline, but you may find consolation in winning the case.

[This article first appeared in the December 1987 issue of *The Advocates' Society Journal*.]

The Conduct of a Non-jury Civil Trial

*Justice William J. Anderson**

[Editors' note: This paper was presented by the Honourable William J. Anderson to a judicial seminar on 20 April 1993, on the occasion of his retirement from the Ontario Court of Justice. It was published with the consent and concurrence of Chief Justice Callaghan.]

There is a saying about advertising, attributed to various magnates in the field of retailing, which goes something like this: "I know half of it is wasted. The trouble is, I never know which half."

When I was a young lawyer I was assiduous in attending sessions devoted to professional self-improvement-sessions put on by the Bar Association, the Law Society, and various groups in the United States. Gradually, a measure of disillusionment set in: I found that a great deal of the time so spent was wasted. I listened to advice I had heard before; I listened to advice that had no bearing on what I did; I was exposed to techniques that I just knew would not work for me. Before I became entirely disillusioned, however, two things became apparent to me. The first was that from almost every such exercise I came away with one or two ideas or techniques that were new to me, were valuable, and were such as I might never have discovered or developed on my own. The sec-

* Mr. Justice William J. Anderson, the Supreme Court of Ontario.

ond — less often, but now and then — was that I came away with a heightened measure of self-confidence, based on the fact that the luminaries who were conducting the courses did not seem to know anything I did not know. So I continued to attend such sessions with the knowledge that much the same thing could be said of them as was said of advertising: half the time was wasted.

I am sure that much of what follows will be already known to you, and that what has worked for me will not necessarily work for you. But perhaps some suggestions will prove useful, and perhaps you will leave, heartened by saying to yourself: he's survived for quite a while without being impeached, and he doesn't know anything I don't know.

And perhaps, in any event, it is a useful thing, once in a while, to review the fundamentals of our calling.

Introduction

This article assumes that the pre-trials have all been concluded, that settlement negotiations have been exhausted, and that the case is to be tried. It does not address the role of the judge as mediator or the intervention of the judge, in the course of trial, to attempt to bring about a settlement. It has been prepared with fairly long trials in contemplation, but the basic techniques do not vary greatly.

Preparation

Try to get the record a reasonable length of time in advance of the opening date of the trial: for a trial commencing on a Monday, I like to have it not later than the afternoon of the Friday preceding.

I first make sure that I have no conflicts. As one's time on the bench lengthens, the probability of conflicts diminishes, but the possibility always exists. The sooner a conflict is discovered, the better. It produces much inconvenience if discovered at the opening of the trial, or worse still, after it is under way. If a conflict appears, I first assess it myself, without help. If I feel the least bit uncomfortable, my rule is simple: if in doubt, get out. If I myself feel that there is no difficulty but that someone else might have a different perception, I raise the matter with counsel at the earliest opportunity. Usually, the problem goes away in the course of discussion. If it does not, I revert to my rule: if in doubt, get out.

I next read the record with a view to assimilating the issues that are disclosed and identifying the role of the various parties. In this latter respect, in a complex action, I sometimes find that a simple diagram is helpful, tracing the claims, cross-claims, and counter-claims, and showing the relationship of the parties to the subject matter of the action. If it appears from the pleadings that a substantial issue of law is raised, and if it deals with an area that is unfamiliar to me (the field is vast), I try to look at a textbook treatment of the subject so that I will have at least a vague idea of what questions may be involved.

At the opening of the trial, I have counsel identify the main issues. I seek to ascertain whether as a result of production and discovery, pre-trial, and so on, any of the issues that appear on the pleadings have been resolved. If any have, I try to get a clear statement for the record from counsel, and also try to make sure that I have it correct in my bench book. At this stage, competent counsel will move for any necessary amendments, and the inquiry may flush out any necessary motions even if counsel are less than competent. It also draws the attention of counsel to something often overlooked: that the pleadings define the issues that the judge will try. Some counsel seem to think of the pleadings as purely interlocutory matters to be largely forgotten by the time the trial commences, rather than as the basic skeleton of the action. If there are issues of law that are unfamiliar to me (after my sneak peek at a textbook), I have counsel enlarge on them.

I inquire whether the estimate of time that has been made by the pre-trial judge and endorsed on the record remains realistic (to the extent that any such estimates are ever realistic) and, if not, to determine what is the present estimate.

I canvass what arrangements have been made for handling documentary evidence: have books of documents been prepared; do they go in on consent; what is the extent of the agreement as to their effect when they do go in? I like to have a set of documents for myself (apart from the one that comprises the official record of the court) so that I can make markings and notes on it, and if I have a law clerk working with me, I like to have one for the law clerk.

I establish the hours during which I propose to sit. I inquire whether counsel anticipate any difficulty with the attendance of witnesses and, if so, whether the sequence and timing of the trial is likely to be affected.

I tell counsel that I would like to have from each of them two documents for my assistance in dealing with the case: a chronology and a factum. As well as making the request orally, either in court or in chambers, I give them a memorandum outlining the request (Appendix A-1). I have little diffidence in asking for the chronology (Appendix A-2). Competent counsel will have one (in some form) in their working papers, and the sooner incompetent counsel prepare one, the better.

In asking for the factum I do have a measure of diffidence, but in time have overcome it. (Some of my detractors say I have a talent for overcoming diffidence.) It adds something to the burden of counsel, but if it is kept brief the added burden should not be onerous. In my view, the rules are deficient in not requiring it. In almost any other proceeding of consequence, the rules provide for a written statement by counsel outlining the substance of the case from the perspective of the party represented. But in a trial — a basic and vital element in any case — a judge must make do with bench notes, with all their frailties. It is of great assistance in giving reasons for judgment to have counsel's own words, not your paraphrase. Although I recognize that counsel expend some time in preparing a memorandum, with some consequent expense to the litigants, I believe it is justified by the contribution it makes to an accurate disposition of the case.

During the Trial

The extent of my intervention in the conduct of a trial varies in inverse ratio to the competence of counsel. In a trial being conducted by competent counsel, I intervene very little, seldom other than to make a ruling when a ruling is required. More than three centuries ago, Francis Bacon said, "An over-speaking judge is no well-tuned cymbal." This terse observation has lost none of its force over the years. Under our system, the conduct of the trial should rest primarily with counsel. That said, however, it must always be remembered that the ultimate responsibility for its conduct lies with the judge. This dictates that when counsel are less than competent, a judge must be vigilant to keep aberrations to a minimum.

From the outset, I seek to impress on everyone (starting with my deputy) that court will open on time and that any recess will not exceed its stipulated duration. The first I do because I think it creates a poor impression on everyone, particularly the litigants and other members of the public, if the opening of court is not prompt. The second I do because the amount of time that can be wasted by twenty-minute recesses, extending to half an hour or more, has to be seen to be believed. (Some of you will remember a former Chief Justice of the High Court with whom a twenty-minute recess could easily last upwards of an hour. There was also a judge who said, of opening court: "When I come into the courtroom, it's ten o'clock, no matter what anyone's watch may say.")

When an objection is taken to the admissibility of evidence, rule clearly, firmly, and, if possible, promptly. I say "if possible" because I do not think one should be inhibited from taking a few minutes, if necessary, to consider a complicated and perhaps vital ruling. I often find that a few minutes walking quietly up and down in the corridor outside the courtroom is much more conducive to arriving at a proper conclusion than seeking to do so while sitting on the bench with everyone looking at me. For any but the most cursory and elementary ruling, some brief reasons should be given.

Avoid the tendency, all too common in non-jury trials, to let everything in, with the intention of sorting it out at the end. To do so will prolong the trial, and sorting it out at the end may be overlooked (I may forget that it was admitted subject to objection) or prove to be more difficult and less satisfactory at that stage than if done when it should have been done. I do not mean to imply that there are not situations in which it is appropriate to admit evidence subject to objection, only that it should be the exception. Where the evidence may be vitally important and admissibility is in real doubt, it may be more satisfactory to admit it subject to objection. A new trial may be avoided. But if this is done, and the evidence becomes critical to the judgment, you must make clear then whether or not you are admitting it as evidence in the case.

There is an excellent article by Ed Ratushny, entitled "Basic Problems in Examination and Cross-examination" [(1974), 52 Canadian Bar Review]. It contains compendious sections on, for example, leading questions, refreshing memory, and hostile and adverse witnesses. On specific points, especially the use of prior statements, it should be brought up to date to include recent enlightenment by the Supreme Court of Canada. However, it remains a useful summary of the topics comprised in the title.

If clearly inadmissible evidence is being led without objection, intervene. Counsel may fail to object through failure to recognize the impropriety, or, less frequently, for tactical reasons. Regardless of what counsel do or do not do, it is the responsibility of the trial judge to assure that only relevant evidence goes into the record.

I terminate, politely, but promptly and firmly, any tendency to verbal exchanges between counsel. I am told that this, and other aberrant behaviour, mostly among young lawyers, is the result of watching television. I can offer no informed opinion as to that, but I do not tolerate it. Counsel should be heard in a courtroom only when questioning a witness or when making submissions to the bench.

If you are in doubt about the direction some evidence is taking, do not hesitate to ask for enlightenment. Different counsel will react differently to such a request. A common ploy (which most of us used at one time or another) is for counsel to say, "If Your Lordship will only allow me to proceed for a few moments, the relevance will become clear." Counsel are entitled to reasonable latitude, but that is a string that you should not allow to be played too often or too long. If it appears necessary, do not hesitate to have the witness stand down, or even leave the courtroom, while counsel explains where the evidence is leading. Usually the time spent in such an inquiry is more than justified.

Opinion evidence can be a quagmire and is increasingly a problem, as the categories of "experts" seem never to be closed. Another article could be devoted to this subject alone. In the context of this article, I think it appropriate to touch on only two areas: the expert report and the facts upon which the expert opinion rests.

The underpinning of the report is rule 53.03, and there is frequently skirmishing over whether a report was served in a timely fashion. I do not propose to discuss that. A more difficult area is the extent to which an expert can expand and amplify his report. Some guidance is to be found in *Thorogood v. Bowden* (1978), 21 O.R. (2d) 385 (C.A.), which indicates that an expert is not to be too narrowly confined to the contents of the report, but may not open up a new field. As in many similar situations, the touchstone is fairness and the absence of prejudice to the other party. I incline to view this question pretty narrowly. Examination, and more particularly cross-examination, of experts is notoriously time-consuming, and frequently the harvest from the time spent is meagre, so the ambit should not be enlarged without good reason.

A second area of difficulty concerns the facts upon which an expert opinion is based. Usually, the report (prepared before the trial) will be predicated upon certain assumptions of fact. These are then put to the witness in the form of a hypothetical question. The facts contained in the hypothetical question must be established by other evidence. Ideally, such evidence is led before the expert witness is called. In this, as in many areas of life, the ideal state does not always prevail. In a proper case, where there is a need for it (for example, because of problems with the availability of witnesses), the expert evidence can be heard on an undertaking to prove the underlying facts that are not already in evidence. Such cases should be avoided, if possible, and in any event kept to a minimum. There are two potential problems: the evidence may not in the end be forthcoming, or — more common and more difficult — it may not be just as the hypothetical question contemplated. Either can create an untidy result.

There is sometimes a brouhaha as to whether the report is to be filed as an exhibit. Strictly speaking, the expert should testify, *viva voce*, in the same manner as other witnesses, and the report does not become an exhibit unless referred to in cross-examination, in which case counsel who called the expert can ask that it be filed. In current practice, many counsel neither know nor care about the proper procedure, and the report is often filed in examination-in-chief, without objection. If no one else objects, I don't. It usually gives a reasonable summary of the expert's opinion.

Protect witnesses from excessive or abusive cross-examination. (This obligation is spelled out in rule 53.01(2).) For many, indeed probably for most, witnesses, giving evidence is a traumatic experience. A feeling that the judge is there to help and protect them does something to make the process easier. However, you should not intervene if, by legitimate cross-examination, a witness is in trouble. In my view, a judge should seldom ask questions of a witness, and only when a good reason and a clear necessity appears. Once more, the primary responsibility is on counsel, and the over-speaking judge is a menace as well as a nuisance. Counsel may have had good reason for leaving some topic unexplored and will not thank the judge for blundering around in it. I make a practice of thanking each witness when he or she leaves the box. We should all remember, counsel and judges alike, that without witnesses the system simply could not function, and that they are sometimes put to great inconvenience and shown scant courtesy.

This is as good a place as any for some observation, no doubt of a highly personal nature, concerning manners in court. We live in an unmannerly age, but a courtroom is a formal setting, and form comprehends manners. I have always deeply treasured the following words of Edmund Burke:

> Manners are of more importance than laws. Upon them in great measure the laws depend. The law touches us here and there and now and then. Manners are what vex or soothe, corrupt or purify, exalt or debase, barbarize or refine us by a constant, steady, uniform, insensible operation like that of the air we breathe.

We all know that litigation is a contentious business and that a trial is not a tea party; neither should it be a bear garden. In large measure, the judge sets the tone of the courtroom by his or her deportment and the manner in which counsel, witnesses, and the court staff are treated. Courtesy is a virtue that induces reciprocity. In large measure, we receive back what we show forth.

Counsel and witnesses are entitled to the same courtesy from the judge that the judge expects from them. Rude conduct by a judge is the ultimate in discourtesy, because it is inflicted on persons who are not in a position to reply in kind. It frequently bespeaks the disposition of a bully. It is usually shown to young and inexperienced counsel. When I was a young lawyer, there were ogres on the bench, man-eating trolls, but I do not remember much abuse being offered to T.N. Phelan, Arthur Slaght, or Frederick Gardiner, to name only a few. Offering abuse to them was just too hazardous. Their response would be couched in the language of deference, but the message would be clear. Rude treatment of counsel is not only discourtesy, it is also rank ingratitude and stupidity. No one but a judge fully realizes how important is the role of counsel and what assistance they can provide. Even if one finds their performance less than adequate in some cases, it behooves us to remember that some litigant has entrusted his or her cause to that counsel.

Counsel have a right to be heard; the right of audience defines the essential status of the barrister, and the right of audience implies the right to be heard: to be heard, I may add, without unreasonable interruption and with an honest and consistent effort at comprehension by the judge. One should always remember that the litigants are usually present in court and will form a most unfavourable opinion of the process if their counsel is badgered or ignored. The late J. Keiler McKay was not a conspicuously great lawyer, but he was a superb trial judge. In part, that was because he had a fund of shrewd common sense and a lively capacity to assess people. Even more important, however, in his stature as a judge, was the dignity that he brought to his courtroom and the unfailing courtesy extended to everyone in that courtroom. No one ever left it feeling that the case had not been fully and fairly heard.

An article in a recent issue of the *Law Society of Upper Canada Gazette* (vol. 25, no. 3, Sept./Dec. 1992), by an Alberta lawyer, is entitled "Judicial Misbehaviour: How Should a Lawyer Handle It?" You may not agree with all of it, but the very fact that it is written and published is a reproach to our calling. I would like to think that such occurrences as the article discusses were unknown in Ontario, but I fear it would be naive to do so. Indeed, I know from casual conversation with the chief justice that he has a considerable flow of complaints. Some can be dismissed as the fulminations of disgruntled litigants, which may occur though the performance of the judge was impeccable, but a significant portion would not have arisen had the conduct of the judge been discreet and appropriate.

We live in an age in which the assertion of rights is a major preoccupation. But the reciprocal nature of rights and duties is frequently overlooked, and the duties are either unrecognized or ignored. A great bishop, preaching a sermon on that relationship, once reduced it to this simple assertion: "You have rights; I have duties." Every person, in every courtroom, has the right to courteous treatment, and it is the duty of the judge to assure that that right is respected.

A caveat concerning humour in the courtroom has been issued many times. Perhaps once more will do no harm. It must be carefully constrained. To the litigants, a lawsuit is deadly serious business, and to hear the judge engaging in trifling exchanges with counsel will not impress them favourably; also, the court sits for their benefit — not for the benefit of the bench and Bar. That is not to suggest that a dour and funereal atmosphere need be maintained. A light touch is sometimes appropriate to relieve the stress, but it is an area in which caution is the watchword.

One must not flag or fail in taking notes. It is frustrating and laborious, but essential. While doing so, a judge must not lose sight of what is happening in the courtroom and, in particular, must not fail to observe the performance of the witness. It is a formidable combination of functions — not made easier as courtrooms increasingly are designed by persons who never saw one in operation and in which it is almost impossible even to see the witness without contortions that make writing difficult if not impossible. And one must not unduly impede the trial by having witnesses slow down to facilitate note-taking.

The witness who talks too fast for the reporter is a pest who is always with us and for whom there is no known remedy. Speech patterns are immutable, and admonition of the witness is fruitless. One can only request counsel to space the questions so as to give the reporter a break. If you have a fast-talking witness and a fast-talking counsel, all you can do is pray for the reporter — and support him or her if he or she eventually has a tantrum.

My personal stance — and I realize not everyone agrees with it — is to give no indication, while the evidence is being heard, of my view of the case. I adopt this stance for three reasons: first, because I think it is an element in keeping an open mind throughout the trial; second, because my view may change and I do not wish the change to be advertised; and third, because I do not wish the litigants, especially the one who may lose, to have a perception that the case was not fully and fairly heard.

I dictate at the end of each day, or on the following morning before court opens, a summary of the evidence with notes as to exhibits and page references to my bench book so that I can quickly locate from the summary the more extended notes taken during the trial. I find that making these summaries requires more self-discipline than almost anything else in connection with the conduct of a trial. I also find it vital. In making the summary, when I come to any bench notes that are even less legible than usual, I try to fill them out while my recollection of the evidence is fresh. If I am unable to set the matter to rights in that fashion, I make a note in the margin of my bench book; and if the point ultimately proves material I ask the reporter for help. Ordering portions of transcript should be done only very rarely. I have the reporter bring in his or her notes and make the necessary amendments or additions to mine. For what limited value it may have, Appendix B appears as a copy of a typical page from one of my summaries (names camouflaged). In a complicated case, I prepare a topical index in which I list the citations (in my summary) to the evidence of each witness on each of the critical issues.

There are many advantages in the use of such a summary. The very making of it tends to implant some salient points in the memory. It greatly reduces the bulk of bench notes and is much more easily read. (I find that typically I make about forty pages of bench notes per day of trial. These are reduced to ten pages or less.) This facilitates easy reference to the evidence when such reference is required, and a cumulative review as one of the last steps before the judgment takes final form.

In a case in which counsel have made the necessary arrangements for daily transcript, it is no less necessary to make notes and summaries as usual. To have the transcript available for checking specific passages is helpful and reassuring, but the judge who depends on it in place of bench notes will end up a sadder and wiser person.

At frequent intervals during the trial — usually every day — I record very briefly my impressions of the trial at that stage: which issues appear to be assuming importance, which are emerging as strong or weak points in the case, which witnesses are faring well or badly, and so on. As with the summary of evidence, the recording of such impressions serves several purposes, one of them consisting in the mere exercise of writing them down, which requires a concentrated look at how matters then stand. I put these notes as they accumulate into a looseleaf binder, as I do also with my summary of evidence as it is typed up. (Frequently, by the end of the trial I will have two or three looseleaf binders on the go.) I find that a review of these impressions is helpful in arriving at a judgment. In the case of a written judgment, it is also useful to review it as the judgment goes through its various drafts.

I get from the registrar at intervals throughout the trial and invariably at the end a copy of the registrar's list of exhibits. This I put in the front of the notebook that contains my summaries of evidence, so that I can tell at a glance whether my references to the exhibits are correct. Where books of documents are not provided, or where exhibits appear that are not in the books, I have the registrar make a photocopy for me, and those also go into a looseleaf binder. To the greatest extent possible, when the trial is concluded and I go to work on the judgment, I like to have a complete set of my own working papers and to refer as little as possible to the official records. This is so I can mark them up with notes and cross-references.

When the evidence is complete, I do not insist that the argument commence at once. As a general rule, I think that by doing so a judge only short-changes himself or herself. A reasonable interval for preparation will usually be of benefit to all concerned. What constitutes reasonable time will, as always where that phrase is used, vary with the circumstances of the case. It may be minutes, it may be hours, in a very complex case it may even be a day or more. During that interval, I expect counsel to be working and I also work. This is one of the occasions when I find that the accumulation of notes made of impressions as they arose during the trial is of value. I identify and outline those aspects of the case that appear to be most difficult and concerning which I will be most in need of assistance from counsel. I try to think then of the questions that will otherwise occur to me after counsel have gone and I am left alone with the task of preparing the judgment. During argument I have less inhibition than when the evidence is going in, about indicating where I think the strong and weak points in the case may be, although I try to avoid being precipitate in reaching conclusions and to avoid the impression that I have done so. However, it is only fair to counsel to indicate where you find difficulty in the case, so that argument may be appropriately focused.

During the argument, I make notes even if I have been provided with a memorandum of fact and law. The notes may be quite attenuated, but I try to get down what appear to be the salient points. I find a review of those notes helpful during the preparation of the judgment.

If case books are provided (and if the case is of any complexity they should be), as cases are cited, I mark the passages to which reference is actually made. I do this even though counsel may have marked them in advance. I use a series of coloured pencils so that I can ascertain, when I am looking at the case later, which passages were relied on by which parties.

If, in the course of argument, issues of fact or law are conceded or agreed, make sure you have the concession or agreement accurately recorded. If in doubt about it, ask counsel to prepare a brief memorandum and submit it as a working document.

Judgment

There is a tendency in some quarters (which I shall not identify) to consider a case concluded when the evidence is in and the arguments are over. This, of course, is a fallacy. A case is not concluded until the judgment is delivered: if in doubt, ask the litigants. It is for that reason (and not entirely because I have a few pet theories on the subject) that I include some remarks on the subject of judgments, which may at first blush seem out of proportion in a paper dealing with the conduct of a trial. I do so because the judgment is the culmination of the trial, and the elements that go into its making should be present to the mind of the judge throughout the trial, from the first day to the last.

My preference is to give an oral judgment if at all possible. There are many reasons why this is desirable, most of which I need not recite for you. The first and most cogent is expedition. The litigants want to know the result and are entitled to know it as soon as reasonably possible. A second reason, almost as cogent, is that generally speaking the shorter the interval between the conclusion of the evidence and argument and the delivery of the judgment, the better the chance that the judgment will accurately reflect what happened at the trial. I am always deeply sceptical about the judgment delivered months later. It may be an elegant legal and literary essay, but I always wonder how much relationship it bears to the dynamic process which is the trial of an action on *viva voce* evidence. A judgment reserved and written at leisure will be preferable from a literary standpoint, but I am not persuaded that it is any better, in substance, than one delivered orally while all the impressions, including those that are largely inchoate, are fresh. Prompt oral judgment has the added advantage that all the loose ends, such as interest and costs — increasingly onerous factors — can be tied off at once, rather than weeks or months later when the whole case must be laboriously called back to mind. So I do it orally if I can: now.

Very few judges have the gift of being able to give a tolerably coherent judgment immediately following the conclusion of the argument. (Chief Justice Gale was one who could.) Most require some period of reflection: it may be a matter of minutes, hours or, in rare instances, days. My own practice is in that interval to prepare a skeleton of the reasons in the form of notes. The technique is almost identical to that which I followed as counsel in preparing for argument. I use these notes in delivering the reasons. The opening paragraph, and any particularly important or difficult conclusions, I may write out fully so that I will know exactly what I intend to say (rather than waiting until I have said it to find out).

Before commencing to deliver oral reasons, I invite counsel to note any patent errors: dates, names, numbers, and so on, and to draw them to my attention when I have concluded. (Any more subtle and substantial errors must be raised elsewhere.)

In a case of any substance or complexity, I obtain from the reporter a transcript of the reasons as dictated. This is advisable on a number of scores. I wish to check for patent errors. I may wish to tidy up the grammar and the syntax. I consider that entirely legitimate. In some cases, I may wish to amplify or vary slightly what I have said. Again, I consider this fair game, as long as the substance of the reasons remains the same. Finally, there is the matter of paragraphing, which frequently is very important to an understanding of the reasons. A reporter can hardly be expected to get this right, and it should be corrected by the judge.

If you must reserve, the first rule of survival is to do something immediately. My own practice is to dictate a short memorandum outlining what seem to be the salient issues and giving my tentative conclusions as to their proper disposition. This gives me, if some lapse of time occurs before I am able actually to work on the judgment, something that has been put down while all the impressions were fresh in my mind. I make every effort to make that lapse as short as possible. Specifically, I try to have at least a full outline, or preferably a rough first draft, within a week after the argument. I am particularly concerned to have dealt promptly with the facts. Questions of law and literary fly-specking can wait, always remembering, however, that the litigants want to know the result and are not at all concerned with the quality of my writing.

Constructing the Judgment

I spend some time composing a brief opening paragraph (not in the mode of Lord Denning or some of his less talented imitators) defining concisely the issues that the judgment must decide. This will be helpful to anyone who reads the reasons, but, of even more importance, it is helpful in framing them. If it is carefully done, one is a long way on the road to an orderly, coherent judgment.

I then follow with an outline of those facts that are admitted, not disputed, or are such as may appear from the relevant evidence as the only rational conclusion. Such an outline has several useful purposes, not the least of which is that it is the essential background against which disputed issues should be decided. They should not be decided as a matter of intuition, but, as far as possible, as a result of logical thought. One of the most valuable processes is to determine which of the conflicting hypotheses best accords with the undisputed facts. In preparing this outline, the chronology and the memoranda from counsel will be of great assistance.

For years I used to complain to myself about the labour of preparing a detailed outline of facts. After all, said I to myself, the parties know all this, why do I need to be telling them? Over the years, however, it was borne in on me that there is a useful discipline in the exercise. It compels a consideration of the whole framework of the case, and it is in that framework that the disputed issues must be reviewed and decided.

The cardinal function of a trial judge is to make findings of fact; it is also the most demanding and the most difficult function, calling for attention, patience, and industry. It is the cardinal function because, of the judges to whom a case may come for consideration, only the trial judge sees the witnesses, hears all the evidence, and considers the whole record. The findings of fact of a trial judge, unless they manifest some egregious error, are not usually varied upon appeal; if they involve matters of credibility they are practically immutable. A trial judge must, of course, deal also with matters of law, but in most instances they are not either difficult or novel. If they are, and the case is one of any substance, the final word on such matters will be said by someone else.

When I come to deciding disputed issues of fact, I try to do so clearly and unequivocally. It is not necessary always to use the formula, "I find as a fact...." Any assertion of fact in a judgment, which has obviously been made on conflicting evidence, will be taken by an appellate court to be a finding of fact. I try to avoid basing findings on credibility unless the circumstances of the case drive me to it. When driven to it, I try to make the process rational and not intuitive. I am offended almost beyond coherent speech (and quite beyond any which would pass in polite company) by the judge who says something like this:

> Having listened carefully to the evidence, and having attentively observed the demeanour of the witnesses in the witness box, I prefer the evidence of A and B to that of C and D, and when their evidence is in conflict I accept that of A and B.

Truth may occasionally come so neatly packaged, but not often — about one case in a thousand, I would guess. More often the situation reflects an exchange between Oscar Wilde and Sir Edward Carson, during Wilde's cross-examination:

Q. Why do you not tell the truth; the pure and simple truth?

A. Sir, the truth is seldom pure, and never simple.

Such judges, in my view, are on a par with those who, fifteen minutes into a trial, conclude that the plaintiff's case has no merit, or, alternatively, that it is of such obvious merit that there can be no defence, and in either instance proceed to hear the rest of the trial with a closed mind. For such, I am persuaded, there is a special place reserved in one of the inner circles of Hades.

I have always found making findings based on credibility to be difficult, onerous, and, in some respects, distasteful. It smacks of omniscience where omniscience is plainly lacking. For an honest person to be disbelieved in a court of law must be a distressing and disillusioning experience. In cases where I must make findings based on credibility I try to buttress them in every way with considerations such as consistency with admitted facts, capacity to observe, memory and other available indicia, relying as little as possible on my subjective assessment of the witness. In cases in which I feel more than usually apprehensive that I may be discrediting someone wrongly, I insert what is almost an exculpatory paragraph (Appendix C). I have also attached as Appendices D, E, and F three passages, two from judgments and one from a speech by an English judge, each of which, at various times and in various ways, I have found to be most helpful.

I try to say nothing in my reasons that I do not have to say and decide nothing that I do not have to decide.

It is my practice, when a written judgment has come close to a final draft, to have it read by a law clerk. I do this, not because I want any help from the law clerk in deciding the case; that burden is imposed on me by the Constitution. (One hears horror stories, which I hope are either gross exaggerations or complete fabrications, about judges who delegate their function. That is wrong and dishonest.) But there is a measure of insurance in having a draft judgment read by another lawyer who is a stranger to the case. Things that may be perfectly obvious to the writer of the judgment, having a long familiarity with the case, may not be apparent at all to a stranger. Also, there may be gaps in the narrative or unexplained sequences in the statement of conclusions. All of this is beside the assistance to be had in such mechanical matters as checking citations. My final precaution is to review, with the draft judgment in mind, my summary of the evidence, my notes of impressions made during the trial and of the arguments of counsel, especially of counsel for the losing party, to see that no matters of significance have been overlooked.

I offer, quite gratuitously, my own personal philosophy as to the place in the thinking of a judge, while working on a judgment, of the possibility, or the probability, or in some cases the virtual certainty that the judgment will be reviewed on appeal. The primary function of a trial judge is to deal with questions of fact. To perform this function honestly and carefully is an obligation not only to the appellate court, but also to the parties to the action. In discharging this function, a trial judge is between Scylla and Charybdis. On the one hand, facts must not be slanted or distorted in an effort to attain a certain result or to shield that result from review. On the other hand, having decided the case in favour of a certain party, that result ought not to be obscured or jeopardized by careless or inaccurate work.

I have never been able to understand the indignation that some judges generate when reversed by an appellate court. A case that is brought to trial by rational litigants, represented by competent solicitors and counsel, almost always has a good deal to be said on both sides. If a trial judge prefers one side and the appellate court another, it is nothing to become exercised about. If a trial judge has done an honest and workmanlike job, his or her concerns should end there.

Indeed, a trial judge should take a measure of comfort from the fact that appellate review is available and that serious errors can be corrected. Apropos of this I think always of two incidents within my own experience. Shortly after the late Chief Justice Laskin was appointed to the Supreme Court of Canada I found myself in Ottawa and went to his chambers to pay my respects. In the course of our conversation I asked the almost inevitable question as to how he liked his new job. All these many years later I still recall his reply, and I think I have the words almost verbatim:

> Bill, I like it just fine. Except that in a very hard case I sometimes look over my shoulder and there is nobody there.

No trial judge need have a similar concern.

The second episode involves the Honourable Mr. Justice James Huggeson, who at the time of occurrence was the Associate Chief Jus-

tice of the Superior Court of Quebec. While he was at the Bar, he and I
had been engaged in a number of professional activities and had con-
ceived a liking and respect for each other. This was exhibited by the fact
that he came to Toronto to be present when I was sworn in as a judge of
the High Court. There was a large and bibulous dinner party at my
house that evening, during which Jim took me aside and said:

> Bill, if you ever find yourself feeling dissatisfied with the job, just
> remember that the Court of Appeal is better than any insurance policy
> you ever carried, and you pay no premiums.

I offer a final gratuitous observation concerning the process of construct-
ing a judgment. At some stage in that process, the judge becomes an advocate
for the successful party. Whether this be good or bad is a question that it is not
useful to debate. It is inevitable, given our training and given the adversary
nature of an action at law. But in order to remain honest, two cautions should
be observed: the stage at which one becomes the advocate must be deferred
as long as possible, and when it is reached it must be remembered that there
is then no one to speak for the loser and that his or her position must be fairly and squarely reflected.

I do not intend to offer any extensive comments on the writing of a
judgment. Many courses and much learning have been devoted to that
topic. I offer only a few of my favourite prejudices.

- Think carefully before using an adjective, and then, as a general
  rule, don't.
- Avoid such assertions as "I have carefully examined the evidence." One hopes that you have examined the evidence and that
  you have done so carefully.
- Avoid legalese, but at the same time do not fail in accuracy and
  completeness of expression by being overly concerned about
  "plain English."
- If in doubt concerning the necessity or propriety of any portion
  of your judgment, leave it out.

Conclusion

In reviewing my notes for this article, I was struck by two things. The
first was that in describing what I conceive to be the proper role of a

judge in the conduct of a trial, I had used a great many words to say what could be said in four: Shut Up, And Listen.

The second was that I have used "honest" and "honestly" a number of times. Many eminent writers have sought to identify and define the qualities that should be possessed by a judge. To enumerate them would be, simply, to catalogue almost all the virtues. (Perhaps chastity, for example, is not greatly required.) In my own assessment, I think honesty comes first; honesty, not in the obvious sense of being unwilling to accept bribes or to be affected by other improper influences, but honesty of the kind that impels one to recognize one's own biases and prejudices, and to set them aside as much as possible (and recognize it is never possible to do so completely); of the kind that impels one to work when one is tired, and of the kind that always remembers that there are two sides to every case.

In the years when I tried criminal cases, I almost invariably concluded my charge to the jury by drawing attention to the words of the jurors' oath. I did so because I knew of no more effective way to impress upon them the weight and solemnity of the burden that rested upon them when they went to the jury room. The words have about them the flavour of years unnumbered, and of juries and verdicts beyond all counting or telling. You have all heard them many times:

> ... you shall well and truly try and true deliverance make between our sovereign lady the Queen and the accused at the bar whom you shall have in charge and true verdict give according to the evidence.

Each of us, before entering upon the duties of our office, also took an oath:

> ... that I will faithfully and to the best of my skill and knowledge, execute the duties of a judge ....

Implicit in that oath is the assumption of a burden no less onerous than that which is made explicit in the splendid simplicity of the jurors' oath, to give a true verdict according to the evidence.

Appendix A-1

Ontario Court of Justice
Doe v. Roe

Memorandum to Counsel

I should like to have from counsel for each of the parties a chronology, in the form attached, of the salient events in the sequence which gives rise to the action, with reference, where appropriate, to a document or exhibit. If counsel are able to agree on a common chronology, that will be desirable. If not, I will be content to have one from each party and will make any necessary reconciliation.

I should also like to have a brief memorandum of fact and law. This is not intended to be a written argument, but a brief outline of the important elements of the case from the perspective of the party submitting it.

I should like to have these documents if possible before the argument commences and, if not, as soon as it concludes. They are to be working documents, intended only for my use, and they will not form part of the official record of the court. Counsel will, of course, exchange memoranda.

Appendix A-2

Ontario Court of Justice
Doe v. Roe

Chronology

Date   Event or Document   Ex. # if Applicable

Appendix B

Ontario Court of Justice
Doe v. Roe

Evidence

Bench Book
Page:

363 J.Q. BLANK

Officer of the plaintiff company — doesn't know whether he is an officer and director.

Plaintiff is a lender on real estate — witness has been thirty-odd years in the mortgage business.

The Jones mortgage was for $250,000 originally — one year.

Property inspected and appraised.

Exhibit 1, appraisal report, produced 11 July 1989.

Retained solicitor Smith in Smithville.

364 There were 3 advances on the Jones mortgage.

Exhibit 2 is the report of August 18 concerning the advances.

All funds were advanced — there was default under the mortgage — cheques bounced — issued a power of sale and a writ of possession,

There was an offer to settle — Jones was to put up extra security — his partner was to put up his house — the partner was Roe.

I visited the Roe property with Peter Grey — don't recall the exact date.

Was greeted by Roe who was sitting there with Jones — there was no discussion — we did not indicate why we were there — we went through from room to room with Roe — there was no conversation.

365 Mrs. Roe was not present.

Appendix C

A trial judge is seldom more conscious of his or her responsibilities and frailties than when it is necessary to make findings of fact upon conflicting testimony and when the conflict must be resolved largely upon conclusions as to credibility. The judge is aware that such findings will in most cases be final, and is likewise aware that a judge has no special insight, nor any supernatural power such as to make it possible, unerringly, to discover truth and to detect falsehood. If the judge errs, it is entirely likely that one or more of the participants in the trial will know that he or she has done so and will be understandably dismayed. None of these considerations, forbidding though they are, can relieve the judge of the responsibility imposed by the nature of the office. He or she must proceed, with care and humility, to use to the best possible effect such skills as training and experience have given and to express conclusions accordingly.

Appendix D

... They may have been imposed upon and duped by the artful misrepresentations of Mr. Harding, they may have suffered their vigilance to be lulled, and their penetration to have slept, and after having embarked in the transaction, and after their characters were in some measure implicated, they may be under a strong bias to support and give effect to the act. Under that bias very honest persons (such is the infirmity of our nature) often deceive themselves without being aware of it: they fancy impressions to have existed, nay they sometimes even suppose facts to have taken place, because those impressions now exist, or because those facts might or ought to have passed, in order to support their impressions. Hence this strong bias will often give a false colour to a transaction, without the witness intending to speak falsely or to suppress the truth. Without, therefore, in the slightest degree suspecting any thing of conspiracy or wilful misrepresentation, on the part of these gentlemen, it may be necessary to examine their evidence upon those other principles which have been just stated; for it was correctly said by the leading counsel for Mr. Tyrrell, and it cannot be expressed in better words, (if I have taken them accurately) "even persons of high character may fail to do their duty when nearly connected."

[See *Marsh v. Tyrrell et al.* (1828), 2 Hagg. Ecc. 84 at 111–112. Sir John Nichol, in the Prerogative Court of Canterbury.]

Appendix E

The credibility of interested witnesses, particularly in cases of conflict of evidence, cannot be gauged solely by the test of whether the personal demeanour of the particular witness carried conviction of the truth. The test must reasonably subject his story to an examination of its consistency with the probabilities that surround the currently existing conditions. In short, the real test of the truth of the story of a witness in such a case must be its harmony with the preponderance of the probabilities which a practical and informed person would readily recognize as reasonable in that place and in those conditions. Only thus can a Court satisfactorily appraise the testimony of quick-minded, experienced and confident witnesses, and of those shrewd persons adept in the half-lie and of long and successful experience in combining skilful exaggeration with partial suppression of the truth. Again a witness may testify what he sincerely believes to be true, but he may be quite honestly mistaken. For a trial judge to say "I believe him because I judge him to be telling the truth" is to come to a conclusion on consideration of only half the problem. In truth it may easily be self-direction of a dangerous kind.

The trial Judge ought to go further and say that evidence of the witness he believes is in accordance with the preponderance of probabilities in the case and, if his view is to command confidence, also state his reasons for that conclusion. The law does not clothe the trial judge with a divine insight into the hearts and minds of the witnesses. And a Court of Appeal must be satisfied that the trial Judge's finding of credibility is based not on one element only to the exclusion of others, but is based on all the elements by which it can be tested in the particular case.

[*Faryna v. Chorny*, [1952] 2 D.L.R. 354, O'Halloran J.A. at 357.]

Appendix F

I question whether the respect given to our findings of fact based on the demeanour of the witnesses is always deserved. I doubt my own ability, and sometimes that of other judges, to discern from a witness's demeanour or the tone of his voice, whether he is telling the truth. He speaks hesitantly. Is it the mark of a cautious man, whose statements are for that reason to be respected, or is he taking time to fabricate? Is the emphatic witness putting on an act to deceive me, or is he speaking from the fullness of his heart, knowing that he is right? Is he likely to be more truthful if he looks me straight in the face than if he casts his eyes on the ground, perhaps from shyness or a natural timidity? For my part I rely on these considerations as little as I can help.

This is how I go about the business of finding facts. I start from the undisputed facts which both sides accept. I add to them such other facts as seem very likely to be true, as, for example, those recorded in contemporary documents or spoken to by independent witnesses like the policeman giving evidence in a running-down case about the marks on the road. I judge a witness to be unreliable if his evidence is, in any serious respect, inconsistent with these undisputed or indisputable facts, or of course if he contradicts himself on important points. I rely as little as possible on such deceptive matters as his demeanour. When I have done my best to separate the true from the false by these more or less objective tests, I say which story seems to me the more probable, the plaintiff's or the defendant's, and if I cannot say which, I decide the case, as the law obliges me to do, in the defendant's favour. The plaintiff has failed to discharge the burden of proof.

[From a paper read at University College, Dublin, 21 February 1975, by Sir Brian MacKenna. Quoted with approval by Patrick Devlin in *The Judge.*]

[This article first appeared in the September 1993 issue of *The Advocates' Society Journal.*]

Oral Advocacy in Matters Argued before Superior Court Judges

Justice Robert A. Blair[*]

The following is attributed to one of my favourite philosophers, Winnie the Pooh:

> Pooh was puzzled. Actually, he wasn't so much puzzled as he was confuzzled. Confuzzled was almost the longest word Pooh knew, and he hadn't known that until Christopher Robin explained that it meant sort of mixed up and baffled.[1]

Good advocates do not leave the judge in a state of confuzzlement.

Trial Advocacy

Trial advocacy, the nature of a trial, and Jell-o

This is true whether the judge is a trial judge, a motions or applications judge, or an appellate judge (at whatever level). Given the more open-ended nature of the trial process, however — as opposed to the "closed-record" characteristic of other forums of advocacy — the task of counsel

---

*   Mr. Justice Robert A. Blair, Court of Appeal for Ontario.

1   R.E. Allen, *Winnie-the-Pooh on Management: In Which a Very Important Bear and His Friends are Introduced to a Very Important Subject* (New York: E.P. Dutton, 1994) at 21.

in leaving the trial judge (or judge and jury) with a clear and manageable understanding about their client's case poses particular challenges. Effective advocacy requires an ability to adapt one's style and approach both to the subject at hand and to the court or type of proceeding in question. Good trial advocacy stretches that ability to its limits.

In an article entitled "A Survivor's Guide to Advocacy in the Supreme Court of Canada," Justice Ian Binnie notes that "the key to advocacy is focus." This is equally so, of course, at the level of first instance. A trial, however, features an important dimension that is absent on an appeal and makes the exercise of focusing additionally tricky: not only must the advocate search for what attracts the attention and favour of the judicial mind; he or she must do so in the context of a delicately developing and often shifting target known as "the evidence." Justice Binnie also speaks of the skill required in "nailing the forensic jelly to the wall in a particular case." Every trial has its "nailing jelly to the wall" aspect. There is jelly, however, and there is jelly — or, "Jell-o" (if I may be permitted to shift the analogy ever so slightly, but not substantively, for purposes of discussion about trial).

Justice Binnie says you nail the jelly to the wall by formulating the question on appeal in the way in which the court is likely to be most attracted to your arguments. At trial, though, counsel and the trier must deal with a more elusive jelly or Jell-o-like concept before even getting to argument — the metamorphosis of evidence into proven and found facts. You will have a pretty good idea what the issues are from the pleadings — or at least what you hope they will turn out to be — but you will not be able to pursuade the trier to your version of them until you have been able to nail down those pesky, slippery, and sometimes wobbly, facts.

The crux of the difficulty lies in the lingering uncertainty that continues to exist in the factual and legal underpinning of the case until the evidentiary support for it has been poured and shaped and has been properly set by the fact-finding exercise at the end of the day. No one can say for certain what the ultimate shape of the Jell-o will be until it has set. The job of the advocate is to facilitate the pouring and shaping of the evidentiary base in the way that is most conducive to the success of the client's case, and to ensure that the judge is assisted effectively in finding the facts — or setting the foundation — which will assure that end. Leaving the judge in a state of confuzzlement, during the development of the evidence and at its conclusion, will not accomplish that goal.

What does the skillful advocate do to achieve the goal, then? I suspect that nothing I can say will be new or startling on this subject. Hopefully, however, the following observations on what helps to make an advocate successful and effective through the eyes of at least one superior court trial judge will be of passing interest, at least. They are offered in the context of an era in which trials — both civil and criminal — are becoming more and more complex, more and more document-laden, and lengthier and lengthier.[2]

Preparation, distillation, and focus

I take "competency" — and what it entails in terms of knowledge of the law and procedure, and in terms of technical skills — as a given requirement for capable advocacy. It goes without saying that a good advocate is able to cross-examine and to conduct an examination in chief adroitly — I have always felt that the latter is a more difficult exercise than the former — and knows when to, and when not to, make evidentiary objections.

Leaving those basic characteristics aside, however, I start with the universal need for preparation and the ultimate distillation of the evidence and the materials into a focused presentation for the court. While this observation may seem trite, the importance of these elements of effective advocacy cannot be overstated or too frequently emphasized.

This facet of the work of counsel can hardly be summarized better than in the following comment by that great Canadian counsel, the late John J. Robinette, epitomizing, as it does, the very traits that he extoled:

> You win by preparation and drudgery. You do research and you read. The actual appearance in court is often like the tip of the iceberg. [You] try to be succinct. [You] formulate your argument as concisely yet as effectively as possible, getting down to the point of the case, avoiding red herrings. Sometimes it means weeks of preparation.[3]

The ability to ferret out the real issues and to organize the presentation of the evidence and documents, with some focus on those issues, is an indispensable quality for an effective advocate. Hours, sometimes

---

2   Some of what follows was first expressed in an address by the author to The Advocates' Society Fall Convention in October 1992, entitled "Effective Advocacy in Commercial Cases: A View from the Bench."

3   John J. Robinette Q.C., *The Globe and Mail*, 26 November 1979.

days, of court time can be wasted when counsel are unable to, or refuse to, do this. The court will be eternally grateful, and much better equipped to deal with your issues on the merits, when you do. A little hard work can go a long way in this regard.

It helps to give the trier of fact some idea of where you are going. Evidence is much more easily understood, absorbed, and retained if it is received in a context. This is often difficult and sometimes impossible in a trial setting. Occasionally, cross-examination strategy will militate against telegraphing to the witness where you are going, but you should remember that you are not cross-examining the judge, who does not need to be left in the dark! You will know what the issues are, from the pleadings, and it doesn't hurt to remind the trier where you are in that story, in terms of the evidence that is being and has been led, and the evidence that is to come.

It is also helpful, at least by the stage of argument, to distill the case into the few important issues that are key to your success. Insisting, for example, that there are thirty or thirty-five issues to be decided in the trial (fifteen of which have three or four sub-items!) is not generally productive (or persuasive). That is rarely, if ever, the case, and the judge is lost by the time you are on issue ten. Counsel sometimes confuse "issues" with points of fact established (or to be established) by the evidence. Successful counsel deal with the evidence and conclude by outlining to the trier the particular "facts" that they wish to have the trier "find" on the evidence. They then relate those facts to the half dozen or so "issues" that must be determined. If the decision in the case is likely to be reserved, a list of the findings sought and a written summary of the points in argument will assist the judge greatly.

The list of findings of fact that the trier is asked to make, and their relationship to the issues, is exceptionally important in cases where alternative findings are possible. These situations are ripe for judicial confuzzlement — not to mention advocate confuzzlement — and good counsel anticipate and meet the situation with a clear identification of what it is they seek.

I digress here to make an observation about reserved decisions. Good counsel will appreciate that if the decision in the case is reserved, although counsel's job is finished, that of the trial judge is not. Moreover, in all likelihood the judge will not be proceeding directly to a leisurely several days of contemplation of the case that has just been reserved. Rather, the judge will be embarking the next day on another case, or series of cases, and will be returning to a consideration of the reserved decision — perhaps along with a number of others that are under reserve — when he or she is able to carve out some time from a busy schedule to do so. One of the big problems for the judge in this exercise is the "mental retro-fitting" required on each return to the task, after having dealt with intervening matters and perhaps weeks of other work. The easier and more time-effective it is to re-enter the decision-making process, the faster the judgment can be rendered and the more likely it is that the decision, when finally released, will be a sound one. Hence, the advantage and utility of providing a road map in the form of a written summary setting out counsel's position and of any other effective type of *aide-memoire*, such as compendia and summaries of law that can be prepared, cannot be overemphasized.

In more complicated cases particularly, the organization of exhibits and documents is crucial. Examining numerous bound document books — each containing thirty or forty tabbed documents — is cumbersome and difficult. I do not find the marking of document books with an exhibit letter, for purposes of identification, and subject to later proof of individual documents, very helpful. Indeed, where there is any significant number of such document books, it becomes quite confusing (and sometimes impossible) to sort out after a long trial just which documents have become evidence for the proof of the truth of their contents, or which have been entered for some other purpose, or which have not been entered at all and must therefore be disregarded. Counsel should endeavour to minimize the need for the formal proof of documentation in order to save time at trial, and should prepare joint exhibit books where that can reasonably be done. Where a joint document book is not feasible, counsel tendering the document books should try to ensure that most of the individual documents in a given book are admitted into evidence by agreement or proved in a fashion that is readily identifiable at the end of the day.

The use of a compendium is becoming more and more prevalent, and rightly so. The compendium is a book of excerpts from documents, pleadings, and so on that are central to the case. Justice Farley calls them "yellow tag specials," a binder of materials "shaved down to something that even a cervically cranky judge could carry around with him or her." That is, a compendium contains all of the pages in the brief that counsel will have marked for reference to the judge, but not the rest of the (sometimes voluminous) documentation, which may be necessary for purposes of context and the record but which are not essential for purposes of the argument and the basic understanding of the case. Paragraph 47 of the Commercial List Practice Direction[4] describes the compendium in this fashion:

> In appropriate cases, to supplement any required formal Record, counsel are requested to consider preparing an informal Compendium of the key materials to be referred to in argument (fair extracts of documents, transcripts, previous orders, authorities, etc.) to assist in focusing the case for the Court. (See *Saskatchewan Egg Producers' Marketing Board v. Ontario*, [1993] O.J. No. 434.) It will be helpful to draw the attention of the court to pertinent information about each document (e.g. the date, the deponent of an affidavit, the parties to a contract, the significance of a particular passage or provision, etc.) by appropriate commentary in the index of the Compendium or on the first page of the document or both. Relevant portions of the Compendium should be highlighted or marked. Counsel are urged to consult among themselves in the preparation of a joint Compendium, if possible. The Compendium should contain only essential materials. The use of a loose-leaf format is particularly helpful to the court both for conducting hearings and for writing decisions.

Case law and excerpts from texts may be summarized in a compendium as well. I prefer to have the case law and authorities in a separate book, as it is frequently necessary to examine both the law and the documentation at the same time. However, different judges differ on this aspect of the use of a compendium. The important thing is to recognize the utility of the concept and to use it effectively. As Mr. Justice Finlayson points out in his article on appellate advocacy, providing the compendium as early as possible in the process is a good idea.

Candour, courtesy, and common sense

Apart from the basic skills of an advocate and the essential elements of preparation, distillation, and focus, the alchemy of effective advocacy calls for a nice mixture of a number of other important ingredients, of a

---

4   (1995), 24 O.R. (3d) 455 at 466.

more general underlying nature, as well. I look for candour. I look for courtesy. I look — perish the thought! — for common sense.

It may seem somewhat gratuitous to place "courtesy" and "candour" at the top of this list of ingredients. I do so not because they are ingredients that are lacking in most counsel — in my experience they are not — but rather to emphasize their central importance to the advocate's role in a particular case and to the advocate's reputation as a consummate professional in the long term. The fight is not between counsel, or between counsel and the clients, or even between counsel and the bench. The exercise of common courtesy and civility among those participating in the litigation does wonders to enhance the process, particularly where the issues are complex, the evidence lengthy, the documentation voluminous, and the emotional tension between the parties high. Open squabbling among counsel is not a helpful contribution to that process.

"Candour" is particularly important in a counsel. An advocate must display honesty and forthrightness in dealing with the court, other lawyers, and clients. This point is well stated by Earl Cherniak at the outset of his excellent article, "The Ethics of Advocacy,"[5] in this way:

> The most important attribute of an advocate is reputation, for it is that which wins him or her the respect of colleagues, the receptive ear of the court and, ultimately, clients. While reputation depends on many factors, the single most important one, without which the advocate cannot function, is that of fairness and honesty in dealings with the court and fellow lawyers.

An advocate must make a careful and realistic assessment of the case and is responsible for conveying that assessment to the client. He or she is also responsible, in my view — as part of the advocate's duty as an officer of the court — to ensure that there is at least a passing connection between that assessment and the presentation of the case in court.

I do not mean to suggest by this latter comment that counsel must "give up" in a weak case. Nor do I mean to suggest that counsel should decline to pursue a line of inquiry or argument simply because he or she feels it will not succeed. As has often been said, the judge may find the

---

5   Earl A. Cherniak Q.C., "The Ethics of Advocacy," *Advocacy in Court: A Tribute to Arthur Maloney, Q.C.* (Toronto: Canada Law Book, 1986).

argument and the evidence more persuasive than counsel does. The test is whether the line of inquiry or argument has any merit. It if does, then it ought to be pursued; if it does not, it should not be pursued.

It is one of the realities of our times that the demands on our increasingly scarce judicial resources do not permit us any more the luxury of the "day in court" — or week, or month, or year — for every client, no matter how hopeless and without merit the cause or defence. The court is entitled to, and does, look to counsel to cut through the irrelevancies and the impossiblities in order to concentrate on the genuine issues. As Lord Templeton noted, in *Ashmore v. Corp. of Lloyd's:*[6]

> The parties and particularly their legal advisers in any litigation are under a duty to co-operate with the court by chronological, brief and consistent pleadings which define the issues and leave the judge to draw his own conclusions about the merits when he hears the case. It is the duty of counsel to assist the judge by simplification and concentration and not to advance a multitude of ingenious arguments in the hope that out of ten bad points the judge will be capable of fashioning a winner. In nearly all cases the correct procedure works perfectly well. But there has been a tendency in some cases for legal advisers, pressed by their clients, to make every point conceivable and inconceivable without judgment or discrimination. In *Banque Financière de la Cité SA v. Westgate Insurance Co Ltd.*, [1990] 2 All ER 947 at 959, I warned against proceedings in which all or some of the litigants indulge in over-elaboration causing difficulties to judges at all levels in the achievement of a just result. I also said that the appellate court should be reluctant to entertain complaints about a judge who controls the conduct of proceedings and limits the time and scope of evidence and argument. ... In his judgement in the Court of Appeal Ralph Gibson LJ recorded that the plaintiffs had resisted the application to Gatehouse J by Lloyd's for a determination of preliminary issues on many grounds in addition to the two specific grounds of objection to which I have referred. Mr. Lyndon-Stanford repeated the arguments in the Court of Appeal and as Ralph Gibson LJ remarked: "He claimed in particular that it was wrong thus to take the conduct of the proceedings out of the hands of the plaintiffs and thereby to disappoint the plaintiffs in

---

6   [1992] 2 All E.R. 486 at 493.

their legitimate expectation that the trial would proceed to a conclusion upon the evidence to be adduced."

Ralph Gibson LJ thought that there was "considerable force in those submissions." My Lords, I disagree; the control of the proceedings rests with the judge and not with the plaintiffs. An expectation that the trial would proceed to a conclusion upon the evidence to be adduced is not a legitimate expectation. The only legitimate expectation of any plaintiff is to receive justice. Justice can only be achieved by assisting the judge and accepting his rulings.

On the criminal side, the Ontario Court of Appeal has affirmed the judge's duty and obligation to control the trial and the proceedings: see, for example, *R. v. Kutynec*[7] and *R. v. Loveman*.[8] In the latter case, Justice Doherty, writing for the court, recognized the trial judge's inherent power to control the proceedings in this statement:

A trial judge must control the trial proceedings so as to ensure fairness to all concerned and preserve the integrity of the trial process. The specific situations in which the trial judge must exercise that power are infinitely variable and his or her order must be tailored to the particular circumstances.

Judges and counsel are more and more faced with situations that call for the exercise of this sort of restraint and skill. Successful counsel will be those who recognize those situations and adapt their presentations to work within the foregoing parameters.

Motions and applications

Arguing motions and applications involves many of the skills that are common to all advocacy, of course, but the exercise is more akin to appellate advocacy than to that of the trial. The record is fixed and already in place. It's what counsel does with the record that counts. There is not the added dimension of having to worry about the creation of the record at the same time.

It is important to condense and to clarify what is in the record in a fashion that focuses the judge's mind on what it is necessary for him or her to decide. This requires counsel to be as brief and to the point as pos-

---

7   (1992), 70 C.C.C. (3d) 289.
8   (1992) 8 O.R. (3d) 51.

sible in oral argument, without missing anything essential to their case. It requires that they take advantage of organizing and writing skills in the form of such things as the use of compendiums and, in particular, that they make effective use of written advocacy's most powerful tool: the factum.

Justices Finlayson and Laskin have covered much of this ground in their excellent articles published in this issue of the *Journal,* and many of their comments are equally applicable to motions and applications. Make no mistake about it, however: many more motions and applications are won or lost in the writing of the factum than in oral argument. The factum is the best chance to tell the judge your client's story. It must be readable. It should be as interesting as possible. Remember that a factum is not a trust indenture!

Keep in mind, as well, that motions and applications are generally argued as one of a large number of other similar proceedings on a daily list. It should not be assumed that the judge will find the matter sufficiently enthralling or important to reserve his or her decision. Time and workload factors do not afford the judge at the Superior Court level the luxury of doing this in very many cases. Therefore — as others have said — if you want the judge to be aware of, or to read, something, take the judge to it. The trick is in knowing what to burden the judge with in that respect, and what not to. Stick to essentials. Avoid surplusage.

When the judge does reserve, your case will not likely be the only one occupying the "deliberating" time available to his or her mind. It will be one of a number in a lineup. The judge may not get to it for several days, or weeks, or even months — if it is complex and the judge has a long list of reserves (which happens with increasing frequency). It is important, therefore, that the judge be left with a record that is clear and understandable and that enables him or her readily to re-grasp the issues and the facts.

Finally, the judge may be somewhat more interventionist on motions and applications than is the case at trial. He or she will have had the opportunity to review the materials in advance, and will have done so, at least with respect to the factum (again, the importance of that written story) and the key document or decision in question. It is inevitable, and quite appropriate, that the judge will have formed some tentative views about the case in advance of oral argument. You must be prepared to respond to questions.

While you will not likely face the full range of questioning "fire" that Justice Binnie describes in this issue of the *Journal* as characteristic before "the mother of all juries," the Supreme Court of Canada, you may well become engaged with the judge in a lively exchange about the issues. Nor should you necessarily read anything particularly sinister into this sort of "judicial activism." While it may indicate the judge has certain reservations about certain aspects of your case, it identifies for you the matters of concern that must be addressed. It lets you know clearly "where the judge is coming from" and, therefore, what you need to respond to. Moreover, this sort of intervention is, as often as not, simply the judge's way of probing and testing questions that he or she wants answered. It is not unusual — at least before some judges — for counsel who have faced the toughest questioning to emerge as the victor! Effective counsel on motions and applications are able, with adroit responses to questions, to make the best of their situation and turn the case to their client's advantage (if, indeed, it is a case that can be turned to their client's advantage).

Conclusion

The keys to effective trial advocacy, and much of the foregoing, can be summarized in these simple suggestions: Be organized. Be clear. Keep things as simple as possible. Be adaptable, yet resolute in pursuit of your client's interests. Be willing to make the tough decisions about what need not, and should not, be pursued, and stick to those decisions. In the end, and above all, remember to tell your client's story.

To the extent that counsel are able to accomplish the foregoing, they will leave the judge with a clear and manageable understanding of their client's case rather than "sort of mixed up and baffled." Advocacy is the art of persuasion.

Good advocates do not leave the judge in a state of confuzzlement.

[This article first appeared in the Summer 1999 issue of *The Advocates' Society Journal*.]

Advocacy in Jury Trials

John A. McLeish[*]

The members of the jury panel were crowded into the courtroom. Some sat in the hard wooden seats and in back of the courtroom, and others stood along the walls. As the court registrar called their names, they shuffled uneasily and acknowledged their individual presence. Each potential juror had been observing, in a discreet way, the lawyers sitting at the tables in front of the courtroom. None had failed to notice a significant difference in appearance and attitude between the two camps of lawyers. On one side sat two neatly groomed individuals; erect and attentive, they seemed to be studying the panel members' every move and gesture. On the other side, two lawyers seemed intently engrossed in some private joke. One slouched in his chair, had his hand cupped over his mouth as he whispered to his colleague between chuckles. Studying these two warring camps, the anonymous audience began to observe more differences.

Some days later, twelve pairs of eyes cautiously studied the lawyers standing before them. As the plaintiff's lawyer presented his final summation, his words were lost in the blur of impressions that had largely been formed during those first few moments at the beginning of the proceedings.

---

[*]   John A. McLeish, McLeish & Orlando LLP, Toronto.

"Ladies and gentlemen of the jury, we have appreciated your service and attention as jurors." [Sure you have, that's why you've been joking with your co-counsel and client in the courtroom and hallways at every break or recess.] ...

"We've tried to bring you this evidence in a straightforward manner." [When you could find the exhibit, when you could decide what question you wanted to ask, when you stopped rambling from point to point.] ...

"My client [and that's all he is to you — just another fee] demands strict justice." [You'd better think again if you think you've got the right to demand anything from me for the way you've presented this case.] ...

"We ask that you give my client the fifty thousand dollars in damages that we have asked for." [Who does he think we are, some Ottawa bureaucrats running a welfare program?] ...

"We made a bond during opening statements, and my client and I now call on you to live up to your part of the bargain." [Now he's going to try and shove down my throat some bargain that he claims we made, that I had nothing to do with formulating, and that he believes he advanced with his tricky lawyering.] ...

"We have established the defendant's negligence." [What was the legal definition of that term the judge read a few minutes ago? What does all this legal jargon mean anyhow?] ...

"You will recall that the first witness we called was my client, Bill Jones. Mr. Jones testified...." [He's not going to go through each witness's testimony in chronological order!] ...

"The next witness we called was the investigating officer, Patrolman Gilbert Holloway." [He's going to do it. He's going to summarize every witness's testimony in chronological order.] ...

"The next witness we called was Dr. George Truman, the plaintiff's treating physician." [I think I'm getting sleepy. I'd better not eat at the hamburger joint tomorrow.] ...

"In summary, ladies and gentleman, we believe the evidence demands you give us your verdict." [What verdict? The judge read us a bunch of legal definitions and questions. What did it all mean? What are we supposed to do when we go back to the jury room? Maybe the defence lawyer will explain it so we can understand what's going on.]

Later, out in the hall during jury deliberations, the plaintiff's lawyer was asked how the case went. "Oh, I don't think the case went that well," he conceded, "but I think I pulled it out in final argument."[1]

The foregoing is not a fantasy. Scenes like this take place in Ontario courtrooms almost daily.

A common belief among many lawyers is that a trial lawyer is someone who was born with a silver tongue. Some believe that advocacy is an inherent talent that cannot be learned. Nothing could be further from the truth: Advocacy is a learned skill. Eloquence may be borrowed and techniques may be acquired.

This article will attempt to enhance the trial skills you already possess and to help you to "empower the jury" to give an adequate award to your client.

General Trial Techniques

Creating a case theme

Before counsel walks into the courtroom, it is imperative to develop a case theme. A good case theme will motivate the jury to give an adequate award to the plaintiff. Some factors counsel should keep in mind in developing a case theme are as follows:

1) The theme should be short and simple. It is preferable that it be stated in ten words or less. If the theme is short and simple, the retention value is higher and the theme can easily be repeated throughout the trial. Consider, for example, advertising themes that we all hear: "The Real Thing" (Coca-Cola), "The Pepsi Generation" (Pepsi), "We Try Harder" (Avis), and "Fly the Friendly Skies" (United).

2) The theme should be bigger than the case itself. For example, in a case involving a drunk driver who injures your client, your theme could be keeping our streets safe from drunk drivers.

3) The theme should present the underlying facts and theory of your case.

4) The theme should be delivered early in your opening. It can be introduced by giving your case a title. For example:

---

1   This is from J.M. Perdue, *Who Will Speak for the Victim: A Practical Treatise on Plaintiff's Jury Argument* (Austin: Bar of Texas, 1989) at 3, with changes to fit the Ontario context.

> On 13 May 1992, Lily Smith's car was struck by the defendant drunk driver and Lily was seriously injured. As a result, her life has been changed forever. This case is about a person's right to drive on our streets free of drunk drivers.   .

There are two themes here — a liability theme: "a person's right to drive on our streets free of drunk drivers," and a damages theme: "Lily's life was changed forever."

Or, in a death case:

> On 13 May 1992, John Smith was killed. The issue in this case is the value of human life in this community and the standard of care required to protect human life. If human life is to be valued, then a high standard of care is needed to protect it.

Again, as in almost every case, there are two themes: the "value of human life" and the "high standard of care needed to protect it."

In a medical negligence case, tell the jury that the issue is not simply whether a particular plaintiff should recover damages. While this issue is certainly important, it is too small. The real issue goes beyond the case: it is the standard of medical care that people in the community have a right to expect, and by their decision the jury will set that standard.

More often than not, lawyers are so busy preparing other aspects of the case that they do not have time to develop a winning case theme. This is a mistake. It is well worth spending the time to create a well-thought-out theme.[2]

Developing a courtroom image

While the content of a case is important, a plaintiff in a personal injury action cannot win a case in the face of unfavourable impressions created both at the outset of trial and during the trial. Cases are won more on impressions than on facts.

One of the first things jurors unconsciously do when they first come into the courtroom is form an impression about counsel. The jurors' formation of an impression of counsel is an ongoing process throughout the trial, but first impressions are key. The following factors are critical in helping you develop a favourable courtroom image and a rapport with the jury.

---

2   For a good article on building a case theme, see D.B. Baum, "Creating a Theme" (March 1994) 30:3 Trial 67.

Dynamism

As counsel for the victim you should be animated, energetic, and dedicated to the victim's cause. You should move about the courtroom in a purposeful, confident manner and not be shy, uncertain, or restricted.

Jurors do not listen continually in the courtroom; they tune in and out. Accordingly, it is very important to keep everything moving, interesting, and novel. If you want jurors to listen, you must develop dynamic qualities and present the case in an interesting way.

Dynamism involves activity and motion, which means varied gestures, a varied voice, and varied movement patterns. Most speakers do not allow their full personality to come out during a presentation; they hold back. The best trial lawyers do not hold back, and that is what makes them dynamic. What they are saying and doing is no longer an "act." The presentation is straight from the heart. If you genuinely have a passion for justice in the case, it will be manifested in your presentation.

You must, however, still be your own person. You can borrow techniques and strategies from another person, but never try to copy anyone's style or be someone you are not. Use styles and mannerisms that are basic and innate to your personality.

Confidence

There is a difference between being confident and portraying confidence in the courtroom. One's level of confidence varies, but a skilled trial counsel must portray confidence during the entire trial, regardless of how poorly a case may be going. Counsel must never show any concern to the jury. Even when a witness's answer is damaging, a skilful trial counsel will continue as if nothing has happened and counsel's words, demeanour, and mannerisms will continue to portray an attitude of unconcern and confidence.

Credibility

Jurors are more easily influenced by those they perceive as credible. The perception of credibility affects the persuasiveness of your message. Jurors are more receptive to arguments from a source they consider credible. If you are dynamic, if you portray confidence, if you are trustworthy, and if you demonstrate competence and expertise, you will go a long way in enhancing your credibility.

Competence is the lawyer's skill and knowledge of the case. Trustworthiness is established by counsel delivering information in a fair and unbiased manner, not overstating his or her case, being forthright and fair in dealing with adverse witnesses, and not engaging in arguments or analysis that appear spurious or too clever.

The use of impact words and powerful speaking enhance credibility and make it more likely that counsel will be perceived as intelligent, likable, and believable. Techniques such as repetition and the use of metaphors, similes, analogies, and rhetorical questions can also build counsel's credibility in the jurors' minds.

The technique of jury empowerment

Jurors cannot be allowed to be mere observers of the legal proceeding. In order for you to obtain adequate compensation for your client, jurors must not only understand their power, they must be motivated to exercise that power. They must know that they are the ones who decide the case and that they are not just bystanders in the elaborate machinations of a trial. One of the most critical tasks during a trial for you as the plaintiff's counsel is to instill in each juror a sense of his or her power. Jurors individually and the jury as a whole must be comfortable with their function, their importance, and their power to render a full verdict. Jurors have the power to determine the outcome of the trial, to make someone's life whole again, to speak for society, and to send a message to other potential defendants. They must be made aware that by providing your client with an adequate award they are performing one of the most important functions they will ever perform. When properly instilled, the power of the jury is virtually unsurpassed.

Empowerment of the jury should be introduced into the trial proceedings in the same manner as a case theme. Empowerment begins with the opening statement and continues through to the end of summation.

Opening Statement

Explain your theory

The opening statement is the first opportunity you have to put your theory to the jury. Your opening statement must be geared to what you will ask the jury to find in closing argument.

One of your goals in the opening statement is to position your case as best you can. Studies have shown that jurors usually make up their minds about liability in a case after the opening statement and do not change their minds 80 percent of the time. In a contentious liability case, the opening statement could possibly be the most important part of the trial. An effective opening on behalf of the plaintiff can put the defence in a hole out of which it is difficult to climb. It is an opportunity plaintiffs' counsel does not want to miss, and a great deal of time should be spent on preparing an opening statement. The last thing you want to do is stand up and give a few personal details about your client, talk about the "accident," and then refer to your client's injuries and losses. If you present your opening this way, you will be putting yourself into a hole out of which you may never emerge.

Primacy and recency

Remember the doctrines of primacy and recency — people remember best what they hear and see first and last. This includes jurors' first impressions of the lawyers. The opening statement is not a time to hide behind a podium and mumble some details of the accident as you shuffle through some notes. Stand in front of the podium and, with no notes or only a brief reference to notes, talk to the jury in a conversational tone as though talking to someone in your living room. If you type out your opening a week or so before trial and practice it aloud at home two or three times, you should have no trouble with it.

Studies also tell us that we have the jurors' rapt attention for the first four to six minutes, and a modicum of attention for another twenty minutes. After this, it is very difficult to get jurors to listen to what we are saying. Therefore do not waste time telling the jury about trial procedures, such as "Under our system the plaintiff's lawyer speaks first and therefore I will address you about the case and then the opposing lawyer will have his turn." The judge has already done this. You want to catch the jury's attention quickly and get in as much in the first four to six minutes as you can.

Start with an attention-grabber

Consider the contrast between two ways of starting an opening:

> My name is John McLeish, and I act for the plaintiff. My friend, Mr. Wheeler, acts for the defendant, Mr. Jones. Under our system ... blah, blah, blah ... . This case involves a motor vehicle accident in which the plaintiff was seriously injured because of the defendant's negligence. Mr. Jones was intoxicated at the time of the accident.

Or:

> On 13 May 1992, Lily Smith's car was struck by the defendant drunk driver and Lily was seriously injured. As a result her life has been changed forever. This case is about a person's right to drive on our streets free of drunk drivers.

What you say is not evidence

When you start to speak to the jury, do not tell the jury that what you say is not evidence. The judge has already done this. You want the jury to indeed think that what you are saying is evidence.

Speak in the present tense

When you "tell the story" about how the traumatic event occurred, speak in the present tense so that the jury can be right along with your client as events unfold. Following is an example of how you might do this:

> What happened to bring about this disaster? That is the subject of this lawsuit. Picture yourself with Howard that evening. Howard is on his way back from work. He looks ahead and sees a curve in the road. Howard drives carefully. It is a narrow, winding street and he is on his own side of the road. The curves are so numerous and the road so narrow that he is travelling at a crawl. Howard has no idea at this instant that his life is about to change forever. As he travels around one curve on his own side of the road, he sees something ahead of him which alarms him. Coming around the curve from the right is the defendant's thirty-two-foot-long, fourteen-ton truck. The truck is on the wrong side of the road, heading right at him in blatant violation of the laws of the Province of Ontario. The truck begins to turn to go back to its own side of the road, but it is too late. Howard watches in horror as the cab of the truck comes straight for him, and then he sees the underside of the truck coming for the driver's side of his vehicle. He lurches to the right side of the passenger seat to avoid this oncoming truck. He flings his body off to the side and ironically, it is during this twisting and turning before the collision, that the rods, which had been inserted in his neck just ten months earlier, come loose and Howard's life of pain begins. The truck never does get back on its own side of the road and crashes into Howard's car.

Handling weaknesses

You must confront your weaknesses. If a weakness comes first from the defence, it will be somewhat of a shock or surprise to the jury. If up to that time you have built the jurors' trust, they will be disappointed with you and you will have let them down. You told them in opening statement that you would be fair, and you have not been fair. An example of how you may wish to handle a weakness in the opening statement is as follows:

> In the interests of fairness, and holding nothing back, I must tell you that Dr. Jones's clinical notes and records will show that in the past, Lily has smoked marijuana. That has nothing to do with the fact that she was seriously injured by the defendant's drunk driving.

Emphasize your opponent's weakness

Point out any fundamental flaw in the defendant's case. Avoid, however, the temptation to simply mention some unattractive but unimportant fact that is of no consequence to the case. For example:

> The defendant says he was not negligent that night, but I want you to pay particular attention to how many beers he drank before he got into his truck that night.

Forewarn the jury about conflicts in the evidence

If you know there will be conflicting evidence, tell the jury candidly about this in your opening. It is a mistake to suggest there is only one version of events when you know the jury will hear more than one version. Explain why your version should prevail.

Basis of liability

After you have told the liability aspect of the story, state in a forceful manner — and, in the right case, a somewhat indignant manner — the basis of liability and why your client is entitled to succeed. For example, you may want to say:

> Ladies and gentlemen, the evidence will show that the defendant was impaired by alcohol at the time, was not keeping a proper lookout, and crossed the centre of the roadway.

Anticipating and refuting defences

From examinations for discovery, you will know the defence's position. You will know the defences that probably will be put forth. The defence does not have the burden of proof and is not obligated to present evidence and, accordingly, you cannot refer to evidence you expect the defence to call. You can, however, state positively that a defence to the defendant's position does exist. You in no way want to allow the defence to define the issue. You could say something like this:

> Lily was driving her car at sixty kilometres per hour in a sixty kilometre per hour zone. She did everything that a careful and prudent person would do in the circumstances.

Rhetorical questions

A rhetorical question directs the jury's attention to an important issue in the case where the answer is self-evident. For example:

> If the defendant truck driver was not negligent, as his lawyer wants you to believe, why did he plead guilty to impaired driving in Provincial Court?

Rhetorical questions can also be used in summation.

Humanizing the plaintiff in the opening statement

Humanize your client during opening statement. Do not refer to him or her as the client or the plaintiff. Say the plaintiff's full name, once at the beginning of the opening — for example, "Lily Smith" — and after that refer to your client as "Lily."

During opening, when referring to your client, look at and if possible stand by him or her, and in the right circumstances be seen touching your client. You want the jury to like your client; if the jury sees that you like your client, this will increase their chances of liking your client.

At the same time, you want to dehumanize the defendant. Rarely refer to the defendant by his name. Refer to the defendant as "the defendant" or "the corporate defendant," and use abrupt movements. In the right circumstances, use a despising tone in your voice and look on your face.

Introduce the plaintiff in opening

When you introduce your client in opening, try to accomplish several things:

- Describe your client so that the jury members will identify with him or her.
- Describe some admirable qualities of your client.
- Set up a before-and-after picture of your client.

With these objectives in mind, your introduction of the plaintiff may go something like this:

> During the trial, you will have an opportunity to meet Lily. Before the collision, Lily was a healthy, active, and energetic young woman. She had a life filled with hard work, sporting and recreational activities, and pride in her ability to maintain her home and garden. All of this has changed as a result of the collision. Lily can no longer work at her job as a legal secretary the way she used to; she can no longer do aerobics or go to Blue Jays games without pain and discomfort, and she can no longer maintain her home and garden the way she would like. There has been a dramatic, drastic, and completely permanent change in Lily's life. The defendant's drunk driving ended Lily's old life and started her new life, a life dominated by pain — overwhelming, constant, intractable pain. However, Lily is a gutsy, brave, and courageous young woman who will never give up and is doing the very best she can to live a normal life.

Canadians love underdogs and love to see the underdog triumph. The reason for this is that most people see themselves as underdogs and can readily identify with an underdog. Jurors are always ready to strike a blow for the underdog. If you can portray your client as an underdog in your opening statement, you will gain an advantage.

The same is true for a person who never gives up, despite all odds. Your client may have a badly injured neck, but somehow he continues to fight to lead a normal life. This picture of your client as a person who is trying to function as best he or she can is especially useful if you know that the defence has surveillance evidence of your client doing things such as shovelling snow. You may want to say something as follows:

> Notwithstanding that Lily is a "neck cripple" she continues to try to lead a normal life, to try to do the things she did before. Although it causes her pain and discomfort during the activity and for a period of time after, she still attempts to do some things around her house like trying to shovel the snow. She can only do it occasionally and for brief

periods and pays the price afterward, but this is the kind of person she is — she never gives up.

Mention important witnesses and evidence

In most cases, a particular witness or document will be the focal point of your position. You want to get the jury ready for this witness or piece of evidence. For example, if an orthopaedic surgeon is going to be your main medical witness — and, for purposes of this example, assume that you have hired the surgeon and hence he or she is not a treating orthopaedic surgeon (although it is easy to avoid this by having the family doctor or rehabilitation consultant make the referral) — you may want to say something like this:

> During the trial, you will have the good fortune of hearing from Dr. Armstrong. Dr. Armstrong is a very skilful and experienced orthopaedic surgeon at Etobicoke General Hospital and, in fact, is the head orthopaedic surgeon at Etobicoke General Hospital.
>
> To assist you in deciding this case fairly and coming to a just result, I asked Dr. Armstrong to do an assessment of Lily. He saw Lily on two occasions. You will hear Dr. Armstrong's opinion that the injuries to Lily's neck are permanent and that repetitive bending or ...

Introduce the medical theory of your case

At some point during your opening statement — for example, after you have told the story as to how the collision occurred — you have to tell the jury in vivid detail what happened to your client medically. For example, in a rear-end collision, you might want to say:

> Lily did not know it then, but when her car was suddenly rammed from the rear without warning and knocked into the car ahead of it, the muscles, ligaments, and tendons in her neck were stretched beyond their physiological point of movement to the point where they were ripped and torn. Over the next few days, the healing process started and the muscles, ligaments, and tendons healed with the formation of scar tissue. The evidence will show that Lily has permanent scar tissue in her neck and that while the acute symptoms of severe pain have abated, Lily will have problems with her neck and limitations on her lifestyle for the rest of her life. She no longer has a normal neck. She has scar tissue in her neck, and it is permanent. In essence, because

of the negligence of the defendant in rear-ending Lily's vehicle, she has become a "neck-cripple."

Deal with complicated evidence

If your case involves complicated or technical matters, use the opening to make sure that the jury will not be afraid of these matters and not tune out such evidence when it comes up. You can tell the jury that you too found it confusing at first, but that it was not as complicated as it seemed after you heard an explanation. Or you can tell the jury that an expert witness will explain the technical aspects of the evidence.

Mention damage figures in opening statement

There is a great debate as to whether the economic losses being claimed should be mentioned in opening statement. Some argue that a jury is not ready this early in the trial to deal with large numbers. My feeling is that I want to get the numbers out as early as possible, for a number of reasons:

1) The jury will become conditioned and not be shocked later on to hear that I am asking for $300,000 rather than $30,000.
2) The jury will know that the case is a serious one and a large one right from the beginning.
3) If I have created a favourable courtroom impression from the beginning and the jurors perceive me as being honest, credible, and competent, they may think that what I am saying is evidence and accept my suggestions from the outset.

A possible way in opening statement to deal with a request for a large sum of money is as follows:

> Ladies and gentlemen, we are going to ask for a substantial sum in this case on the basis of the evidence — $610,000 for loss of income alone. And I ask you this: if there is clear, convincing evidence of serious, lifetime injuries and clear, convincing evidence that Howard cannot go back to his old job, and if this evidence adds up to a very large sum, do you feel you will be able to make an award consistent with the proof of the injuries and damages? Do you understand that I am not asking you for a blank cheque in advance? I would be foolish to do that. I am merely asking you if you can award an amount of money to

fit the seriousness of the injuries and the effect those injuries have had on Howard's ability to earn a living.

Jury empowerment in the opening statement

The opening statement is the first real opportunity counsel has to empower the jury. Somewhere in the opening you may want to empower each juror by saying something like this:

> Howard has entrusted his case to me to present, but the hardest work of all will be done by the six of you. Your job is far more difficult and far more important than anyone else's in this courtroom because the six of you are the judicial system in this case.
>
> For most of you, it is the first time you are going through this process. You are being asked to make a momentous and consequential decision — a decision that will affect someone else's life forever.
>
> Only the six of you have the power to right a wrong. Only the six of you have the power to award fair and full compensation. Only the six of you have the power to give a full cup of justice.
>
> I am sure each one of you is saying to yourself right now, "My goodness, we have never done this before. We want to do the right thing. How do we do the right thing?" You can and will do the right thing if you decide this case on the evidence and the evidence alone. You must not decide this case based on what you have read in the newspapers or seen on television or the movies or what people might have told you about a case they heard about from a friend of a friend. If you decide this case in accordance with the law given to you by the judge and the evidence you will hear, the six of you will come to a verdict you can all be proud of.
>
> You took on an obligation when you became a juror and that obligation was to do justice. If the six of you do not do justice for Howard, he simply cannot get justice. The only thing that I ask of you is that you use the enormous power you have to dispense justice fairly.

Closing the opening

There are many ways of closing the opening. I prefer to remind the jury of how fair I am and make a plea for justice. Others prefer to summarize the issues. An example of the method I use is as follows:

Either now or later in the case, the defendant's lawyer will talk to you. I want you to listen carefully to what the defendant's lawyer says and then make up your own minds as to which side is really supported by the evidence.

At the end of this case, I will have an opportunity to speak with you again, and at that time I will remind you of some of the things I have said here today. At that time I will ask you for one thing, and one thing only, and that is fair and reasonable compensation for Lily.

Maintain eye contact

As part of the ongoing process of developing a favourable courtroom image and developing rapport with each juror, you have to look at each juror during your opening. You cannot devote your time to one or two and avoid the rest.

Cross-examination

Although cross-examination is probably the area in which counsel gets the most satisfaction in a trial, few cases, if any, are won on cross-examination. The case is won on its structure from beginning to end. Nevertheless, successful cross-examination is a key component of winning a case, and much can be done from an early stage in the case to maximize your chances of successfully cross-examining defence witnesses.

Early preparation for cross-examination

You can position yourself for an effective cross-examination at trial by using certain techniques at examination for discovery and by exploiting the full potential of a summons. Some of these techniques are listed below.

Commit the deponent to the answer given

You can make inconsistencies between discovery and trial more dramatic by asking a few standard questions at examinations for discovery — several at the start and several at the end. At the start of an examination for discovery, ask a question similar to the following:

> If there is any question you do not understand or any question that
> needs clarification, please let me know and I will explain the question
> or clarify the question for you.

At the end of the examination for discovery, ask a question like the
following:

> Have you understood all the questions I have asked, and have you
> answered them truthfully and correctly? Is there any answer you want
> to modify, clarify, or expand upon in any way?

If at trial when you are cross-examining on inconsistencies you read
the above few questions and the answers to the witness, you will have
made it much more difficult for her or him to explain away any inconsistencies. You will also make yourself look like a very fair-minded person
and one in whom the judge or jury should have great trust and confidence.

Names and addresses of witnesses, and summaries of their evidence

Rule 31.06(2) of the *Rules of Civil Procedure* reads:

> (2) A party may on an examination for discovery obtain disclosure of
> the names and addresses of persons who might reasonably be expect-
> ed to have knowledge of transactions or occurrences in issue in the
> action, unless the court orders otherwise.

There is no reason why any counsel in any civil trial should be going
to trial without knowing the name and address of every witness who is
going to be called by the other side and a summary of every person's evidence. It is not a proper question on examination for discovery to ask for
the names and addresses of witnesses and a summary of the evidence
each person has. It is a proper question, however, pursuant to Rule
31.06(2), to ask for "the names and addresses of those persons who
might reasonably be expected to have knowledge of the transactions or
occurrences in issue in the action." Under the case law, you can then ask
for a summary of the evidence of each person. This is a broader question
than asking for the names and addresses of witnesses. The opposing
party is obligated to give to you even the names and addresses of persons
he knows might harm his case. Follow up this question by asking, "If
you become aware of any additional people in the future, will you provide
me with their names and addresses and a summary of their evidence?"

Findings, opinions, and conclusions of opposing counsel's expert

With respect to expert witnesses other than defence medical doctors who have conducted a defence medical examination, under Rule 53.03 an opposing party does not need to deliver an expert's report until ten days before trial. However, under Rule 31.06 at examination for discovery you are entitled to the expert's findings, opinions, and conclusions if the expert is going to be used at trial. In a situation in which the opposing party does not have an expert by the time of examination for discovery and you are quite certain that he or she will retain one before trial, you can ask these questions:

Q. In the event that an expert is retained, will you forthwith deliver a copy of the expert's report to me?

A. No.

Q. As soon as you receive any report from any expert (either in writing or orally), will you provide me forthwith with that expert's findings, opinions, and conclusion, or in the alternative, deliver an undertaking not to call the expert as a witness at trial?

If the answer to the last question is "no" you can bring a motion if the issue is going to be an important one. Most, but by no means all, opposing counsel will deliver an expert's report in a timely fashion rather than ten days before trial. If the subject matter upon which experts have been retained is a complex one, it is sharp practice or very close to sharp practice to deliver an expert's report only ten days before trial.

"Clean-up " questions at examination for discovery

Near the end of an examination for discovery, you would be well-advised to ask the following series of questions:

Q. Have I now received all of the facts and all of the evidence in support of the allegations contained in paragraph six of the statement of defence?

A. Yes.

Q. If you learn of any further facts or further evidence in support of the allegations contained in paragraph six of the statement of defence, will you please provide me with full details of these facts and evidence before trial?

A. Yes.

Use of summonses to adduce documentary evidence

There are a number of instances when a summons can assist you with cross-examination. Remember that service of a summons on a person obligates that person to do two things. First, it compels that person to attend as a witness in court to give oral evidence, and, second, it compels production of documents from that person.

> The procedure for using a summons is uncomplicated with a witness who is to give oral evidence. The witness is served personally with the summons and witness fees in accordance with the *Rules of Civil Procedure*. Counsel makes appropriate arrangements with the witness, who then attends as required. The witness takes the oath and is [guided] by counsel through the oral testimony, subject to any claim for privilege.
>
> A summons may also be used at trial to compel production of documents from a non-party who has custody.[3]

It is this latter use of a summons that is helpful for cross-examination. Here the procedure is different. The summons commands the custodian of the documents to attend at the outset of trial with the documents specified in the summons. Before the trial starts, but with the witness and his or her documents in the courtroom, the witness is asked whether he or she has any objection to producing the documents. If the witness has no objection, the documents are placed in the custody of the registrar of the court and the witness departs. The documents are not marked as exhibits, nor is the individual sworn. The documents are then available for the inspection of counsel before trial, and they can be used by either party in chief- or cross-examination of witnesses. At some point the documents must be formally proved.

Using the summons to compel production of documents from a non-party at the outset of trial is known as "calling the witness on his summons." Counsel would make use of this technique in the following circumstances:

---

3   G. Farrell, *The Use of Summons in a Civil Action* (Ontario Trial Lawyers Association, 30 October 1993) at 2–3.

- When the documents are useful to your case, but the oral evidence of the custodian may be dangerous to your case.
- When the onus to call the witness who must prove the documents is on the opposing party, you have an opportunity to look at the documents beforehand and to prepare for cross-examination and ultimately to cross-examine the witness.
- Where the document must be put to a witness in cross-examination before you can put your case in, such as in the use of a prior inconsistent statement.
- To avoid calling a defence witness when defending in a jury action, to maintain the right to address the jury last.[4]

Basics of cross-examination

Aims of cross-examination

Some of the potential aims of cross-examination are:

- Discrediting the testimony of the witness being examined.
- Using testimony of the witness in the witness box to discredit the unfavourable testimony of other witnesses.
- Using the testimony of the witness in the witness box to corroborate the favourable testimony of other witnesses and to contribute independently to the favourable development of your own case.

The dos and don'ts of cross-examination

1) Do not "wing it" with pointless cross-examination.
2) Do not prejudice the judge or jury against your client by showing a quick temper, by showing an offensive personality, or by using seemingly unfair tactics.
3) Do not ridicule or be sarcastic with a witness or treat every witness as if he or she is a perjurer.
4) Do not misrepresent the facts or use false innuendo.
5) Do not argue with a witness; it is usually a sign that the cross-examiner is receiving damaging answers.

---

4   The preceding section borrows heavily from G. Farrell, *The Use of Summons in a Civil Action* (Ontario Trial Lawyers Association, 30 October 1993) at 2–3, quoting J. Dunn, "Subpoena Duces Tecum" (1983) 4 Advocates Quarterly 94.

6) Do not become angry, except when, as a tactical and strategic matter, righteous indignation is appropriate.

7) Do not ask the question "why" unless you do not care what the answer is.

Asking a question on cross-examination without knowing the answer

It is often said that a cross-examiner should never ask a question unless he or she knows the answer. There are several reasons why that rule should not be considered absolute.

First, the question may be far more important than the answer, and you may not really care what the answer is. For example, you may have bloodied and bruised a defence neurologist who says that notwithstanding the fact that your client suffered periodic dizzy spells, he can still go back to work as a pipe fitter even though this involves working at very high heights on small platforms. You could ask, as your last question before you sit down, something like this:

> Doctor, do you want these members of the jury to believe that notwithstanding the fact that the plaintiff suffers from periodic dizzy spells and notwithstanding the fact that he works at great heights on platforms and notwithstanding the fact that if he has a dizzy spell while working on one of these platforms, he could fall and kill himself, he should still go back to work as a pipe fitter? Is that what you want this jury to believe?

The second exception is to ask some preliminary questions, the answers to which cannot hurt you before you get to the main question, the answer to which is crucial to the outcome of the case. In other words, creep up to the very important main question by asking preliminary questions that will give you a feeling or an idea about what the answer to the main question will be.

Finally, if you feel that the odds favour you getting the answer you want and you are prepared to take the chance, go ahead and ask. Before doing so, however, you must weigh the potential gain from the answer you want against the potential harm of getting the wrong answer, and then decide whether to ask the question.

Unnerve the witness at the beginning

With many witnesses, there are going to be one or several facts about which you know and with which you can unnerve them. An example of this may be several major inconsistencies between trial testimony and examination for discovery testimony. It is often advantageous to begin cross-examination with these strong points in order to make the witness as uncomfortable and as co-operative as possible.

More advanced techniques

Handling the witness who will not directly answer a question

In almost every trial you do, you will encounter at least one and probably several witnesses who will not answer your questions. They will either beat around the bush or they will give in their answer far more than you were asking. For example, you may ask a simple question as follows and get a very long-winded and speech-making answer not at all responsive to the question:

> Q. Did the plaintiff tell you he suffered from headaches?
>
> A. Yes, the plaintiff did tell me this, but in my view, the headaches were not serious, could easily be controlled by medication, and would probably disappear in about three months.

There are several ways of dealing with this. You can say:

> Dr. Jones, I will ask the question again. I want you to listen carefully to the question and simply answer what I am asking. If you do that, we will get through this a lot quicker, you will get to go home sooner, and the jury will get to go home sooner.

Or you can say something like this:

> Dr. Jones, under the rules that govern the conduct of civil proceedings, I am entitled to ask questions and you are obligated to give answers that are responsive to those questions. Do you understand that, and will you please try to be responsive to the questions asked?

If the witness still insists on speech-making, you can ask for help from the trial judge and say something like this:

> Your Honour, the witness is not being responsive to the questions asked. He is engaging in speech-making and is wasting a lot of the court's time. I ask that you direct him to confine his answers solely to the question asked.

Often, at this point, opposing counsel will get up and say that the witness is entitled to give a complete answer to the questions asked and that is all he is doing. Some judges will make a witness answer strictly the questions being asked, and others will give the witness such a wide latitude that the witness can make speeches.

Another way of attempting to control the witness is as follows:

> Witness, I am going to ask you a series of questions that in my view can be answered yes or no. I would like to reach an agreement with you and ask that either you answer the questions I ask you yes or no or, if you feel you cannot answer yes or no, you tell me and I will try to rephrase the question so that it can be answered yes or no. Do we have that agreement?

This latter method has not, however, been terribly effective.

Watching the clock

There are many reasons why your cross-examination will be interrupted: a recess, lunch, or the end of the day. If possible, end on a strong point that the jury will remember. If there are a few minutes to go before the end of a day and you have made a particularly good point with the witness, suggest to the judge that you break for the day because you are going to enter upon another major area of inquiry. If, on the other hand, the end of the day comes, you feel that you are about to make a point, and the judge suggests that you end for the day, ask the judge if you can continue until the end of this area of inquiry.

If you end strongly, the judge or jury will remember it and your momentum will not be broken. If you finish a particular topic, rather than have it interrupted part way through, you will not give the witness an opportunity to collect his or her thoughts or speak to others.

Use of examination for discovery transcripts at trial

At virtually every civil trial there is an opportunity to cross-examine the opposite party on inconsistencies between what the party said at trial and what he or she said at examination for discovery. The correct procedure to impeach the witness at trial if you prefer the answer given on examination for discovery is as follows:

Q. Do you remember being examined for discovery at the office of Bay Street Court Stenographers by me on 23 September 1990?

A. Yes.

Q. And before you were examined for discovery; you swore on the Bible to tell the truth.

A. Yes.

Q. And before the examination for discovery, you met with your lawyer and prepared for the examination for discovery.

A. Yes.

Q. And you remember at the examination for discovery being asked certain questions and giving certain answers under oath.

A. Yes.

(To the judge) Your Honour, I direct your attention to page 31, question 434 of the transcript.

Q. Witness, on page 31 and specifically starting at question 434, do you recall being asked these questions and giving these answers:

Q. 434: "And did you see the other vehicle before the accident?"

"Yes."

Q. 435: "What speed was it travelling?"

"Approximately thirty-five kilometres per hour."

Q. Do you recall being asked those questions and giving those answers at your examination for discovery back on 23 September 1990?

A. Yes.

Q. And here today at trial, you say that the other vehicle was travelling sixty-five kilometres per hour.

A. Yes.

Q. Which is the true answer — the answer you gave here today, where you say the other vehicle was travelling sixty-five kilometres per hour, or the answer you gave on 23 September 1990, when you said the other vehicle was travelling thirty-five kilometres per hour?

A. Well, the answer I gave here today is more accurate.

Q. Isn't it fair to say that because the time the examination for discovery took place was closer to the events in question in the accident, your memory would be fresher at the examination for discovery?

A. Yes.

Q. That being the case, is the answer you gave on examination for discovery on 23 September 1990, most probably the correct answer?

A. Yes.

The impact of this exchange will be even greater if at examination for discovery you made the witness commit herself or himself to the answers given there by asking the above opening and closing questions.

Attacking the factual underpinnings of an expert's opinion

It is virtually impossible for any expert to know all the facts of a particular situation on which he or she is going to base an opinion. Sometimes the expert will not know very important facts; at other times, he or she will not know less important facts. The way to attack the factual underpinnings of an expert's opinion is set out below.

The first example is a cross-examination of a plaintiff's orthopaedic surgeon when he did not receive an accurate history from the plaintiff.

Q. Doctor, you took a history from the plaintiff?

A. Yes.

Q. And you relied on that history in coming to your conclusions, did you not?

A. Yes.

Q. And if the history you received was incorrect or incomplete, can that throw off your conclusions?

A. Yes.

Q. It can make them wrong, can it not?

A. Yes.

Q. Doctor, did you know that five years before this accident, the plaintiff had another accident in which she injured her neck and had physiotherapy for six months?

A. No, I did not know that.

Q. Would you agree that you received an incorrect history from the plaintiff?

A. Yes.

Q. As you indicated earlier, this can throw off your conclusions. It can make them wrong.

A. Yes.

Q. And in this particular case, it may be that the plaintiff was attempting to deceive you?

A. Yes.

Q. It might well mean that the plaintiff is not telling the truth on other important matters?

A. Yes.

The second example is a cross-examination of a forensic accountant who has given evidence on behalf of the plaintiff and does not have all the facts:

Q. Mr. Joyce, you have relied on certain facts and made certain assumptions in coming to your conclusions that the plaintiff's loss of income, both past and future, is $325,000?

A. Yes.

Q. And one of those assumptions was that the plaintiff's injuries prevented him from climbing ladders, is that not correct?

A. Yes.

Q. Did you know that the plaintiff was seen climbing a ladder not three weeks ago at a friend's home when he was helping that friend clean out his eavestroughs?

A. No, I did not know that.

Q. And did you know that four months ago the plaintiff used a ladder to climb up the side of his own house to remove screens?

A. No, I did not know that.

Q. It would appear that a major assumption you made in concluding that the plaintiff has suffered a loss of income of $325,000 is simply not correct?

A. Yes, that would appear to be the case.

Q. And, if in fact what I am suggesting to you is correct, you would agree with me that your opinion that the plaintiff has lost $325,000 is probably wrong?

A. Yes.

Q. And in fact, the plaintiff may not have suffered any income loss whatsoever?

A. Yes.

With respect to the second example, a good plaintiff's lawyer should be able to avoid this type of cross-examination. It is incumbent on the defence counsel who made suggestions about the ladder-climbing to the plaintiff's accountant to then call the person or persons who saw the plaintiff climb the ladders — usually a private investigator. If you were using the *Rules of Civil Procedure* to full advantage, you should have obtained the names and addresses of those persons who might reasonably be expected to have knowledge of the transactions and occurrences in issue in the lawsuit as well as a summary of their evidence. You should also have received an undertaking to receive future names, addresses, and evidence. If the defence counsel has information that your client was climbing ladders, you should know about it in advance of trial pursuant to your discovery questions.

Closing Argument

Closing argument is the last opportunity you have to communicate with the jury. Accordingly, it is imperative that your closing express your position and the reasons why you should prevail logically and forcefully. If the defence has presented evidence (and your overall game plan should have forced the defence to do so, if it is otherwise a case where the defence might not have to call evidence), you have the opportunity of speaking last. As with the opening statement, where you have the opportunity to take advantage of "primacy," in the closing statement you have the opportunity to take advantage of "recency." You want to make the very best of this opportunity.

Your closing argument should be prepared in advance of trial and should be constructed so as to parallel your opening and your examination-in-chief. This parallel construction can only be achieved if you organize and plan in advance of trial.

Discussing evidence

You have to discuss the evidence in your closing, but under no circumstances do you want to give a long-winded recitation of the evidence. You want to selectively pick and emphasize those portions of the evidence that tie the case together and that will give the jury the impression that you should win. This includes clearing up any confusing or conflicting evidence.

The use of emotion

Whereas the opening statement must, for the most part, be delivered in a conversational style, this is not true of summation. The issue regarding summation is whether to make a logical appeal to the jury through a discussion of the evidence only, or to make an emotional appeal as well. Defence counsel will be limited to a discussion of the evidence, as they do not have a sympathetic side to their case that would lend to an emotional argument. Not so with plaintiff's counsel. You should inject as much emotion as possible into your closing.

My preference is to discuss the facts as I have noted above and thereafter concentrate on making an emotional appeal. Just before I deliver my summation, I think of the saddest things that have ever happened to me (the death of close family members), and I very quickly get into a mood where I have no difficulty making an emotional appeal. The emotions I try to convey are those of sympathy for the plaintiff and righteous indignation at the conduct of the defendant or the position defence counsel has taken with respect to the plaintiff's case — for example, not admitting liability when the defendant was impaired.

The use of exhibits

Using exhibits in closing argument performs two valuable functions: corroborating and highlighting the main points of your argument, and providing breaks for the jury. Regardless of how effective a closing argument you have prepared or how well you are delivering it, a juror's attention span is limited. If you drone on for fifteen minutes, you will lose the jury. You have to have a juror yawn just once when you are in the middle of what you think is one of the best closings you have ever given to realize this. Using exhibits during your closing provides a refreshing change of pace and allows you to recapture the jury's attention.

Capitalize on the judge's charge

You know what law the judge is going to explain to the jury in his or her charge. By telling the jury that the facts, as well as the law that the judge will instruct them on after your closing, support your position, you can use these instructions to your advantage. The key to using this technique is to discuss the facts and then immediately follow with what the law will be in the judge's charge so that the association is firmly fixed in the jurors' minds. An example of this technique is found below under the headings "Use of Analogies" and "The Burden of Proof."

Introductory line

Before the closing argument is the part of the trial where good trial lawyers develop a cold sweat on the palms of their hands. The reason for this is that the closing argument is the part of the trial where counsel must use almost all of the advocacy skills he or she has developed to communicate with the jury.

Most experienced trial lawyers have standard lines as a crutch or icebreaker. There are as many different introductory lines as there are trial lawyers. One I use quite frequently is as follows:

> Counsel for the defendants have just finished speaking with you, and
> they have spoken with great eloquence. I may not measure up to them
> in eloquence, but I ask you not to hold that against my client, Lily. I

have done my best for her, just as I would for any one of you, if any of you were my client.

Another possibility is as follows:

> I want to thank you for spending the last five days with Lily and myself. I know that I am not the only one that has gone home at night thinking about this case. I thank you, for without you, the jurors, the whole system would fall into disrepair.

Handling defence counsel's sympathy argument

Both the defence lawyer in closing and the judge in the charge will warn the jury not to decide the case based on sympathy. A possible way of dealing with this is as follows:

> Ladies and gentlemen, the defence lawyers warned against sympathy for Lily. I agree. Don't look at Lily with sympathy. Believe me, she has received plenty of sympathy. She has received enough sympathy to last ten lifetimes. We are not here about sympathy. We are here about justice.

Adding emphasis by using trial transcripts

If there is an important bit of evidence in a trial, you can help draw the jury's attention to it by ordering that part of the transcript during the trial and reading from it during your summation. For example, you may say:

> Do you remember when the doctor hired by the defendant's lawyer took the stand and I questioned him about the formation of scar tissue in Lily's neck? Do you remember me pointing out to him that he had not made any mention of the formation of scar tissue in the report he delivered to the defendant's lawyer, and then at trial he admitted it? The formation of scar tissue in Lily's neck and the effect of it on her is very important and is the most important medical issue in this case. Several days ago I asked the court reporter to type this part of the transcript, and I now have copies. (Your Honour, I have a copy for you. May I distribute copies to each of the jurors. [Yes.] Thank you.) (And then going to the jury box.) Mrs. Jones, would you please take a copy and pass the rest down to the other jurors? Thank you very much. (And then counsel reads from the trial transcript.)

Q. Dr. Slanger, there is no mention of the formation of scar tissue in your report.

A. That is correct. I did not think it was important.

Q. And yet, you just told us a minute ago that this scar tissue will interfere with the sliding and gliding of the muscles, ligaments, and tendons in Lily's neck.

A. Yes.

Similarly, if defence counsel said in opening that he or she was going to call a certain witness or demonstrate a certain fact and has not done so, order the transcript and read from it in summation to bring added emphasis to the defence lawyer's "broken promise."

Use of analogies

An analogy is a form of comparison. It makes something clear by comparing it to something else and brings out an idea that is difficult to express. The use of analogies is one of the most powerful tools that can be used in closing argument. There are many kinds of analogies that can be used in closing argument. Following are some examples.

The burden of proof

At the end of trial, His Honour will direct you on the burden of proof. I would like to say a word about that now. The plaintiff has the burden of proof, and all the plaintiff needs to do in a civil case such as this is prove her case by preponderance of the evidence or a balance of probabilities. Now, what does that mean? Here are the scales. (Hold your hands up in front of you.) All the plaintiff has to do is tip the scales ever so slightly, and that is a preponderance of the evidence or balance of probabilities. It does not have to go like this (indicating with hands one scale very high and the other very low). It does not have to remove every doubt. Just the tipping of the scales ever so slightly is all that is required in a definition of preponderance of the evidence. Otherwise, someone could negligently injure you and you would have to come to court and remove every possible doubt in a juror's mind. That is not the law. So you can have all kinds of doubt and if you think about something and say, "Oh, it is probably correct," then Lily succeeds on that point.

And with the chance of something happening in the future, such as the chance that Lily will lose income in the future, the burden of proof is even less. His Honour will tell you that if there is a real and substantial "possibility," and I say "possibility" rather than "probability," that as a result of the injuries suffered by Lily, her capacity to earn income in the future has been reduced or she will lose income in the future, you as a jury "must," not "may," "must" review this evidence and must fix a monetary value in respect thereof. This is a very important point, and I want you to listen carefully to His Honour's instructions on this.

The standard of care

We allege that the defendant, Maria Evans, was negligent. Let's look at the standard of care imposed on the defendant. His Honour will tell you that the standard of care depends on the amount of risk. What does that mean? If you were loading potatoes into a wagon in the field, you would pick them up with a shovel and heave them toward the wagon. You would not be much concerned if one potato fell off, would you? One potato is not worth much, and if it fell off, it would not hurt much. But suppose you were loading nitroglycerine. Then how carefully, gingerly, you would carry it and place it in someone else's hands, wrapped in foam and cotton, and protect it against vibration. Both acts will be done with ordinary care. Ordinary care in handling danger that is nitroglycerine and ordinary care in handling non-danger, potatoes.

In this case the defendant was handling a lethal object — a car in a residential and school area with children playing. With what care should the defendant have handled this car? I say, with extreme care. And how did she handle it? I submit, carelessly.

The effect of a disability on ability to earn income

When considering the effect of a disability on a person's ability to work and earn income, I suggest that you not look at what has been taken away from a person but what is left. Let me give you an example of what I mean. Now, I know that Lily is not an automobile, but if you have a brand-new automobile and it has a flat tire and you can never fix that flat tire, then that flat tire renders the automobile 100 percent useless as a means of transportation. While a human being is a machine of marvellous efficiency, you cannot write to the factory and get a replacement part. Lily's leg is similar to an automobile tire. It does not work the way it is supposed to. And while Lily will still be able to work, she will not be able to work as efficiently and productively as she would otherwise be able to. Any job that involves repeated lifting, bending, or crouching will aggravate her leg injury.

Handling non-pecuniary general damages

There are many ways of dealing with non-pecuniary general damages in summation. An argument you may wish to make can go something like this:

> We have dealt with all of the blanks of His Honour's questions with respect to damages except one — the blank with respect to general damages. By filling in all of the other blanks with the figures I asked, you have not yet given Lily anything. All you have done up to that point is replace what the defendant took away from her. You have simply given her money to compensate her for expenses and losses she has incurred or will incur.
>
> You have given her nothing for general damages. General damages are damages for two things — pain and suffering on the one hand and loss of enjoyment of life on the other. How do you arrive at a figure for this? How do you perform bookkeeping for pain and suffering and loss of enjoyment of life? It is hard to conceive of, isn't it? And yet, that is your obligation, that is your responsibility, your duty. To the extent that I can be helpful to you in assessing general damages for pain and suffering and loss of enjoyment of life, I would like to do so.

Under Bill 164, I may talk about a third category called "loss of amenities."

> There are two ways of assessing general damages. One of them is to go into the jury room and make your best guess. You just might be right, but you will probably be wrong. I do not think that any one of you would like to simply guess at a figure for general damages. Another way to assess general damages is to go into the jury room and use a methodical and logical approach following the law and the evidence. What do I mean by this? Well, there are two separate and distinct categories of general damages for which Lily is entitled to be compensated. The first is pain and suffering, and the second is loss of enjoyment of life.

Let's consider, first pain and suffering. You cannot feel another person's pain. Pain is a cruel monster. It is almost impossible to describe. People in pain pray for death. No one has ever prayed for pain. Lily is still a young girl, and she is going to suffer from and live with pain for the rest of her life.

Let's consider the second aspect of general damages — loss of enjoyment of life. You are going to have to measure what human life is all about. Lily is no longer free to spend her days and enjoy them as she desires. She will no longer be able to run. She will no longer be able to play with her friends the way she used to and enjoy sports the way she once did. Think of the inconvenience. Think of the unhappiness. Everyone in this courtroom has feelings, hopes, and dreams, and Lily is no different. You are going to have to measure the effect of these injuries on Lily's feelings, hopes, and dreams.

So those are the two categories of general damages — first, pain and suffering, and second, loss of enjoyment of life.

What is the next step in the methodical and logical approach to assessing general damages that I was telling you about? We know that this unfortunate incident occurred three years ago. Consider the pain and suffering that Lily has been through from the day of the incident up to the present time without regard to her loss of enjoyment of life and without regard to anything that takes place in the future, and come to a figure for this pain and suffering. Then do the same thing for loss of enjoyment of life. If you add these two figures together you will have arrived at a figure for pain and suffering and for loss of enjoyment of life from the time of the incident up to the present time.

From the actuary, we know that Lily's life expectancy is another sixty years. Accordingly, Lily is expected to live for another twenty three-year periods. You have decided on a figure for the first three years, and this should help you in arriving at a figure for the next twenty three-year periods. You can add up these figures and you will have applied a methodical and logical approach to assessing general damages, and you will have avoided simply guessing at a figure.

If you use this methodical and logical approach, you will come up with a large sum of money. From my experience, I can tell you someone in the jury room may say, "Oh, that is a lot of money. We'd better pare that down." Some of you on the jury may reject it simply because it is too large. Those of you who do that will not be following the law.

That would be unfair to Lily. I am going to have to ask some of you on the jury to hold out for the right principles, not to give in, but to hold out for being fair, for being right, for being a person of principle. When you compromise, when you give in and agree to less than what is fair, you, as a juror, will not be giving 100 percent justice. And to the degree that the figure is compromised whether it be by 10 percent or by 20 percent, remember that anything less than 100 percent justice is an injustice.

Something you may want to use in a scarring case, especially involving the threshold, may go like this:

And what about the scarring? A scar is small if it is on someone else's face, but if it is on your own face it might be the biggest, ugliest-looking thing you can imagine. We live in a world where beauty is supreme. None of us in this courtroom started it, but we are bombarded with it every day, in school and on television. People write poems about beauty. Sunsets are beautiful. A full moon is beautiful. The most beautiful painting is the Mona Lisa. Lily did not start all of this concern for beauty, but now she must learn how to live the rest of her life without it.

Another possibility regarding a pain and suffering argument may go like this:

Let's first consider pain and suffering. You cannot feel another person's pain. It is almost impossible to describe. People in pain pray for death. No one has ever prayed for pain. Lily is still a very young woman, and she is going to have to suffer from and live with pain for the rest of her life.

Jury empowerment in closing argument

In summation, one way in which you may want to attempt to empower the jury in a drunk driving case may go something like this:

The power of your vote today is enormous. This is not like voting in an election. Here you truly dictate justice. Justice not just for the parties in this case, but for the many other victims of drunk drivers and many other potential victims of drunk drivers.

How many people must be maimed and killed before we realize that we have the power to stop this? It is an epidemic. We have the power to stop this from happening again. You have the power, by your verdict, to prevent this from happening to hundreds and even thousands of other victims. You have that power, now you must take that power and you must exercise it because drunk drivers won't do it themselves.

Your verdict must send a message so strong and so loud that it gets to all drunk drivers and would-be drunk drivers. Your verdict must say, "Enough is enough. We will stand for no more. We the jury in Lily Smith's case will not accept another tragedy that could be prevented." You have the power. Use that power.

Another way of empowering the jury is make sure the individual jurors know that they are the conscience of the community. For example:

You are the conscience of the community. What do I mean by that? You are not six individuals, you are a jury, and the jury system in this country is 120 years old. By your decision you are going to set standards in this community. Not only for the parties in this case, but for everyone in your community. For your neighbours, your friends, your relatives, and your family. By your decision, standards are established, and hopefully by those standards the quality of life improves and continues to improve. That is the power of your verdict, and it is an awesome responsibility.

Another example is as follows:

Ladies and gentlemen, it is only you who have the power to render full and complete justice for this courageous young woman. There is only one cup of justice, and it should be full — not one drop less. The six of you have the power to balance the books, to pay back a debt, to right a wrong.

Evidence not called by the defendant

Even if the defendant puts in all the evidence that he or she should, in almost every case you try you still have an opportunity to bolster your case and make the defence look bad by referring to evidence that was available to defence counsel to call, but which was not called. For example:

I want to say a few words about the evidence you did not hear. You have seen the great skill of counsel for the defendants in cross-examining the witnesses and the great skill with which he addressed you. So you have a mystery. A mystery which, to a large extent, will help you in deciding this case fairly. The mystery is that of the missing witnesses.

For do you, for one solitary moment, think that if there had been any evidence favourable to the defendants to demonstrate that the defendant was not negligent or that the injuries to Lily and the losses to Lily were not truly devastating, this evidence would not have been called by the defence? A human being does not live in a vacuum. Lily has friends, schoolmates, workmates, relatives. Counsel for the defendants have not summoned to court any of these people to show that the effect of these injuries was anything other than devastating. You waited patiently to hear this evidence, you have the right to hear this evidence, and you did not hear it, because it did not exist.

Avoid having the plaintiff punished for overreaching

If you have asked for hundreds of thousands of dollars in future loss of income, there is always the chance that the jury will think the plaintiff is overreaching and asking for too much. Under no circumstances can you afford to have your client look greedy because then the jury surely will punish your client with a lower award of damages in other areas, such as non-pecuniary general damages. One way to handle this is as follows:

I am asking you, ladies and gentleman of the jury, to return a verdict of hundreds of thousands of dollars. I submit that the figures I have asked for on behalf of Lily are just and fair and in accordance with the evidence. But if you disagree, if you feel I am overreaching, if you feel I am asking for too much, please do me one favour. Do not take it out on an innocent person, namely my client Lily. You decide what amount to give her. It is your decision.

Use of biblical passages

The nature of the population has changed dramatically in the last thirty years, particularly in large urban areas. In these areas there will be jurors who are agnostic, are atheist, or subscribe to different faiths, so if you are going to use references to the Bible, consider your audience. References to the Bible may be offensive to certain jurors in certain communities. However, the Bible (including the Apocrypha) is a work of great merit quite aside from theology, and it contains many gems for the trial lawyer. A biblical quote I use often is as follows:

Something was written in the book of Apocrypha, chapter 30, verse 16, which is as true today as it was when it was written five thousand years ago: "There is no riches above a sound body."

Certainly good health is a person's most precious asset. But you cannot give Lily back the body she had. What you can give her is a reasonable semblance of human dignity to replace what she has lost.

There is no tomorrow

The jury has to understand that the plaintiff cannot come back to correct an inadequate award. If the jury is going to err in the amount of its verdict, you want it to err on the side of giving your client too much, not too little. A possible way of dealing with this is as follows:

> You have seen the attitude of the defence — at all costs to minimize your award — every question designed for that purpose and to that end. Because of this attitude, Lily has come to you humbly. The amount we are asking for is substantial, there is no question about it. But remember this. Remember the pencil I wrote with during this trial is susceptible to error (hold pencil in front of the jury). However, you can see that my pencil has an eraser. But members of the jury, the pencil with which you write is completely different. Do you know why? (Snap pencil in half). Because, members of the jury, the pencil with which you write has no eraser. If you make a mistake and fail to take into consideration some aspects of Lily's damages, that mistake can never be erased. It can never be corrected. Lily cannot come back to you a year from now, five years from now, or thirty years from now, and ask you to correct an inadequate award. This is the only time — today is the only day. So please, be sure that when you are filling in the various amounts for damages in His Honour's questions, you do not make a mistake.

Closing thoughts on closing argument

The final thought that counsel wants to leave with the jury may require minutes or seconds to deliver. This is the point in closing where you should speak more slowly and use a lower tone of voice. Dramatic pauses can be particularly effective at the end of the closing. An example of the closing of a summation is as follows:

> When you walk out of here, this case will just be a memory to you. Perhaps pleasant, perhaps unpleasant, but you will be out of this court-

room and finished with this case. But Lily will live with your decision every single day, every single hour, every single minute, for the rest of her life. She comes to you, six members of the jury, because she has nowhere else to go. You have an inescapable responsibility. You are called upon in this case to do the highest task known to humanity — to do justice. It is a truly godlike task. I know you will not let me down.

After completing your closing, stand for several seconds and do not move. Give the jury an opportunity to think about your thought-provoking and incisive argument.

Other Tools of Courtroom Communication

Avoiding admissions of liability

If you have outrageous liability facts, such as drunk driving by the defendant, under no circumstances do you want to allow the defendant to admit liability. The reason for this is that as soon as liability is admitted, evidence of the defendant's drunkenness becomes irrelevant and hence inadmissible. You then lose a golden opportunity to have the jury "punish" the defendant by a higher award of damages than otherwise might be the case. Two ways to avoid admissions of liability are, first, to claim in the statement of claim an amount exceeding the defendant's insurance limits, and second, to claim punitive, exemplary, and aggravated damages which are not covered by an insurance policy.

Controlling space

Canadians equate the greater accumulation of space with status and dominance. For example, the larger your house, the more cars you own, the higher up you are in a hotel or apartment building, the greater the perception of status. The same is true in a courtroom. Jurors will perceive you as having greater power and confidence if you have greater control and ownership of the space in a courtroom. Some ways you can control and dominate space in a courtroom are as follows:

- Continually move about the space, from your chair to the end of the jury box to the witness stand to where the registrar is sitting.
- Use gestures that are natural to you.

- Stay physically exposed to the jurors. Do not deliver your opening or your submissions behind the podium, and always be in full view of the jurors.
- Prevent the defence lawyer from controlling the space.
- Avoid invading territory that belongs to the jurors.

As counsel, you are permitted to move around the courtroom and to stand in locations that you feel are most strategic. This is important in controlling space and maximizing the effect of your various examinations and addresses to the jury.

You should conduct examinations-in-chief from location A on the accompanying schematic drawing of a courtroom. One reason for this is that when the witness is looking at you, he or she will also necessarily be looking at the jury. Another reason is that you want the jury's attention directed toward the witness and not at yourself, and by standing at location A you will be as unobtrusive as possible.

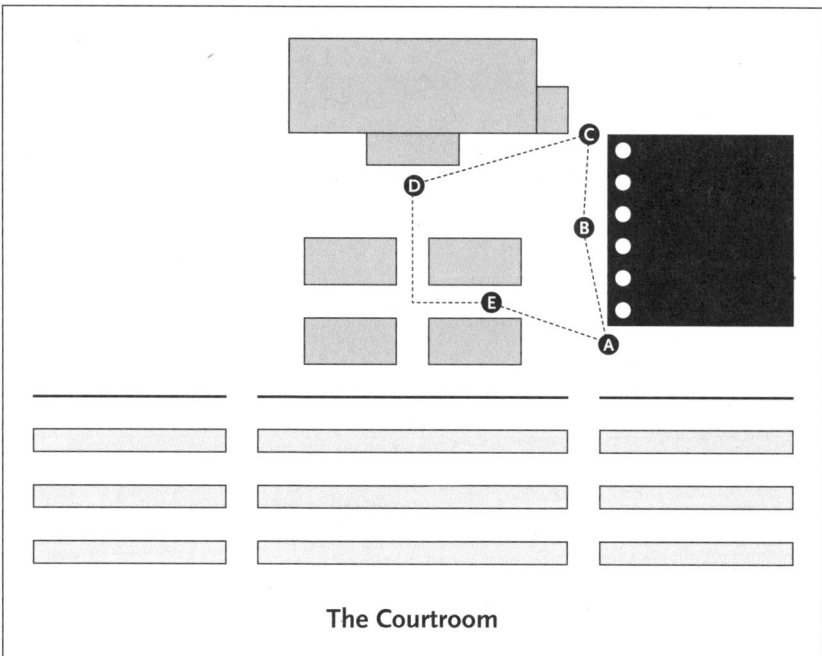

The Courtroom

You should conduct cross-examination from location B. The reason for this is that you want to be the dominant physical presence during cross-examination and you want to be the centre of the jury's attention. If you stand directly in front of the jury, you will force them to watch you and listen to your questions. The jurors will also be able to see any facial expressions you want to make while asking a question or listening to an answer.

You should also open and close from location B. You can easily make eye contact with all the jurors and make gestures and do all of the other things necessary to build trust and rapport with the jury from this location. If you stand closer to one end of the jury box than to the other, it will seem as though you are favouring those to whom you are standing closest.

Location C is where you should be when you are dealing with exhibits with the witnesses, and location D is where you should be dealing with exhibits with the registrar.

Location E is where you will be sitting when you are not examining witnesses, addressing the jury, or dealing with exhibits. You can see that during the trial, if you stand where you should, you will be controlling the space from location A all the way to location E and getting the most out of your examinations and addresses to the jury.

Use of impact words and phrases

Do not say "accident" because, after all, "accidents happen." Say instead "crash" or "collision." Do not refer to the defence lawyer as "my friend." You do not want any juror thinking that the defence lawyer is your friend. Refer to him or her as the "defendant's lawyer" or, when the opportunity arises, as the "corporate defendant's lawyer."

Avoid legal phrases

Examples of words to avoid and words to use in their place are as follows:

Avoid	Use
prior to	before
aforementioned	previously mentioned
by reason of	because
cease	stop
in lieu of	instead
on or before	on
said	the
commence	begin, start
endeavour	try
during the course of	during
proceed	go, go ahead
obtain	get
utilize	use

The rule of three

The Rule of Three works effectively because it creates a rhythmic pattern. Read the following sentences out loud, and see which one has the most impact.

- Before the collision, Joe was an open and gregarious person.
- Before the collision, Joe was an open, gregarious, and fun-loving person.
- Before the collision, Joe was an open, fun-loving, gregarious, and happy person.

When read properly, with effective voice tone and emphasis, the second sentence will have the most impact and accordingly, the greatest likelihood of retention by the jurors.

For a slightly more elaborate example of the Rule of Three consider the following:

> The tragic collision of 28 June 1992, was needless, senseless, and endless.
>
> It was needless in the sense that Johnny Brown's death could have been avoided by the exercise of simple care and ordinary prudence on the part of the driver of the corporate defendant's truck.
>
> It was senseless in the sense that, as a result of this driver's negligence, these parents have lost their only son. They have sustained a substantial and tragic loss.
>
> It was endless in the sense that these parents must now face the twenty-five years of life that lie ahead of them without the comfort, aid, and protection that a loving son, like Johnny Brown, would have provided his parents.

The Rule of Three applies not only to phrases and sentences. It also applies to major statements or issues presented in a case.

Parallelism

Parallelism refers to maintaining a consistency in the type of words that are used. Below is an example of three major points that do not have parallel construction. Read them out loud and listen to how they sound.

> Sandy had a zest for education, wanted the best for his family, and was well-known in the community.

Compare:

> Sandy believed in education. He believed in his family. He believed in
> his community.

There are only three words that the jury needs to remember — education, family, and community. A second benefit from this example is the use of repetition: "Sandy believed ...."

The use of repetition

Some of the greatest speeches ever given have used repetition. Will you ever forget Martin Luther King Jr.'s speech in which he said over and over again: "I have a dream"?

Repetition is the key to retention in memory. During the trial your theme and major points should be repeated during the opening statement, examination-in-chief, cross-examination, and closing.

Link to an existing belief system

It is impossible to change people's beliefs, and it is crucial for you as plaintiff's counsel to link up to the jurors' view of the world. For example, a juror's perception may be that low-speed collisions cannot cause serious injury. If you are acting for a plaintiff injured in a low-speed collision, with little or no damage to the vehicles involved, it will be important to create a picture of how your client's collision and circumstances differ from the norm. It is impossible to alter the belief that low-speed collision cannot cause serious injury. Therefore you need to do three things:

1. Acknowledge the existing belief system. This does not mean that you validate the existing belief system as being correct, but it does mean that you acknowledge its existence. You might say:

> I know that we often think that a low-speed impact cannot cause
> injury. This may be because we ourselves have been in a low-speed
> impact and have escaped injury.

2. Link to the existing belief:

> Now in this case, there was a low-speed impact. The defendant's truck
> was travelling at about ten kilometres per hour, and Kelly's car was
> travelling at about five kilometres per hour at the time of the collision.

There was no damage to the defendant's car and only $250 in damage to Kelly's car.

3. Build a new belief:

But this case is different, for five reasons. First, the defendant was driving a truck that weighed over four tons — much heavier than the average car — and Kelly was driving a Honda Accord, a car smaller than the average. Second, Kelly's car was catapulted forward one-and-a-half car lengths, causing her head to whip wildly back and forth. Third, the shoulder part of Kelly's seat belt held her trunk firmly in place, causing extraordinary whipping forces on her neck. Fourth, Kelly has an unusually slender neck, far thinner than average. And, fifth, at the time of impact, her head was turned to the left to allow her to watch for oncoming traffic.

Losing objections

If you lose an objection, do not slump your shoulders forward, avoid eye contact, and look dejected. Instead, stand tall and give a look of approval. Chances are that the jurors will think you got what you wanted. You will be portraying confidence through your demeanour.

The same is true if you are arguing a motion in the absence of the jury. If you lose the motion, when the jury returns you should look confident and try to continue your questions as though you have won the motion.

If you have indeed won the motion, you will want to make sure the jury knows where to direct its annoyance for having to leave the courtroom. When the jury returns, you may want to start your very first question as follows: "As I was asking, before the defendant's lawyer interrupted ...."

You should make objections sparingly and only when absolutely necessary. Jurors think a counsel who is continually objecting has something to hide, and the jurors do not appreciate having continually to leave the courtroom, because they feel they are missing out on something important.

Focusing your message

If you want to draw particular attention to a part of your opening or closing, or even the examination-in-chief or cross-examination, you can say

something like: "The third and final point I want you to consider is ..."
or "Now, this is important ...."

Conclusion

If you try cases, you will lose some cases. There is no shame in losing a
case if you have done your best. The oath of the athletes of the Special
Olympics is as applicable to trial lawyers trying cases on behalf of victims
as it is to the athletes of the Special Olympics: "Let me win, but if I cannot win, let me be brave in the attempt." Losing a case can cause feelings
of self-doubt, but if you thoroughly prepare your cases and apply the
basic skills of advocacy, you will become one of those lawyers who consistently get good results and seem to win more than their share.

[This article first appeared in the August 1996 issue of *The Advocates'
Society Journal*.]

Stranger in a Strange Land: Advocacy Before Administrative Tribunals

David Stockwood, Q.C.*

A lawyer's role is everywhere that "justice" is administered, either to individuals or to organizations. In every area of justice, he must be ready, willing, and trained to act. It is the job of the barrister today to put his client's case not only in the familiar, well-trodden paths of the courts where he has endless models to follow and great traditions to guide him, but also to be ready to put his client's case in any forum where "judgments" are to be rendered.

                                                          – John T. Weir, Q.C.

The above quotation and the sub-title of this article are taken from an excellent lecture by the late Jack Weir, Q.C.[1] Although the paper was published in 1971, most of what he said then is still relevant and too often ignored. The purpose of this article is the same as that of the Weir lecture: to encourage counsel to appear before unfamiliar administrative tribunals and to suggest ways in which they can use their advocacy skills to the greatest effect.[2]

---

*   David Stockwood, Stockwoods LLP, Toronto.

1   *Law Society of Upper Canada Special Lectures 1971* (Toronto: Richard De Boo, 1971).

2   After completing the first draft of this article, my attention was drawn to a 1988 Canadian Bar Association of Ontario panel discussion on the same subject. The panel moderator was Patricia Jackson, and the panelists, in order of appearance, were

Although I do professional discipline defence work, most of my time has been spent as a prosecutor or independent legal counsel. In those capacities, I have had the opportunity to observe many defence counsel, both experienced and inexperienced. While experience helps, it does not guarantee a good defence. Sound advocacy techniques and a sense of one's impact on the tribunal are the keys. Some of the following points may seem obvious, but it is surprising how often those points are ignored. Advocacy is like the game of bridge. Few cases are won by brilliant moves; many are lost by basic mistakes.

To illustrate the points, I shall use the example of a discipline hearing involving a health professional. Such hearings are quite "courtlike," yet the members are non-lawyers. Thus they serve as useful models to demonstrate the similarities and differences of administrative practice. I shall assume that you are defending, as that is the most likely scenario.

Overview

Why do it?

Administrative tribunals have a tremendous impact on all our lives. They deal with the environment, the economy, the way we earn our livelihood, and a host of other issues. In doing so, these tribunals must assess conflicting interests. To be successful, those who seek to advance their interests must persuade tribunals, and persuasion is the natural province of the advocate. Advocates should play a key role in administrative proceedings. Despite this need, many counsel shy away from administrative work. Strangely enough, the things that initially deter them become the very things that attract them if they persist.

Close encounters

Some tribunals deal with broad policy issues. Grappling with these issues can be frustrating; one senior counsel described his experience before a tribunal as "trying to nail jelly to a wall." Yet, it is these very policy issues that can take an advocate beyond the confines of traditional litigation.

Mary Eberts, John Laskin, and Ian Binnie. Many of their ideas coincided with my own, but there also were several other interesting points, some of which I have worked into this article.

The atmosphere at a hearing can also be unpredictable. Some hearings are "courtlike"; others are informal. One Toronto hospital had only two appeals to its board in the span of a decade. By a quirk of fate, I appeared for the doctor in both cases. The first hearing was much like a trial, while the second was informal. We sat around a table with cups of coffee and "chatted" about the issues. This involved a certain flexibility of approach, but the process in each case was both satisfactory and interesting.

Tribunals may take disconcerting forms. If you think that jury trials are tricky, or if you feel outnumbered in certain types of appellate proceedings, try arguing a case before a hospital board composed of twenty-seven members.

These variations in form, atmosphere, and content can be stimulating, but they can also intimidate. A lawyer's natural inclination is to avoid the unfamiliar in favour of the well-trodden path. However, if you are prepared to invest a little time in self-education, you will be able to practice before a new tribunal with a degree of confidence. It is true that certain tribunals are the preserve of specialists, and appearances in those tribunals require a major change in one's practice. Other tribunals may not be as specialized, but prosecutors are selected by governing bodies and defence counsel by professional associations. These lawyers are trained by, and able to draw on, the experience of more experienced counsel. However, there still remain a host of tribunals that are open to freelance counsel with varying degrees of specialized knowledge.

The lay of the land

Assuming that you are prepared to forge ahead, there are a few simple steps that you can and should take to understand the tribunal. Obviously, your new-found spirit of adventure should not lead you to rush in without a map of the terrain. Familiarity with procedure always makes an advocate more effective.

You can start with the governing Act and regulations, which may set out the procedural framework. If they don't, you must look to the *Statutory Powers Procedures Act (SPPA)*.[3] However, legislation will only provide you with a bare outline; it will not tell you what really goes on. Reading tribunal decisions will help, but you really need a live guide: a member of the administration, a regular defence counsel, or a prosecu-

---

3   R.S.O. 1990, c. s. 22.

tor.[4] If you appear for the defence, you may wonder why a prosecutor would want to help you. The answer is quite simple: an inexperienced defence counsel is a prosecutor's nightmare. A half-day "parking ticket" case can turn into a five-day extravaganza in the hands of a novice. Offer to meet your prospective source and you will usually learn more in half an hour than you can with any amount of research.

The best approach is to sit in on a hearing. Seeing the tribunal in action is not only educational, but it eases the natural discomfort that you would otherwise feel when appearing before the tribunal for your first hearing.

Don't bite the hand

If there is a golden rule for this type of advocacy, it is this: *Do not antagonize the tribunal.* This may seem stunningly obvious. However, in my experience, some lawyers who appear before tribunals are totally oblivious to the impact they have on those who hold the professional fate of their clients in their hands.[5] There are five main ways in which lawyers antagonize tribunals.

First, lawyers sometimes behave in an over-aggressive fashion. Tribunal members hate this. They understand that thorough cross-examination is necessary. However, they will not excuse rudeness or bullying in the examination of witnesses.[6]

Second, lawyers are in love with legal points. Tribunals want to hear the facts. They do not want to spend a lot of time on the law. The production of a large authorities book will almost certainly make their eyes glaze over. There may be times when it is necessary to draw their attention to a specific statutory provision or a specific case; if so, they should have a copy of it when you are making your submissions. However, it is far more important to argue general principles than to deal with specific cases.

---

4   Make a telephone call, explain your dilemma, and arrange a brief personal visit; most people are accommodating and willing to help.
5   This comment on alienating tribunals applies equally to juries. When I taught trial practice, the juries at mock trials invariably disliked aggressive lawyers. A fascinating study of the phenomenon is found in *Trial by Jury*, edited by Steven Brill (American Lawyer Books), which leaves the reader with the impression that it is lawyers rather than clients who are on trial.
6   This is the principal complaint of members of tribunals and juries.

Third, lawyers are sometimes obstructive or repetitious. This frustrates tribunal members. They want to get to the point. You may have to go clearly and slowly, but you must not treat the members as though they were slow-witted. While it may be necessary for you to be firm and stand up for your client's rights, you must persuade the tribunal that you are not there to harass and obstruct. You are there to help the tribunal understand your client's case and to put it in a concise, clear fashion.

Fourth, lawyers sometimes behave in a way that would not be tolerated in court, for example, addressing each other rather than the chairperson.

Finally, lawyers antagonize tribunals simply by being lawyers. Many people do not like lawyers. They have a stereotype in mind, and it is up to you to break that stereotype.

Preparation

Assuming that you have familiarized yourself with the tribunal, you can now begin to prepare your case. In doing so, you should bear in mind a number of factors. First, the tribunal before which you will appear will generally be composed of professionals. Professionals do not like to be talked down to, particularly in their field of expertise. In law, they can only decide on the expert evidence before them.[7] In practice, their own expertise, whether justified or not, will come into play. Where it is alleged that your client's conduct fell short of the standard of practice, you may have to rebut their preconceptions with an expert witness.

Second, remember that for all practical purposes, there is no tomorrow. Quite apart from privative clauses, the courts are reluctant to interfere with tribunals on a judicial review application. Even where there is a broad appeal power, the courts will not retry a case.[8]

---

7   *Re Reddall and Ontario College of Nurses* (1983), 42 O.R. (2d) 412 (C.A.).

8   Mr. Justice Reid put the matter this way in *Re Singh and College of Nurses of Ontario* (1981), 33 O.R. (2d) 92 (Div. Ct.) at 93:

> The proceedings of the Committee and its reasons were made on this appeal the subject of a sweeping and detailed attack. Section 13 of the Act confers upon us broad powers of review: see *Re Matheson and College of Nurses of Ontario* (1979), 27 O.R. (2d) 632 at 633, 107 D.L.R. (3d) 430 at 431–2; affirmed 28 O.R. (2d) 611n, 111 D.L.R. (3d) 179n.
>
> However wide our powers are they do not, in my opinion, amount to a

Third, you must be aware of the "political" atmosphere prevailing at the tribunal. For example, health professions are under intense pressure in the field of sexual misconduct, If you are defending a sexual misconduct case, you must tread carefully.

Fourth, you may have to deal with non-parties[9] as well with independent legal counsel to the tribunal.[10] (The subject of independent legal counsel is dealt with by Professor Mullan in his article in this issue of the *Journal*.)

Advice

As in traditional litigation, effective administrative advocacy begins long before the hearing. A lawyer is not a mouthpiece; the first function of the lawyer is to give advice. There are certain cases that must be fought no matter how weak the defence. However, there are others in which a more creative solution can be found. Horace Rumpole's credo, "Never plead guilty," cannot be your guiding principle when appearing before

---

general warrant to retry cases decided by the Committee. As a practical matter that would be impossible. The reasons for this have repeatedly been expressed by Courts of Appeal. An appeal under s. 13 is not a trial *de novo*. Much of the appeal amounted to an invitation to retry this case. That, I think, we must refuse.

Thus, I think that as a general rule we should not attempt to weigh the evidence upon which various conclusions were clearly based by the Committee where no error is suggested other than that the Committee should have reached a different conclusion. Where there was no evidence, or where the evidence was contrary to the conclusion, that would, of course, be a different matter.

9   A discipline panel may allow a person who is not a party to participate in a hearing if (a) the good character, propriety of conduct, or competence of the person is an issue at the hearing; or (b) the participation of the person would, in the opinion of the panel, be of assistance to the panel: *Regulated Health Professions Act* (RHPA), S.O. 1991, c. 181, s. 41.1(1). If counsel for a complainant wants to participate, you should consider the possibility of objecting or arguing that participation should be limited. You do not want your client to be "double teamed." You will usually find that the prosecutor is not too keen to have non-parties involved because their involvement often backfires on the prosecution. You will have to decide on a case-by-case basis.

10 At the College of Physicians and Surgeons of Ontario, independent legal counsel are always present. At the College of Nurses, independent legal counsel are sometimes present and always available for telephone conferences. The practice at other tribunals varies.

discipline tribunals. This is particularly true in modern times, when many tribunals are swamped with cases. An excellent result may be obtained for your client through alternative dispute resolution or "plea bargaining." As well, there are some cases in which a full-scale defence may lead to disaster. There have been a number of cases in which a professional faced with a single complainant participated in a well-publicized and drawn-out hearing that brought out a host of other complainants. In such cases, good defence counsel get their clients in and out quickly, before more harm can be done.

This is not to suggest that a lawyer should "roll over" when his client is faced with a professional charge. In many cases, there is an arguable defence. From this point on, we shall assume that your client has instructed you to defend. Even then, there are different ways of defending a case. In most cases, it is prudent to admit all non-contentious facts and stake one's defence upon the key disputed issues. Even if you lose, the tribunal will be inclined to be more sympathetic if you have not taken days fighting hopeless issues.

In most cases, the jurisdiction of the tribunal to deal with your client will be clear. However, you should always review this issue. You cannot afford to lead your client into a hearing that is, in effect, a scatter-gun attack on his or her entire practice.[11] In most cases, there is a screening mechanism referred to as a complaints procedure. A complainant writes to the professional body. The professional body delivers the letter of complaint to the professional, who must reply. A complaints committee decides whether the case should go on to discipline.

You must hope that your client has consulted you before replying to the complaint. A response denouncing the professional body and all its members does not get things off on a good footing. If your client has delivered such a response independently, you would be well-advised to follow up with a more temperate letter setting out the merits of the defence and explaining that your client was understandably agitated when the complaint was received. In addition, an ill-advised response to the complaint provides fodder for cross-examination. The response

---

11   See, for example, *Kupeyan v. Royal College of Dental Surgeons of Ontario* (1982), 37 O.R. (2d) 737 (D.C.), wherein an appeal was allowed when the Discipline Committee was instructed to "inquire into the actions and conduct of" the appellant.

should address the complaint, and it should be complete. It should avoid any personal attack on the complainant.

Disclosure

In the past, lawyers who appeared before tribunals were often disconcerted because they did not have the safety blanket of discovery. Aside from specific statutory requirements to produce documents, the defence had to rely on the rather broad wording of section 8 of the *SPPA*[12] and the requirements of natural justice.[13] Times, however, have changed. For many years, prosecutors have been giving details of the case,[14] and most discipline committees now order broad disclosure.[15]

Some counsel become involved in motions with regard to particulars. Unless the notice of hearing fails to set out the basic charge against your client, such motions are a waste of time. Discipline hearings are not criminal proceedings, and the courts have held that technical requirements need not be met provided that the professional is not caught by surprise.[16]

However, if you feel that you have not been provided with the information that you need to defend the case, you should move before the tribunal. Hammer away at the basic concept of fairness. Discipline tribunals are acutely aware of the need to fair. Generally, they will strive to ensure that you have the material to defend the case, but they will not permit you to embark on a fishing expedition.

Marshalling your evidence

Preparing evidence for a discipline hearing is much the same as preparing the evidence for any other piece of litigation. I have already mentioned

---

12   Section 8: "Where the good character, propriety of conduct or competence of a party is an issue in a proceeding, the party is entitled to be furnished prior to the hearing with reasonable information of any allegations with respect thereto."

13   The *SPPA* does not eliminate the common law regarding natural justice; it supplements those requirements. In some cases, the common law overrides the provisions of the *SPPA*. For example, in *Lischka v. Criminal Injuries Comp. Bd.* (1982), 37 O.R. (2d) 134, the Divisional Court held that while s. 15(1) of the *SPPA* permits the admission of hearsay and opinion evidence, in some cases the admission of such evidence could amount to a denial of natural justice.

14   This is normally done in writing with "will say" statements being delivered.

15   *Markandey v. Ontario Board of Ophthalmic Dispensers*, [1994] O.J. No. 484.

16   *Re Cwinn and Law Society of Upper Canada* (1980), 28 O.R. (2d) 61 at 70 (D.C.).

the advisability of agreeing to non-contentious facts. Agreed statements are particularly helpful where the witness against you would be a sympathetic one, for example, a grieving widow. From the defence standpoint, it almost always pays to avoid the "technicolour." There are two qualifications. You should not agree to a statement if you need the witness for the purpose of proof unless the other side agrees to have the witness available for cross-examination. Second, agreed statements do not work if they contain partisan arguments as opposed to an objective outline of the facts.

Many of your witnesses may appear voluntarily. However, there is a summons power under section 12 of the *SPPA*.[17] It is also possible to summons a party to produce documents.[18] However, the section only enables you to produce documents in evidence. It is not a discovery mechanism.

Section 15 of the *SPPA* permits a certain latitude in admitting evidence. However, most discipline tribunals can only accept evidence that would be admissible in a courtroom.[19] Apart from specific provisions, natural justice may limit the scope of section 15.[20]

Finally, barring a non-suit,[21] you must call your client. You are not involved in a criminal trial. For all practical purposes, there is no presumption of innocence. The legal onus is on the prosecutor to prove the case on clear, convincing, and cogent evidence. The practical onus is on you.

Experts

Next to your client, your most important witness will usually be an expert. I say "usually" because there are some cases when experts are not required. For example, if your client is a doctor charged with sexual intercourse with a patient, your defence will usually be that the act did

---

17 Section 12(1): "A tribunal may require any person, including a party, by summons, (a) to give evidence on oath or affirmation at a hearing; and (b) to produce in evidence at a hearing documents and things specified by the tribunal, relevant to the subject-matter of the proceeding and admissible at a hearing."

18 *Ibid.*

19 See, for example, s. 49 of the *Health Professional Procedural Code* (the Code), which is schedule 2 to the *RHPA*.

20 See footnote 13, *supra*.

21 While professional discipline hearings are, for practical purposes, a hybrid of criminal and civil proceedings, they are essentially civil in nature and most tribunals use the civil non-suit test. In other words, you are put to your election.

not take place. You will admit that sexual intercourse with a patient is unprofessional. However, in a case involving professional standards, an expert will be necessary. You cannot rely solely on your cross-examining skills to undermine the opposing expert. Remember that, in a discipline situation, you do not have to satisfy the tribunal that your expert is correct. You only have to satisfy the tribunal that there are differing professional views, and thus, no failure to maintain the standard of the profession. To do that, you have to provide them with a professional view that supports your case.

The first step is to pick a strong expert. Do not put up your client's old college chum against the leading authority in the field. Your client may be able to suggest an expert, but you should always check the expert's qualifications with some professional body.

You should also remember that some experts are very useful as information sources but do not have forensic skills. It is conceivable that you will have one expert to explain the case to you and another who will actually appear in the courtroom. Make sure that your expert is an expert in the right field. Do not put a general practitioner up against a specialist.[22]

The expert must understand that the game is played in the black-and-white world of the law. Before you put the expert in the box, you must be satisfied that you will get a clear answer when you ask about your client's conduct. Again, it is not necessary for your expert to testify that he would have done the same thing as your client. It is sufficient for him to testify that your client's actions met the standard. It has been argued that the standard is the same in every location. However, as a matter of practice, a tribunal may expect more of a doctor in an urban teaching hospital than a doctor in a small town. However, professional knowledge evolves, and the standard at the time of the hearing may be far more strict than the standard at the time of the events in question. It is your job to ensure that the tribunal "compares oranges with oranges."

If your expert does not support your case, try another expert. If the second agrees with the first, you may have to reassess your approach to the case.

---

22   A prosecutor sometimes has a more complicated decision. He or she may have to call both a peer and a specialist or face an argument that the professional is being judged by the standards of a specialist rather than by the standard of a general practitioner.

Your expert will also help you to prepare your cross-examination. Generally speaking, you will not meet an opposing expert head on. The normal cross-examination of an expert will involve an attack on the assumptions underlying his opinion. If you do have to attack an expert head on, you will need to be thoroughly prepared by your own expert before venturing into such a confrontation. This is a complicated field, and space does not permit an in-depth discussion of the cross-examination of an expert. Generally speaking, it will be difficult to get an expert to back down from his or her opinion. However, you may be able to undermine the opinion using generally accepted professional texts. At the very least, you may be able to put your expert's opinion to the opposing expert and get the opposing expert to agree that there can be an honest difference of professional opinion.

Finally, you must be aware that some legislation now requires the defence to file an expert report within a certain period of time before the hearing.[23]

Demonstrative evidence

We seem to lag behind our American peers in the use of demonstrative evidence. In certain situations, photographs, drawings, and other demonstrative aids can be extremely useful. In one case, the complainant's evidence of sexual misconduct seemed quite plausible until a scale drawing of the professional's office was produced. The drawing made it clear that it was almost impossible for the alleged event to have occurred.

Character evidence

In most professional matters, character evidence is extremely important. It should be called during the hearing on liability, not during sentencing — after the case has been lost.

Where possible, the witness should be aware of the client's character in the profession and in the community. The witness should also be aware of the case against your client, so that he or she is not caught by surprise.

---

23   Section 42.1 of the *Code* provides that an expert report prepared on behalf of the defence must be delivered at least ten days before the hearing. Note that there is an inadvertent inequity in the legislation. Section 42(2) permits the panel to allow introduction of the expert's evidence even if the prosecutor has not met the ten-day requirement. Section 42.1 contains no such saving provision. Most tribunals take the view that natural justice permits them to relax the ten-day period in any event. Do not take a chance; deliver your report ten days before the hearing.

Most tribunals will permit you to file written character evidence. You will have to make a judgment as to whether or not to call witnesses, even if you are permitted to file written material. If you do call witnesses, it is generally best to call one or two strong witnesses and submit the rest of the evidence in writing.

Law

As mentioned above, most tribunals are not enthralled with legal arguments. Usually your defence will turn on the facts. However, it may be essential for you to use a case or an excerpt from a case to illustrate the point.

You must also be prepared for jurisdictional, evidentiary, and procedural arguments that may arise during the hearing. For those purposes, you will need the specific Act and regulations as well as the general texts that you would take to court.[24]

Mechanics

As in a trial, it is important to have copies of all your documents and authorities for all parties involved in the proceedings. This means that you should have a copy for the reporter, the witness, members of the panel, independent legal counsel, and your opponent.

In many cases, there will be an agreed document book. It is usually wise to agree to a document book, but you should bear in mind the distinction between agreeing to the admission of a document and agreeing to the truth of its contents. There may be certain situations in which you will agree to a document book provided that your opponent produces a particular witness for cross-examination. If that agreement is not forthcoming, you may have to insist on a document being proved so that you have an opportunity to examine the witness.

Summary

As you close your preparation, go back to the basics and ask yourself:

1.   Do I understand the tribunal?
2.   Do I have an overall game plan?

---

24   My personal choices would be Sopinka, Lederman, and Bryant on Evidence and Adair on Trial.

3. What is the applicable standard of proof?
4. Have I obtained all necessary disclosure?
5. Have I admitted all non-contentious facts?
6. Have I thoroughly prepared my general, expert, and character witnesses?
7. Do I have all the documents, law, and demonstrative aids necessary to prove my case clearly, concisely, and smoothly?

The Hearing

At this point, I shall assume that you have thoroughly prepared your case and have arrived at the hearing room well ahead of time, so that you know what conference rooms are available for the preparation of witnesses and have a chance to set up and show your witnesses the hearing room. This is very important. If you walk the witness through an empty hearing room, you will eliminate some of the intimidating impact he or she may feel when called to testify.

Introduce your client to the opposing counsel. Introduce yourself to the opposing expert and introduce your client. It is very much in your interest to have them see your client as a human being rather than an object. This is particularly important as far as the opposing expert is concerned. Very few experts can meet a fellow professional without thinking: "There, but for the grace of God, go I." If you have not already done so, discuss procedure and protocol with the prosecutor. For example, it is not a good idea to remain lolling in your seat if the prosecutor gets up on his hind legs when the members of the tribunal enter the room.

Motions

If you have motions going to jurisdiction, you must bring them before the plea. Other motions, such as the exclusion of witnesses, should also be dealt with at the start. As previously discussed, you should bring motions only if absolutely necessary. Try to give the motion an air of informality by saying something to the following effect: "Could I just deal with a few house-keeping matters before you take the plea?"

The plea

Waive reading of the plea; it is time-consuming and unnecessary to have the gruesome details read aloud. Prepare your client for the plea. For some reason many defence counsel appear totally stunned when asked to respond to the plea, and whisper to their client. Have your client prepared to respond "Not guilty"[25] in a strong, clear voice when asked to plead.

Openings

Never miss the opportunity to open. Remember that the tribunal has no pleadings or record before it. It has not had the issues framed; it only has the allegations against your client. This is your chance to tell them about your case, and you should do so even if the prosecutor decides not to open.

As in any other litigation, it is unwise to open high. Use phrases such as: "I anticipate that the evidence will be ...." If you come to a controversial part of the evidence, you might say, "You will hear Dr. X deny the allegations against him."

Make sure that you begin your opening with a description of your client. As discussed, your aim is to make the tribunal see your client as an individual, not just a statistic. In complex cases, a written opening submission is useful, particularly if you need to set out a chronology of events.

Direct examination

Direct examination before a tribunal is much the same as direct examination in a courtroom. It is permissible to lead on uncontentious items and then switch to non-leading questions on issues that are in dispute. Make sure that you "qualify" your professional. Although he or she may not be an expert in the case, that does not mean that you should speed through professional credentials. You should place particular emphasis on professional work, teaching, and charitable activities. Everything should be directed toward the same end. If there is an ethical issue, you must convince the tribunal that your client is an unlikely person to have committed an ethical breach. If you have a standards case, you must convince the tribunal that, at the least, your client was acting conscientiously and professionally.

---

25   In some cases, the member now "denies the allegations" rather than pleading guilty; e.g., the *RHPA*.

Objections

The general principle is quite simple. Keep your bottom in the chair unless you simply have to object. If you do object, state your point clearly and concisely. Remember that you must address your objection to the tribunal but that they will probably call upon independent legal counsel, if present.

Cross-examination

Although I have already dealt with the issue of aggression, it is so key that I must mention it again. It is almost always disastrous to cross-examine a witness aggressively. You may have to be firm; you may have to show indignation. But you must not bully or browbeat the witness.

Remember that every member of the tribunal identifies with the witness, not with you. The key to most cross-examinations lies in the complainant's original statement. Do not nit-pick, but make sure to bring out any major inconsistencies or omissions.

When dealing with experts, be respectful but firm. Your key weapon is an expert's sympathy for your client's plight. Unless it is absolutely necessary, do not box experts into a corner, where they must live and die with their opinion or else lose face. Always leave them a way out, such as: "That is what you would do under ideal conditions. If Dr. X did something else, you might disagree with him, but you would accept that he was following his best professional view."

Another key point to emphasize is that the expert has had the benefit of the "retroscope." He or she has been able to look back with the benefit of hindsight and has had all the time and resources to deal with the situation that your client may have had to deal with on the spot, under extreme pressure.

Re-examination

This is always a dangerous area. You cannot lead, and you run the risk of making matters worse. Do it only if it is essential.

Questions by the tribunal

This part of the hearing makes lawyers turn prematurely grey. The tribunal has a chance to ask questions, and, technically, its members should ask them to clarify difficult points. In fact, they may well be dying to commence an inquisition.

It is bemusing when a member of a tribunal asks a question that has been avoided by both the prosecutor and the defence because the answer could end the case one way or the other. The member putting the question inevitably has an expression on his or her face that seems to ask, "How can both these idiot lawyers have missed the key to the whole case?"

You may suffer the torments of the damned when the members start to ask questions. Unless the question is completely out of line, however, you will simply have to grin and bear it.

If a tribunal member wanders into an area that is grossly prejudicial to your client and irrelevant to the case, you would do well to use the following formula when addressing the chairperson: "I do not want to hamper questioning by the committee, but I am concerned that we are venturing into an area that is outside the scope of this hearing."

The committee will inevitably ask counsel if they have questions arising out of the committee questions. Use the same guideline as you would use on reexamination. Only ask clarifying questions if you are certain of the answer, or if the case is lost if you leave the matter as it is.

Argument

This is your chance to pull the whole case together. As in opening, consider the advisability of a written argument or outline. Emphasize the onus and the standard of proof. (A smart prosecutor will already have dealt with this.) Do not waste time on uncontentious facts or red herrings. Get straight to the point and summarize your position. When arguing, keep in mind the policy issues that drive the tribunal. Keep your argument concise. If you go over a certain time limit or if you repeat yourself, you will lose the tribunal. There is a simple way to determine if you have their attention. If they are taking notes, they are listening to you. If they put down their pens, you are losing them.

Providing the tribunal with a factum or other means of outlining your argument is almost always beneficial.

Waiting for the decision

Unless the decision is reserved, you will now enter a period of torture. This is the worst part of the case for your client, and he or she needs your moral support at this time. If the tribunal has indicated that it will be out for only a short time, go for a walk or otherwise distract your client. Then return to the delirium of victory or the agony of defeat.

Sentencing

If things go well, you will never come to this phase of the hearing; you and your client will have waltzed off in triumph. On the off-chance that this has not taken place, due (obviously) to the tribunal's failure to grasp your compelling arguments, you must be prepared to deal with sentencing.

Most tribunals deal with the sentence on the spot. In rare cases you may have to ask for an adjournment, but in most cases you should be prepared to go ahead.

In reality, your entire case has been preparation for sentencing. All of the arguments you used had a dual purpose: to win an acquittal or to mitigate sentence. Emphasize the impact of the hearing on your client. Emphasize your client's importance to his or her patients or clients if suspension is a possibility. Think hard before you make a proposal that is unrealistically low. If you do this, the committee may simply ignore your submissions and apply its own assessment. You are more likely to have an impact if you make a sensible proposal.

I must emphasize that the above comments are based on personal experience and the wisdom of others, some of whom I have been able to acknowledge in the endnotes and some of whom I have not. I hope these comments will persuade counsel who have been reluctant to venture into this field to take up the challenge.

[This article first appeared in the December 1994 of *The Advocates' Society Journal*.]

Winning Strategies in the Civil Jury Process

Roger G. Oatley and Brennan Kahler*

[Editors' note: This article is the edited text of a paper presented to the Canadian Institute's conference on Civil Procedure and Evidence, held in April 2003 in Toronto.]

A jury provides litigants in a civil action with access to justice determined by a collection of peers. This right is a basic tenet of our modern system of civil justice. It is a substantial statutory right, which our legislature and courts ardently protect. It is a right that is subject to very few exceptions. This article discusses the benefits the civil jury provides. It also examines the civil jury's inherent limitations. It reviews the procedure, and suggests practical strategies, for requiring and striking out a jury. It discusses the role of focus groups in promoting effective jury selection, and it describes and explains persuasive jury communication and presentation techniques. This article concludes with a discussion of recent cases considering current civil jury issues, including judicially imposed limits on counsel's freedom to address the jury and the jury's new and improved ability to award punitive damages.

---

* Roger G. Oatley and Brennan Kahler, Oatley, Vigmond, Barrie.

The Decision to Use a Jury in a Civil Action

As a general rule, we try our cases before juries. Properly educated and sufficiently motivated to help your client, civil juries often award more generous damages than will a judge. That said, a jury is not always appropriate, for both legal and practical reasons. This section describes the circumstances where counsel should seek, or try to avoid, a jury trial. It also discusses some of the differences confronting counsel who are presenting a claim to a judge rather than a jury.

When is a jury appropriate for resolving disputes?

A jury is appropriate for resolving disputes in most cases. But there are exceptions. Juries should be avoided in the following circumstances:

- When the plaintiff is not likeable.
- When liability is very difficult.
- When the theory of damages or legal foundation for your case is difficult to understand.
- When you do not possess the skill or personality to advocate effectively before a jury.

If your plaintiff is not likeable, a jury might be the worst possible trier of fact. Juries do not like people who lie. They do not like people who exaggerate their injuries in personal injury cases. They do not like people who abuse their spouses or their children or shirk their obligations. And they have little sympathy for people who flout the law. Judges are influenced by these factors too, but they are more inclined to be tolerant because they have heard it all before.

If liability is very difficult, think long and hard before risking a trial with a jury. Juries, when properly instructed, will do their duty and throw a case out. Judges, on the other hand, will often bend over backwards to give some relief to a deserving plaintiff even in the most difficult of cases.

If the legal foundation for your case or your theory of damages is extremely hard to understand, you may want to steer away from a jury. The reasons are obvious.

Finally, if you don't know how to present a case to a jury or if you don't have the personality to be effective, don't run the risk. Either retain counsel or don't serve a jury notice.

What differences confront the advocate presenting a claim to a jury rather than a judge?

There are significant differences in the presentation of a claim to a jury. Different presentation techniques must be used, because effective advocacy demands that demonstrative evidence be shown to each and every juror, and that jurors can see any exhibit being referred to by a witness. For example, in a judge-alone trial, the judge and the witness can pore over their own copies of a photograph, but do that in a jury trial and you will lose the jury. The use of demonstrative evidence in a jury trial requires careful planning and the use of presentation techniques that bring demonstrative evidence alive.

Also, the effective jury lawyer must be able to appeal to the juror on every level. The jurors' decision is a much more emotional process than that of a judge alone. It requires careful planning and hard work, combined with the essential skills to appeal to a juror at both an emotional and an intellectual level.

Furthermore, the jury trial must be presented in a very clear, simple, logical fashion. We are not suggesting that these are not requirements before a judge alone. But judges will use their experience to sort out the evidence, no matter what the order in which it is called. Jurors, however, do not possess the judge's experience and training. Therefore, the evidence must be presented in an entirely orderly way.

Finally, jury trials take longer. This is so because opening and closings are much more expansive. Also, the most significant arguments concerning procedure are made in the absence of the jury. Plan on your trial taking at least a third longer if it is before a jury.

The Jury Notice

A party may require a jury trial in most civil actions. It does so by delivering a jury notice.

The *Rules of Civil Procedure*[1] ("the Rules") prescribe the content of the jury notice.[2] The notice recites the style of cause and states the issues the party intends the jury to decide. The party may require the jury to

---

1   R.R.O. 1990, Reg. 194.

2   Form 47(A) of the Rules.

decide all issues of fact and assess all damages. The party may also wish to limit the jury's role. In that case, the notice will state whether the jury is required only to decide matters of fact or to assess damages.

Delivering the notice

Rule 47.01 states that the party requiring the jury must deliver the notice before the close of pleadings. Delivery is accomplished by serving the notice on the other parties and filing the notice, with proof of service, with the court.

Motions to Strike a Jury Notice

Delivering a jury notice does not guarantee that a jury will try the action. As discussed, juries are not appropriate for all matters. Depending upon counsel's position, it may make sense to move to strike the jury.

For example, defence counsel often consider striking juries in cases involving sympathetic plaintiffs facing tough liability cases: this is so because many defence counsel worry that a jury is more likely than a judge to disregard the plaintiff's difficulty in establishing liability where they are motivated to help a vulnerable plaintiff. In such a case, plaintiff's counsel is well-advised to vigorously oppose the defence motion.

Procedure for striking a jury notice

Before a motions judge

Rule 47.02 provides that a party may move before a judge for an order striking out the jury notice. A judge may strike out the notice where delivery of the notice breached procedural requirements prescribed by Rule 47. It is submitted that few judges will strike out a jury notice not served in compliance with Rule 48.01, unless the breach causes the moving party prejudice.[3]

Of more practical importance, a judge may also strike out the notice where a statute requires a trial without a jury. Section 108 of the *Courts of Justice Act*[4] lists a number of proceedings that shall be tried without a jury. Specifically, subsection 108(2) provides that actions seeking the following relief shall be tried without a jury:

---

3   *Ampadu v. Novopharm Ltd* (1998), 27 C.P.C. (4th) 64 (Ont. Ct. Gen. Div.).
4   R.S.O. 1990, c. C.43.

- injunction or mandatory order
- partition or sale of property
- relief under Part I, II, or III of the *Family Law Act* or under the *Children's Law Reform Act*
- dissolution of a partnership
- foreclosure or redemption of a mortgage
- sale and distribution of proceeds of property subject to a lien or charge
- execution of a trust
- rectification, setting aside, or cancellation of a deed or other written instrument
- specific performance of a contract
- declaratory relief
- other equitable relief
- relief against a municipality

Before a trial judge

In Ontario, the trial judge may also strike the jury. In fact, the trial judge possesses significant discretion in determining whether to allow a jury to try a case. This discretion manifests itself in two ways.

Subrule 47.02(3) provides that despite any order, the trial judge retains discretion to try the action without a jury where she determines that a jury trial is not appropriate. The practical result is that a party may move to strike a jury notice in advance of trial. The judge hearing the motion may decline to grant the order sought. Notwithstanding this defeat, the party seeking to strike the jury may still achieve its objective if the trial judge determines that a jury should not try the case.

Subrule 47.02(1) lists the grounds upon which the motions judge may strike a jury notice. However, a trial judge's discretion to strike a jury is not limited by the grounds listed in subrule 47.02(1). Rather, a trial judge possesses broad discretion to strike a jury where she finds that the case is not an appropriate one for a jury to decide.

A trial judge may exercise her discretion to strike a jury notice where the matters in issue are unduly complex. Complexity may result because the subject matter of the action is itself complex.[5] Unacceptable complexity may also result where the action involves difficult questions

---

5   See *Migos v. Zurich Indemnity Co. of Canada* (1998), 28 C.P.C. (4th) 268 (Ont. Ct. Gen. Div.), aff'd 100 A.C.W.S. (3d) 42 (Ont. C.A.); *Ball v. Vincent* (1993), 27 C.P.C. (3d) 148 (Ont. Ct. Gen. Div.).

of mixed fact and law.[6] Our courts will also strike a jury notice where the moving party establishes that the evidence or circumstances surrounding the trial may actually prejudice a party.[7]

The trial judge's discretion is not easily overruled. The Supreme Court of Canada tells us that an appellate court shall not override a trial judge's exercise of this discretion unless she acts arbitrarily or capriciously or where her reasons do not demonstrate that she exercised her discretion on the basis of established principles.[8]

Practical strategies

We deliver jury notices in nearly every action we commence. Our experience tells us that defence counsel are unlikely to move to strike the jury notice before trial. If this issue will arise, it will almost certainly arise at trial.

Materials for use on the motion to strike the jury notice should provide the trial judge with a clear understanding of the law applying to the motion. We like to file a factum or statement of law on all such motions. In these materials, we like to remind the trial judge that she may exercise considerable discretion in making her decision. We set out the established bases for striking a jury and explain how applying those principles to our client's circumstances justifies our position. This is important since, as stated above, our courts tell us that, so long as the trial judge exercises her discretion within the boundaries of established principles, her decision will likely withstand the scrutiny of appellate review.

Selecting a Jury

In a jury trial, the jury occupies the most important position in the court. It will decide whether your client wins or loses. Understandably, you will want to select the jury that provides your client with the best shot at success.

Counsel in Ontario selecting juries face considerable difficulty in identifying panelists who maintain beliefs and values that make them more likely to support a particular side of a dispute. This is so because, unlike our neighbors to the south, counsel in Ontario possess few rights to question or challenge potential witnesses.

---

6   See *Oliver v. Gothard* (1992), 10 O.R. (3d) 309 (Gen. Div.).
7   *Graham v. Rourke* (1990), 75 O.R. (2d) 622 , 40 O.A.C. 301 (C.A.).
8   *Hamstra v. British Columbia Rugby Union*, [1997] 1 S.C.R. 1092.

Identifying persons who will support your client

Once inside the courtroom doors, counsel in Ontario possess little right to identify the values and beliefs of potential jurors. As a result, good counsel identify the sort of people likely to support their clients and their case before trial begins. Counsel do this through the use of a focus group.

A focus group consists of any number of impartial lay-people whom counsel will recruit and to whom counsel will present his case — the good, the bad, and the ugly. The technical and strategic issues involved in selecting and running a focus group go beyond the scope of this article. It is sufficient to say that you will want to enlist the help of at least six, and probably no more than twelve, impartial minds. You will also want to foster an environment in which each person is motivated to explain his or her thoughts and impressions.

After presenting your case (or perhaps only a particularly thorny issue) to the focus group, you will elicit opinions and ideas from these lay-people.

Ultimately, your goal is to identify the sort of person who relates to and likes your client and supports your client's position. For example, and in the best-case scenario, you may find that a person's education, occupation, age, gender, or general social status influences their support for your client. In that case, you will want to identify a jury consisting, as much as possible, of people possessing those characteristics.

Procedure for selecting your jury

A civil jury in Ontario consists of six persons. These jury members must meet the basic conditions concerning residency, citizenship, and age detailed in section 2 of the *Juries Act*.[9]

A jury is selected from a panel of potential jurors assembled in the court by the sheriff. The sheriff will draw six cards from the ballot drum. The persons whose names appear on the card will then stand and face counsel. Counsel must then decide whether to accept the juror or to challenge him or her.

In making this seemingly split-second decision, counsel only has access to the name, place of residence, and occupation of each potential juror. Counsel may ask the court to identify the former occupation of a retired person.

9   R.S.O. 1990, c. J.3.

Counsel may challenge, and ask the court to remove, any juror falling into any of the ineligible categories described in section 3 of that Act. Section 3 states that the following persons are ineligible to serve as jurors:

- every member of the Privy Council of Canada or the Executive Council of Ontario
- every member of the Senate, the House of Commons, or the Assembly
- every judge and every justice of the peace
- every barrister and solicitor and student-at-law
- every legally qualified medical practitioner and veterinary surgeon who is actively engaged in practice, and every coroner
- every person engaged in the enforcement of law
- every person likely to be summoned as a witness or possessing an interest in an action that may be tried at the same sitting
- any person suffering a physical or mental disability impairing his ability to serve as a juror
- any person convicted of an indictable offence not subsequently pardoned

Our case law suggests that these classes of ineligible persons constitute the only basis for challenging a juror for cause.[10] However, counsel may also remove a potential, eligible juror from the panel.

You may remove an eligible, potential juror from your panel by using a peremptory challenge. Counsel uses a peremptory challenge to remove an otherwise eligible but undesirable potential juror.

In a trial involving only two parties, the procedure for using the peremptory challenge is simple. With six potential jurors selected, the court asks one party (normally the plaintiff) if it challenges the juror. Counsel will either challenge a juror or indicate that they consent to the panel. If counsel challenges a juror, the challenged juror is replaced by another person whose name is drawn from the ballot drum. The other counsel is then invited to challenge a panelist. This process of alternating challenges and replacing jurors continues until either both sides consent to the panel or both sides exhaust their peremptory challenges.

The plaintiff, or plaintiffs, have four peremptory challenges. The defendant, or defendants, also have four peremptory challenges.[11]

---

10   *Thomas-Robinson v. Song* (1997), 34 O.R. (3d) 62.
11   Section 33 of the *Juries Act, supra*, note 9; and see *Hrup v. Cipollone* (1994), 19 O.R. (3d) 715 (C.A.).

Practical strategies

As a general rule, potential jurors who are most like your client should relate to your client and support your case. We also look for jury panelists possessing sufficient intellect to understand and feel comfortable working with (and awarding) significant amounts of money. We try to avoid jury panelists we believe are apt to control the outcome — putting all of your eggs in one basket is risky business. Finally, we generally try to keep teachers off our panels.

Using focus groups to identify potentially supportive jurors is not an exact science; you must always rely upon your intuition and apply your common sense. Nevertheless, despite its imprecision, using a focus group improves your ability to select a helpful jury.

Presenting Your Case to the Jury

As jury lawyers we must rid ourselves of the notion that jurors decide cases as we were taught to analyse them in law school. If we are to have any chance of properly advising our clients when to settle and when to push on to trial, and if we are to have any hope of success in the courtroom, we must understand how jurors decide cases. When we understand how jurors decide cases, we can fashion our presentation of our client's case in a way that makes sense to the jury and motivates them to want to help our client.

Key Concepts of Perception and Effective Communication

This section discusses basic principles of perception and effective communication and explains how those principles work in the courtroom.

Perception

The first and fundamental principle of communication is that it is based on perception. This principle holds simply that what a juror learns, understands, and believes is based on what he or she perceives the case to be about.

It is not whether the witness is telling the truth that matters; it is whether or not the juror believes the witness is telling the truth. We may know that the defence witness is misleading the jurors, but if a juror perceives that she is the expert who is credible and authoritative, then that is the witness who will carry the day. Perhaps sad, but nevertheless true. Perception rules.

Belief systems

Jurors bring their own belief systems into the courtroom. These belief systems help them make sense of the world. As lawyers, we must understand those belief systems and develop strategies to deal with them or use them to advantage our case.

Many excellent trial lawyers anticipate and deal with belief systems intuitively, but most of us cannot take the risk that we will overlook a belief system. As trial lawyers, we try to discover what belief systems might be at work, by conducting focus groups and then hoping that the belief systems of the members of our focus groups are representative of those of our jurors. For example, if male jurors are going to think that women with children should be at home looking after their children, that is a pretty important belief system in a case where a thirty-year-old woman cannot work anymore and there is a claim for future income loss. If older jurors think that young people on motorcycles are all reckless drivers, that is an important belief system if our client is a seventeen-year-old motorcyclist.

The time to learn about the specific belief systems affecting your case is before the trial, not when you are analysing a bad verdict. The time to plan strategies for dealing with belief systems is before the trial begins. The time for implementing your strategies is in the opening and throughout the trial. All of us must plan ways to neutralize or to take advantage of particular belief systems.

Biases

Biases are a feature of human nature. We all have them. Biases that are common to litigation, and, in particular, compensation claims, are always at work to some degree. Our task is to understand them and to develop strategies for coping with them. The more common biases are reviewed here.

The defensive attribution bias

Attribution theory in general is a way of explaining the causes of the behaviour of others. This theory begins with the premise that we seek to simplify our understanding of behaviours by making assumptions of general causes. Basic to attribution theory is the fact that jurors will create their own explanations for behaviours unless more compelling explanations are provided. They will resort to bias very early in the trial experience unless they are given the motivation and the information required to reach the explanation we prefer for the occurrence of an event.

Understanding the defensive attribution bias and where it comes from is one of the most important insights a plaintiff's jury lawyer can possess. This bias is so powerful that it can defeat a deserving case. It will defeat a case when jurors find fault with a plaintiff without a shred of evidence to justify their doing so. This finding of fault without justification can at one extreme result in a dismissal of a deserving case and at the other extreme result in a finding of contributory negligence that makes no sense.

The reason for the bias has been expressed in this way: People want to believe they live in a world where good things happen to good people and bad things happen to bad people. The idea that a person has suffered undeservedly is so threatening that people often feel compelled to resort to condemning the injured plaintiff.

The confirmation bias

The confirmation bias refers to the tendency of a juror to cherry-pick the evidence so that the evidence appears to support the juror's belief system or model of the world. The tendency includes the phenomenon of readily accepting evidence that supports the juror's view and critically rejecting evidence that does not. This bias also causes the juror to interpret ambiguous evidence in a manner that supports his or her view. Finally, in support of their views jurors will seize on information that lawyers consider irrelevant or inconsequential if no other confirming evidence is available.

We see this bias at work in our daily lives. Think of the old joke about the amulet that keeps pink elephants away — because there are no pink elephants around, the amulet must work. We all have a tendency to cherry-pick information to support our beliefs.

The belief perseverance bias

The belief perseverance bias describes the tendency we all have to resist changing our minds once we have settled on an explanation for some event. We like to think, not surprisingly, that once we have reached a conclusion it is the correct one. It is disquieting to be faced with information that disturbs the comfort we have achieved with a decision. Some people, described as pigheaded, are especially resistant to new information.

The availability bias

The availability bias describes the tendency of all of us to conclude that because we hear about something often, it occurs frequently. The same tendency explains why all of us "jump to a conclusion"; because we have information (or because it is available to us), we use it to explain why something happened.

This phenomenon can be observed with respect to plane travel. We are all anxious about getting into an airplane because of our belief that planes are crashing all around us, despite statistics demonstrating that it is much safer to fly than to drive. Because crime and air disasters are reported frequently and with much drama, it is our tendency to assume they occur more frequently than they actually do.

How jurors respond in the courtroom

You improve your ability to effectively present your case to the jury by understanding how a jury thinks. Experienced jury trial lawyers understand and learn to control and use to their advantage the phenomena described below.

Jurors try to make sense out of their courtroom experience

Courtrooms are frightening places. Think of a room full of potential jurors during the selection of a jury. Why is there always nervous, often inappropriate, and sometimes embarrassing laughter from every juror in the room in response to some event or comment that usually would go unnoticed by a mature audience? Jurors try to minimize their anxiety by understanding their new environment, the expectations of others, and the case they must decide. Jurors want to get rid of their anxiety as quickly as possible.

It is for this reason that we must be conscious of our behaviour and the messages we communicate from the start. And the start is certainly not the evidence. It is not even the beginning of the opening. It is the moment we walk into the courtroom to pick a jury. Every eye in the courtroom is upon us, searching for clues to the environment.

Jurors form perceptions quickly

This principle may be among the most important of all. As trial lawyers we cannot overstate the significance of this principle for our work with juries, because it puts the theory of primacy into the context of juror decision-making. Juries form perceptions about the lawyers, about the process, and about the case they are to decide very, very quickly.

The consequence is that conclusions about the case are substantially formed early in the trial, probably by the time the first one or two witnesses have been heard. This principle and its implications put into perspective the importance of the opening statement, the effective use of themes, and your choice of the order of witnesses.

Jurors rely on stereotypes to make decisions about fault

The principle that jurors rely on stereotypes to make decisions about fault is, once again, easily observed. It operates within all of us. For example, because the defendant is a teenage male he was probably driving too fast. Or, because the plaintiff is a young mother she probably would not have worked until her children were back in school. Or because the defendant is an old woman she probably could not see where she was going. The stereotypes may or may not be true, but that is beside the point. The point is that we all form perceptions about behaviour based on stereotypes, and so do jurors.

Our task as jury lawyers is to anticipate the juror's reactions to the stereotypes and either to take advantage of the stereotype or to develop a strategy to deal with it. For example, if your plaintiff is an out-of-work teenager, your objective will be to develop a new stereotype that will support your case. Your teenager might also be a volunteer lifeguard at the local YMCA. Your task would be to embed an overwhelming picture of your client as a lifeguard looking after and teaching young kids, so that the more favourable stereotype of the responsible, ever-observant lifeguard — instead of the stereotype of the irresponsible teenager — influences the jurors' decisions about fault.

Jurors tend to see others as similar to themselves

People project their feelings onto others, and as a result jurors tend to see others as similar to themselves.

A jury lawyer who understands this principle of communication will develop strategies to take advantage of this principle. For example, if you have sixty-year-old women on the jury who are homemakers, you will anticipate that these jurors will have some trouble with the suggestion that your female plaintiff would have worked until age sixty-five. Those jurors will see the plaintiff as similar to themselves. Your challenge in such a case is to demonstrate that the plaintiff is just as devoted to her family as the jurors are, but that she expresses her devotion by working to help with its support.

Jurors will transfer feelings about you as counsel to your client

This principle holds that we transfer feelings about one person to another.

Transference is at work in the courtroom. Whenever we consider the importance of identification, it is necessary to keep this phenomenon in mind. If the juror likes you as counsel, he or she will probably like your client. If the juror thinks a counsel is a fool, the chances are good those feelings will be transferred to that lawyer's client.

Jurors believe those with whom they identify and whom they like

If a juror perceives himself or herself as being similar to a certain lawyer, party, or witness, then that juror will be more easily influenced by that person than by someone else who is perceived as dissimilar.

The implications for the importance of identification are extraordinary. If a juror identifies with you and your client, and does not identify with your opponent, who will be the credible source of information? You will be believed.

When people identify with others, they tend to idealize themselves. Jurors will identify with a lawyer who is fair because jurors perceive themselves as fair, even though they might not be, except in the idealized way in which they see themselves. Similarly, jurors will identify with the lawyer who is competent and organized and in control, because that is how jurors see their idealized selves.

On the contrary, jurors do not identify with someone who is tripping over himself or herself looking for documents by thinking to themselves, that's just what I'd be like if I had to run a complicated case like this.

Jurors perceive credibility in proportion to the perception of authority

People are more willing to believe someone whom they view as a legitimate source of authority. This principle is founded of course on our common experience, but it is nonetheless profound in its implications for the jury lawyer.

This principle explains why a judge's interfering in the conduct of an examination can have such a disproportionate influence on the outcome, or why a judge's charge is so important. It also explains why it is essential for counsel to maintain the impression throughout the trial that counsel is a reliable authority where the case is concerned.

This principle also puts into context the significance of an expert's qualifications as an authority and the manner in which the expert is led through his or her qualifications. It is essential to the expert's believability that he or she is perceived to be an authority, because the more authoritative the expert is perceived to be, the more believable the expert becomes.

Jurors decide issues with their hearts

Jurors make decisions, as we all do, first at an emotional level, and then by finding support for their decisions in the evidence presented.

Implications for the advocate

Any jury lawyer who ignores the principles of communication set out here and who trusts in decision-making as a purely rational process will surely be disappointed with the results. No one suggests that decisions in the courtroom are made at a purely unconscious level or purely by emotion. Most jurors, like the rest of us, search for comfort at the intellectual or conscious level that their decision is the right one. On the other hand, no juror will want to make a decision based on the facts and the argument unless it feels right. The lesson for us is that we must appeal to jurors at both the conscious and unconscious levels, or intellectually as well as emotionally. Above all, the decision must feel right first, and we must then supply the information to support it.

Demonstrative Evidence and the Jury Trial

This section describes the crucial role that demonstrative evidence can play in motivating jurors to want to help your client and support your position. Understanding how a jury perceives evidence and reacts and relates to the courtroom experience provides counsel with a great advantage. Our experience with jury trials convinces us that we can maximize this advantage through the use of quality demonstrative evidence.

In the quest for victory in the courtroom on behalf of a client, counsel cannot overlook any legitimate tool of persuasion. One of the most powerful means of influencing a jury is through visual evidence. Oral communication has taken a back seat to visual media; in a society that is increasingly visually oriented, a lawyer's ability to control the visual field of play in the courtroom often makes the difference between winning and losing.

What is demonstrative evidence?

Demonstrative evidence refers to evidence, usually visual, presented to the trier of fact, which is relevant to matters in issue in the absence of oral testimony or circumstantial evidence.[12] There are two categories of demonstrative evidence:

- *Real evidence.* This includes evidence that, in itself, is relevant to determining matters in issue, such as the deficient seatbelt in a product-liability action against a car manufacturer.
- *Illustrative evidence.* This includes evidence that is relevant because it explains testimonial evidence. A chart summarizing the occasions on which an injured plaintiff participated in rehabilitative therapy is illustrative evidence because it explains visually the plaintiff's rehabilitative efforts. The chart itself, however, does not relate to any matters in issue.

The power of demonstrative evidence

Demonstrative evidence is powerful because it increases the likelihood that the trier of fact will understand and remember the evidence you introduce.

People understand things they see. Complicated concepts are made simple through diagrams and pictures. Simple things are better understood.

Further, we live in a visual age in which generally we find things that we look at are more interesting. The more something captures our

---

12   John A. Olah, *The Art and Science of Advocacy* (Toronto: Thomson Canada, 1990), at 11-4.

interest, the more likely we are to want to understand it. The more we want to understand and focus on something, the more likely it is to stay with us.

In addition, people will remember more of what they are told for a much longer period of time when the information is accompanied by a visual aid. Some researchers suggest that when people see something they become involved in a present experience of the evidence. This may make the experience more memorable.

The experiential factor is most present with demonstrative objects, such as spine and brain models. Jurors can touch and manipulate these objects. In so doing, they are involved in the trial process. When your expert then touches the model, the juror can identify with him. This creates liking and makes the whole experience more memorable.

Demonstrative evidence is also powerful because it can summarize and remind the trier of facts of the theme of the case you present.

A theme is a concise statement of the key elements of your case. Effective themes explain why your client should win, and motivate decision-makers to find in your client's favour.

For example, if your client suffered a devastating injury in a car crash, your theme might be: We are here today because when the defendant crashed through the stop sign he ruined John's car and his life; now John has nowhere to turn except to us.

The more memorable your theme, the more likely that it will affect the decision-making process. You can make your theme more memorable by linking, or "anchoring," it to an image. For example, in John's case, a picture of the mangled automobiles perfectly summarizes, visually, the theory of John's case.

By your linking of the demonstrative evidence with your theme every time the anchored image is shown, the jurors are reminded that their role in the proceeding is to give your client deserved justice.

Good counsel also know that juries and judges alike appreciate well-prepared, professional presentations. Quality demonstrative evidence increases both your credibility and the credibility of your experts. This in turn improves the likelihood that the jury will understand, remember, and believe what you and your witnesses tell them.

Counsel cannot overlook the final reason why demonstrative evidence is a powerful ally: as an exhibit, it will be taken by the jurors to their deliberation room.

How to introduce demonstrative evidence to your advantage

Demonstrative evidence should be introduced fairly. Introduce the evidence through the appropriate witness. The material should complement and not overwhelm your witnesses' testimony. Finally, when dealing with a jury, demonstrative evidence should be shown early to let the jury members know their importance and to fully involve them in the learning process.

We give opposing counsel fair warning of our intention to introduce demonstrative aids as soon as we enter the courtroom. Doing so assures opposing counsel and the court that you are open and forthright. It also increases the likelihood that counsel will respond courteously and consent to your demonstrative evidence.

One of the chief advantages of introducing your demonstrative materials through your witnesses is that you can prepare them and ensure that they understand and can properly explain the evidence. Pick a witness with personal knowledge of the demonstrative tool. For example, whenever possible, your client should introduce her treatment chart. Your experts will introduce your medical illustrations.

Understanding the psychological impact of some exhibits on the jury is important. Since many exhibits are informative, interesting, and exciting to the jurors, this will help them to stay focused on the case. Spread your materials out among your witnesses so that you can spark the jurors' interest when you expect things to move more slowly.

Keep in mind that very attractive exhibits may pose a problem during the presentation of evidence (not in the opening statement). Some exhibits draw attention away from oral testimony — they win the battle for the jury's attention. That is why exhibits should complement oral testimony rather than compete with it.

Finally, in a jury trial, the jurors want to be educated and feel involved. They will become frustrated and believe that you think they are unimportant if you do not show them the exhibits as soon as you are able to. Good counsel will avoid this problem by showing the exhibit to the jury as soon as it is made an exhibit. (Obviously, this is not a problem with large exhibits because the jurors can see the exhibits as they are being introduced.)

Conclusion

Counsel should use demonstrative evidence in virtually all personal injury cases.

Its use will improve your ability to communicate your case to the jury. It will simplify complicated issues and make the evidence and case you present more memorable. Used effectively, demonstrative evidence will help you persuade the jury, and, ultimately, help your client achieve a just result.

Current Issues Concerning Civil Juries

Judicially imposed limits on counsel's freedom to address the jury

Counsel intending to deliver a jury should study the case of *Hall v. Schmidt.*[13] In that decision, Justice D.S. Ferguson took great offence at plaintiff's counsel's reference to liability following a clear order that he not do so. It is clearly improper to refer to liability or the facts creating liability once liability is no longer in issue. Once negligence and liability are admitted, the issues of negligence and liability are no longer relevant. However, once the issues are resolved, neither counsel have the right to refer to those issues. Moreover, counsel should never proceed in violation of a ruling by a trial judge. In *Hall*, counsel said:

> This case is about a defendant driver, who negligently ... causes a collision ... which changes the lives of his family members ... We are here because the defendant's negligence has meant that Ben will never see his loved ones again.

To this extent, the opening flew in the face of a direct ruling from the trial judge. Unfortunately, once liability was admitted, the case was no longer about a driver who negligently caused a collision — it was purely about damages.

Having said that, Mr. Justice Ferguson's decision presents a point of view that plaintiffs' counsel must consider when crafting an opening statement. Justice Ferguson took issue with much of the language in the opening statement in *Hall*. In criticizing certain aspects of the opening statement, Justice Ferguson drew what he called "a significant distinction between overt argument and persuasive narrative." While that distinction sounds simple enough, the reality is much more complex. Whether counsel's words amount to "overt argument" or "persuasive narrative" will be the nub of all decisions in this area for years to come.

---

13   (2001), 56 O.R. (3d) 257 (S.C.).

It is important to note that Justice Ferguson reached his decision in
Hall without considering the Court of Appeal's decision in *Creasor v.*
Cadillac Fairview Corp.[14] Also, Justice Ferguson's decision relies on case
law which counsel may argue is properly restricted to the role of crown
counsel in criminal cases.

Plaintiffs' counsel should take heart that Justice Ferguson endorsed
"persuasive narrative." In truth, to admonish persuasion would be to fly
in the face of virtually any respected text on Canadian practice that has
ever been written. However, Justice Ferguson did not admonish persuasion, he endorsed it. In *Hall*, he only expressed concern about the way
counsel goes about persuading. Although Justice Ferguson considered
overt argument as improper, he endorsed the following:

- persuasive narrative
- mentioning a point of law in issue
- describing the anticipated evidence
- explaining how the anticipated evidence will relate to an issue
- anticipating what questions the defence may put forward
- anticipating what evidence the defence may put forward
- posing questions the jury could consider in deciding the issues

Since the decision in *Hall*, the Court of Appeal has decided *Khazza-*
ka Auto Body v. Commercial Union Assurance Co. of Canada.[15] In *Khazza-*
ka, the Court of Appeal considered an appeal against a jury award of
$200,000 in punitive damages. One of the grounds of the appeal was
the nature of plaintiff's counsel's opening statement to the jury.

It is very important, in order to appreciate the significance of the
court's ruling, that we appreciate the language used by plaintiff's counsel. This was an arson case. Counsel's opening used these words as a
theme: "This merely brings us to part three of our story which I have
aptly entitled: Commercial Union's Desperate Attempt to Avoid Paying
a Claim." According to Justice Ferguson's admonition, this theme would
be argument.

Later in the opening, counsel said: "But they weren't only wrong; they
were entirely out in left field. They were on another planet ...." And still
later: "That puts Commercial Union's case on a bit of a slippery slope."

---

14   [2000] O.J. No. 4217 (C.A.).
15   (2002), 162 O.A.C. 293 (C.A.).

The following paragraphs are very important to our understanding the importance of the Court of Appeal's decision in *Khazzaka*.

> At the end of this trial, ladies and gentleman, I will have one further opportunity to speak to you, and by that time you would have seen what I have already seen, and you would have heard what I have already heard, and at that time we will get together again to share the important moments of this tragic story. At the end of that discussion, you will be left on your own to fight the injustices which you perceive and to determine whether Elias' quest for justice will be answered.
>
> In the interim, I sincerely hope that I will be able to bring this story to light and when we meet again, you will understand why I feel so honoured to have been chosen by this man to represent him at this trial.

Mr. Justice Carthy had this to say about the opening statement:

> In fact, counsel's opening, as it related to the claim for punitive damages, quite naturally included some indignation — that is the foundation on which such a claim must be built. And the charge to the jury read in its entirety appears to me to be more than adequate and fair to both sides.

It might also be helpful to restate here the opening words and the theme of counsel's opening in the *Creasor* case:

> If the Cadillac Fairview Corporation had obeyed the law and built a wheelchair ramp that was safe we wouldn't be here and Chris Creasor would be forging ahead with a good life.
>
> You and I recognize [this sign]. It's a symbol that means the same thing everywhere. Doesn't it mean the same thing to all of us? It is a sign of safety: "This access is safe for use by a disabled members of our community." Someone in a wheelchair is supposed to be able to rely on this sign. We are here because Chris Creasor relied on this sign and it led him into a trap which ruined his life. We are here because the defendant Cadillac Fairview gave lip service to this symbol and created a ramp which looked safe, but was dangerous.
>
> If the brain of any person is severely damaged it is tragic, but when the damage is to the brain of an extraordinary person like Chris Creasor it is a catastrophe which I cannot find the words to describe.

This language would offend the admonitions found in the *Hall* decision, but it did not offend the Court of Appeal.

Would the "indignant language" of plaintiff's counsel (to use the appellant's words) in *Khazzaka* be overt persuasion to Justice Ferguson? We would think so, but you will have to decide what is correct for you in each particular case. However, in our respectful view, where the *Hall* case conflicts with the decision in *Khazzaka*, it is not the law.

There is nothing more important than our integrity and our reputation for being honourable counsel. It is our duty as counsel to present a case fairly and according to the rules of court.

The jury and punitive damages in Canada

With its decision in *Whiten v. Pilot Insurance*,[16] the Supreme Court of Canada has introduced a hard-hitting form of consumer protection law that is certain to have a profound impact on the way insurers treat their insureds. *Whiten* has confirmed the role of punitive damages in Canada in any case where suitably egregious conduct offends the court. Because the court, in *Whiten*, sanctions a damages award of $1 million and approves of the award of punitive damages as an independent actionable wrong, claims for punitive damages are certain to become more common in Canada.

We predict with confidence that all of these cases will be tried by juries if plaintiff's counsel have their way. Juries are more likely to identify with the plaintiff. They will almost always be more generous than a judge. Good counsel will consider how it can use *Whiten* to its best advantage in an appropriate jury trial.

In what kinds of actions are punitive damages available?

Punitive damages are available in any case where the egregious conduct of the defendant merits punishment.

In *Whiten*, Mr. Justice Binnie discusses the types of actions in which one may advance a claim for punitive damages. He concludes that "the control mechanism lies not in restricting the category of case but in rationally determining circumstances that warrant the addition of punishment to compensation in civil action."

---

16   (2002), 209 D.L.R. (4th) 257 (S.C.C.).

Justice Binnie also notes that "it is in the nature of the remedy that punitive damages will largely be restricted to intentional torts or breach of fiduciary duty ...." But he finds that punitive damages are also available in negligence and nuisance as well.

Justice Binnie approves the notion that punitive damages "ought to be available whenever the conduct of the defendant is such as to merit condemnation by the court."

What evidence should counsel introduce to the jury to justify a punitive damage award?

Counsel acting in an action involving a claim for punitive damages are well-advised to understand both the relevant factors considered in assessing the punitive damage claim and the issues the trial judge will discuss in his or her charge to the jury.

The Supreme Court of Canada decision in *Whiten* provides a valuable review of circumstances previously meriting an award of punitive damages. Specifically, the court suggests that the following factors are relevant to a punitive damage award:

- whether the conduct was planned and deliberate
- the intent and motive of the defendant
- whether the defendant persisted in the outrageous conduct over a lengthy period of time
- whether the defendant attempted to conceal or cover up its conduct
- the defendant's awareness that what it was doing was wrong
- whether the defendant profited from its misconduct
- whether the interest violated was known to be deeply personal to the plaintiff
- the financial or other vulnerability of the plaintiff

Good counsel will investigate the file scrupulously and identify facts supporting these and other relevant considerations. There is no doubt that the foundation to establishing the punitive damage case relies upon thorough documentary and oral discovery. Understanding your client's case and reviewing all of the documents supporting it will help you determine the most effective means to assemble your punitive damages.

In *Whiten*, the Supreme Court of Canada listed issues that a trial judge should discuss in her charge to the jury. Counsel are well-advised to tailor their submissions to accord with these instructions. Specifically, the court notes that in charging the jury, the trial judge may comment that:

- Punitive damages are very much the exception, rather than the rule.
- Punitive damages are imposed only if there has been highhanded, malicious, arbitrary, or highly reprehensible misconduct that departs to a marked degree from ordinary standards of decent behaviour.
- Punitive damages should be assessed in an amount reasonably proportionate to such factors as the harm caused, the degree of the misconduct, the relative vulnerability of the plaintiff, and any advantage or profit gained by the defendant.
- Regard should be had to any other fines or penalties suffered by the defendant for the misconduct in question.
- Punitive damages are generally given only where the misconduct would otherwise be unpunished or where other penalties are or are likely to be inadequate to achieve the objectives of retribution, deterrence, and denunciation.
- The purpose of punitive damages is not to compensate the plaintiff but to give a defendant his or her just deserts, to deter the defendant and others from similar misconduct in the future, and to mark the community's collective condemnation.
- Punitive damages are awarded only where compensatory damages, which to some extent are punitive, are insufficient to accomplish these objectives.
- Punitive damages are given in an amount that is no greater than necessary to rationally accomplish their purpose.
- Although the state would normally be the recipient of any fine for misconduct, the plaintiff will keep the damages as a windfall.
- Judge and juries have usually found that moderate awards of punishment, which inevitably carry a stigma in the broader community, are generally sufficient.

Ultimately, a well-selected jury hearing persuasive evidence establishing that a powerful and resourceful defendant abused a vulnerable plaintiff will identify with the plaintiff and award significant punitive damages.

Conclusion

Civil juries provide counsel with an opportunity to achieve a fair verdict for the client. When managed ineffectively, civil juries also pose the very real risk of failure.

Counsel undertaking a jury trial are well-advised to understand the rules and procedures regarding the entitlement to, and selection of, a civil jury.

Understanding the procedural rules governing the use of a civil jury is necessary, but that knowledge alone does not ensure success. Counsel should also seek to understand how a jury will view their client and the case. In Ontario, focus groups provide counsel with the best chance of predicting how a jury will view a client, and these groups help counsel identify the sort of juror most likely to support a client's position.

Achieving excellent results in a jury trial requires counsel to present evidence persuasively and memorably. This is accomplished by understanding how a jury thinks and employing compelling communication and presentation techniques.

Jurors want to do the right thing. They want to reach a verdict that is fair. As advocates, we best serve our client's interests when we appeal to that desire to be fair. Meticulous preparation, coupled with an understanding of how jurors make decisions, will help us achieve that result.

[This article first appeared in the Summer 2003 issue of *The Advocates' Society Journal*.]

Appellate Advocacy

Justice John Sopinka[*]

During the twenty-three years that I practised litigation, I had many appeals, and I thought I knew the subject well. However, after my experience on the bench, I know that I was looking at it from one perspective, that is, that of counsel. I tried to put myself in the judges' shoes, but since I have been on the Supreme Court of Canada, I have decided that I did not do that very well. I have revised my thoughts on appeal advocacy to reflect the different perspective that one gets from the bench.

The Decision to Appeal

The first aspect of an appeal is the decision to appeal. In many cases that decision is purely tactical. In other words, you do not expect to win. You may appeal in the hope of forcing a settlement. What I have to say does not apply to that kind of an appeal. My comments apply to appeals "on the merits."

An appeal can be very costly, and the client looks to you for advice as to the chances of success. That advice should not be given the day the judgment comes down, as the decision could be made in anger. You should take a few days to regain your composure and then consider the

---

*   Mr. Justice John Sopinka, Supreme Court of Canada.

following. Is the judgment wrong? Even if it is, is it the kind of case in which the Court of Appeal will interfere? I have found increasingly that not only the Supreme Court of Canada, but also courts of appeal, are mesmerized by findings of fact. In the Supreme Court of Canada, if the case is basically a factual case, that is almost a guarantee that you will not succeed.

In a *Charter* case, it is very important to consider whether or not there was a factual base to be established at trial and whether the *Charter* argument was raised at trial. Particularly in our court, we have had a number of cases raising serious issues where we refused to deal with the matter because there was not a sufficient factual base on which to make the decision. If the crown fails to adduce evidence under section 1, it would seem unfortunate to strike down a statute because some lawyer made a fundamental error. A decision can affect the whole country, and sometimes the court knows that there is a better justification under section 1 than has been put forward in the evidence. That is the reason why, in *Charter* cases, it is very important from the court's standpoint that the controversy be a live controversy and also that there be an adequate factual base.

Notice of Appeal

The notice of appeal is not that important a document. The most important thing about it is to get it filed and to make it as general as possible so that you have included every possible ground of appeal. Some people think that the grounds should be very precise. This is a mistake. If a point is not covered in the notice of appeal but is in the factum, the court will give the notice of appeal the most general interpretation. Courts are not very keen on throwing something out as long as there has been adequate notice in the factum. However, being too precise in the notice of appeal may put you out of court.

The Factum

The importance of the factum is apparent when you consider that it is the central document at all stages of the appeal. Before the argument, it is the principal source from which the judges derive their information. During the oral argument, it is the blueprint and the framework for counsel's argument. After argument it still serves an important function. Some judges do not take notes. In the Supreme Court of Canada, we now receive a transcript, and it is a great relief not to have to take notes. Even so, the factum often elaborates the argument fully. The argument cannot always be delivered, particularly where there are time limits. Judges constantly go back to the factum when writing the judgment. Perhaps the greatest impact of the factum is that it provides the court with its first impression of the case and of you as counsel.

What about the style of the factum? This is very much a function of the rules of court. In the United States, some appellate courts decide cases entirely on the basis of the written argument. Moreover, in cases where they permit oral argument, such as those in the federal courts, only fifteen minutes per side is allowed. Therefore the factum is a substitute for oral argument. In these circumstances, the factum must include not only the points of argument, but the development of the argument.

In England, the filing of written submissions is a recent phenomenon. It wasn't until 1983 that the Master of the Rolls suggested that counsel might consider providing the Court of Appeal with a skeleton argument on paper prior to the oral argument. In 1989, the skeleton argument became mandatory in all civil appeals. The purpose of the English version of the factum is to identify, and not to argue, the points.

In Canada, the rules call for a factum that is, as in so many things, a compromise between those two positions: the American, which is much fuller, and the English, which is simply in point form. In Ontario, rule 61.10 requires "a concise statement of the law and authorities relating to the issues." In the Supreme Court of Canada, rule 37 provides for a statement of the argument setting out briefly and concisely the points of law or fact to be discussed. Notwithstanding the slight difference in wording, I don't see any difference in the application of those rules as far as the drafting of the factum is concerned. They call for, and permit, a terse version of the argument, leaving something for oral argument.

The terms employed in the rules are sufficiently flexible to permit some variation in the amount of detail devoted to argument. When there is a page limit on the length of the factum, this imposes its own restraints. Apart from formal restraints, there are technical restraints. Judges are apt not to read an overly long factum. One of the judges of the United States Supreme Court told me: "I do not care about page limits. I do not worry about them because I stop reading at page thirty." Time limits are becoming the order of the day in appeal proceedings. We have them in the Supreme Court. As you know, we permit an hour per side. No doubt time limits will be adopted in the provincial appellate courts.

A time limit on the oral argument has a significant bearing on how you should draft the factum. When you are drafting your factum, you should decide which points you will argue orally, which points you will just touch on, and which points you will not argue at all. With respect to the points that you intend to argue orally, do not develop the argument with respect to those points. Leave something for the oral argument. Fully develop the points that are going into your factum.

The first step in drafting the factum is to understand the points in issue. If the points in issue are drafted first, then this will achieve that objective. They should be carefully crafted until they express, with tight precision and economy of language, exactly what is intended.

Having mastered the points in issue, turn to a review of the evidence. I recommend the preparation of a summary, which can now be done on computer. Before anyone mastered computers, the technique usually adopted was to go through the transcript and note, opposite the line and page where the witness stated a point that was relevant to an issue, what the substance of the point was. This could be done fairly quickly. Then a secretary or a student could read through the transcript the notations on the right-hand blank page and prepare a summary referring to the page and line, the name of the witness, and the point. The product of this exercise became very useful in the later preparation of the concise statement of facts.

The main rule with respect to the facts is that you must be scrupulously fair and candid in presenting them. Misrepresenting the facts can not only ruin the case, it can ruin your reputation. The worst thing to have in an appellate court is a reputation for not being trusted with respect to stating the facts. Do not be put in the position with regard to anything you say where the court will ask, "Where do we find that in the record?"

Generally, unless counsel is seeking to reverse a finding of fact, the statement of facts should be based either on a finding of the trial judge or on facts that are not in dispute. When setting out a finding of fact, state what the trial judge found to be the fact and give reference to the reasons for judgment. You may go on to state that this finding of fact is supported by the evidence and give a reference to the evidence. On the occasions when it is necessary to deal with disputed facts, both versions should be summarized.

The factum contains a concise statement of the law as it relates to the facts. These are not two ships passing in the night. They must be woven together so that each supports the other. Avoid citing too many authorities. It may look good in the factum, but it annoys the court because they think they have to read all the cases and then find that half of them do not have anything to do with the point. If there are cases directly on point, just cite the highest authority. If there are two cases of equal authority, cite them both but do not multiply cases in the factum just for filler. If a short passage in the case states the ratio of the case, and if it is particularly applicable to your case, quote it in the factum right after the case reference.

In *Charter* cases, your review of the authorities should not be limited to Canada. You should look at other jurisdictions, including the European courts. Moreover, in *Charter* cases, the court is often ploughing new ground, and the opinions of academic writers are most helpful. It is amazing the impact that people such as Professor Hogg have had on decisions under the *Charter* because there are no precedents.

This is a piece of mundane but very important information: check your citations; carefully. There is nothing more annoying for a judge working at night who finds a reference to a case that seems important, checks it, and cannot locate it because the citation is wrong. Books of authority help in this regard, but they should contain only the key cases, not cases used as a passing reference in the factum.

Finally, the rules require a statement of the relief requested. This can often be quite technical, so spend some time on this. Although there is a tendency just to ask that the appeal be allowed or dismissed, often there are alternatives, depending on your degree of success.

In a recent case in our court, the crown was very embarrassed. In an entrapment case, the trial judge had found entrapment with respect to three charges and therefore entered a stay. The crown appealed successfully to the Court of Appeal, and the Court of Appeal lifted the stay and directed a new trial. The accused appealed. The crown lawyers resisted the appeal and asked that instead of a new trial there be a conviction. They did not have anything about this in their "nature of order requested," so they had obviously not turned their minds to it.

It turned out that, if they had, they would have found that the crown cannot appeal from a judgment from a Court of Appeal that overturns an acquittal but directs a new trial. The crown was very embarrassed when it was pointed out that they did not have the request in the factum. They asked to amend and were even more embarrassed when it was pointed out that they could not amend because there was no such right of appeal.

Oral Argument

It is wise to observe the formalities of oral argument. You should start with "My Lords and My Ladies." Try to avoid endless repetition of this phrase throughout the argument. "May it please the court" may be a useful substitute.

Different people take forms of address in different ways. I am reminded of the story about one judge, Mr. Justice X, who considered the form of address very important. He took himself so seriously that his wife was sometimes called Mrs. Justice X. There was a trial before Mr. Justice X, and the plaintiff had spent most of his time in police court, where they used to call the magistrate "Your Worship." He kept calling Mr. Justice X "Your Worship." So Mr. Justice X, at the noon recess, said to counsel, "Mr. Y, would you please instruct your client as to the proper address to one of Her Majesty's Justices of the High Court?"

Counsel went out and said, "You dolt, I told you not to forget to call him 'My Lord'. Do you want him to know where you spend most of your time?" The plaintiff seemed to take the lesson to heart. They went back in the afternoon, and it was apparent that he wanted to undo the harm that he had done and was waiting for a question from Mr. Justice X. Finally, the question came. He replied, "Yes, Your Majesty." Apparently, he won his case.

I have always considered that the appropriate structure for an oral argument is as follows:

1) An opening
2) A statement of the points in issue
3) A review of the evidence
4) A review of the law as related to the evidence
5) A conclusion

The opening of an appeal is much shorter than the opening of a trial. The issues are now much more concentrated, and the court does not have to be given a road map of the evidence to be called, as is done at trial. The purpose of an opening statement on an appeal is to capture the essence of the case in words that will excite the interest of the court. Appeals are often dull, and you would be surprised how welcome a little bit of drama is.

I will not say that this won the case or that it is the most perfect opening, but I thought I would look up my opening in the Supreme Court of Canada in *Nelles v. The Attorney General.* In this case the issue was whether or not the attorney general and his agents, the crown attorneys, were immune from the suit in a malicious prosecution action. The Court of Appeal said they were. The Supreme Court of Canada allowed our appeal and said they were not.

My opening statement was as follows:

> My Lords and My Ladies, in this case the Court of Appeal has decided that crown attorneys enjoy immunity from civil suits. That makes them unique among public servants. The common law has uniformly refused to recognize any protection from civil liability for a public servant who has acted maliciously, but the Court of Appeal has said there is this one exception.

After making the opening statement, state the points in issue. These may already be apparent. If there is a time restraint, you do not have to repeat them, although it is desirable to do so. If you have drafted them as I have suggested in the factum, then just read them from the factum. You have now got them in exactly the form in which you want them. Furthermore, when you deal with some of them, if they are not too numerous, give the court a little preview as to the way in which you are going to argue these points. A little blueprint helps, because the court always looks for a framework within which to fit the mass of material that has been filed and the oral argument that they are going to hear. This is the time to drop any points that you are going to drop. That will always be welcome.

If there are several counsel, you should announce how the argument will be divided. In the *Ontario-Quebec Railway* argument in the Supreme Court of Canada, we argued the appeal for four days. On our side we had about three different counsel, because there were a number of parties, and on the other side Pierre Genest had even more lawyers. At the beginning of his argument, the court asked, "How are you going to divide the argument, Mr. Genest?" He replied, "My Lords, unless I drop dead, I'm going to do it all." Mr. Justice Beetz, who was presiding, turned to Mr. Justice Estey and said, "What did he say?" Justice Estey, who was always quick, replied, "He has reserved the right to die."

Following the points, you will review the evidence. The extent to which this is done depends on the nature of the appeal. As I have said, in the Supreme Court of Canada the findings of fact of the trial judge are almost sacrosanct. If there is a finding of fact on a point sought to be made, there is virtually nothing to be gained by referring to the evidence. Subject to time restrictions, this aspect of the argument should simply consist of a reaffirmation of the findings of the trial judge.

One of the important issues on an appeal is to ensure that you and the court are on the same wavelength with respect to the facts. It is impossible to persuade them of the law if they have a different idea of the facts. So whether you deal with the evidence or not, make sure you are on the same wavelength on the facts.

Even when appeals do not involve an attempt to change the findings of fact, I am still amazed at how the atmosphere can be changed by the reading of key passages in the evidence. This is especially so if you have former counsel or trial judges on the court. Suddenly, the drama of the courtroom comes to life when some dramatic passage of the evidence is read. So, it is not a bad technique to read a particularly good passage in the evidence that supports your position.

In the Court of Appeal, appeals are frequently concerned with facts. In such a case, the review of the evidence must be much fuller. It will be designed to show that the findings of the trial judge were clearly wrong in that he or she misapprehended the evidence or failed to consider material evidence. Judges of appellate courts would often say to me, "We do not retry cases." In fact, that is unrealistic. If there is an appeal on a finding of fact, it is true that the court does not retry the case, but it cannot decide if there is a patent error in the facts without reviewing the evidence. In order to avoid impatience, your review must be a tightly knit exercise. A rambling attempt to rerun the trial will bring forth the rebuke that I have already mentioned.

The facts in a *Charter* case require special treatment. They include not only what we normally consider fact, but also a great mass of material that is loosely described as legislative facts. The rules are almost non-existent as to the proof of this material, which includes things such as reports of commissions, studies, foreign studies, reports from United Nations committees, and statistics. These things are neither pure fact nor pure law. The rules as to how they can be introduced into the record are very vague. They are frequently, without objection, filed with the books of authorities.

After dealing with the facts, review the law. This is not simply a recital of the cases. At this point the issues have been firmly established, and the court should be on the same factual base as counsel. It is now necessary to add the principles of law that you say dictate the result. Unless there is a binding authority on all fours in your favour, do not lead with the cases. Lead with the logic of your argument, which will be supported by the cases: show the court that what you are saying makes sense. Text writings and academic writings are helpful here because very often they address the subject not just from the aspect of whether or not it is covered by *stare decisis*, but whether it makes sense. If you do have an appellate case on all fours, you naturally lead with that case.

When citing cases, use the following format. First, tell the court why you are citing the case. There is nothing worse than having somebody ramble through a long authority without knowing why, so state the proposition for which you cite the case. Ordinarily, you do not have to give the full name of the case because you give the court the tab number in your book of cases. If the facts are relevant, state them briefly and then state what the court decided with particular reference to the proposition you are advancing. Finally, illustrate the point with a brief quote. If you have to read a great deal, you may summarize it, and then wrap it up by explaining how it advances your case.

In *Charter* cases, it is usually necessary to cite not only Canadian decisions but legislation and writings from other countries. These materials are relevant to show whether the legislation under attack is rationally connected to the government objective that the impugned legislation is designed to achieve. And here, I must say, the government frequently does not do a very good job in putting forward what is a government objective. This does not have to be found within the four corners of the statute; the government can file other material. But I know from my own experience that it is like pulling hens' teeth to get a government official to swear an affidavit as to what is intended by legislation and how it achieves the object. Very often that would save the legislation.

As an example of the type and breadth of material that can be filed, the material for a recent case that we heard with respect to whether or not the public service should be entitled to participate in partisan political activity (*P.S.A.C. v. A.G. Canada*, released 21 March 1991) included the legislation of every country in the Western world that dealt with this subject and also studies as to how it worked.

With regard to the conclusion, it's hard to say much because it is such an individualistic thing. It should briefly sum up the main thrust of the appeal. It may contain some comment about the nature of relief requested. Try to finish on a carefully-crafted statement that tends to simplify and not complicate the issues.

Delivery

The basic rule is that you have to be true to your own style. You cannot be somebody else; that just seems phony. Some counsel have the gift of eloquent language. I recently saw a videotape of Arthur Maloney in action. Here was an example of a counsel who had a great gift of language. Such counsel are apt to rely less on substance and more on form. Others, without this gift, rely on their mastery of the law and on the logical force of the argument. Both methods are effective. A little humour often provides welcome relief, but not everybody can get away with it. Also, there has to be an opening for it. Often it falls flat when you are dealing with something that is deadly serious and nobody wants to be funny.

One of the last appeals I had was for the City of Windsor. It involved a strip club called the Latin Quarter. The city was trying to get rid of these clubs on a street it was trying to beautify. The city, therefore, passed by-laws, and these by-laws were attacked by the Latin Quarter on the ground, *inter alia*, that they violated section 2(b) of the *Charter*: freedom of expression. Nowhere did the material contain any detail of exactly the expression for which they were seeking protection. Reference was made to dancing, but there was no evidence of it in the record.

We decided to have an official from the City of Windsor, acting beyond the ordinary course of duty, view one of their shows. That he did, and a stripper came out and did her act, all sorts of gyrations on the stage, all of which he recorded in an affidavit. That was in the record, but counsel for the Latin Quarter did not refer to it.

My argument was fairly long, and on a boring afternoon I said, "Now My Lords, I come to an aspect of the evidence which is somewhat more stimulating than your Lordships are used to in this court." I told them the story and read them the affidavit. This was a point in the appeal in which humour was welcome, and it certainly didn't hurt the case. We won.

What use should be made of the factum, and how does the factum fit in with your argument? There are basically two methods that I have seen used: arguing from your notes, and arguing from the factum. If you argue from notes, they should be keyed to the factum. That does not necessarily mean that you have to follow the order of the factum, but you should always let the court know where you are in the factum because some judges are more used to acquiring information by reading than by hearing. If they have lost the point and did not quite follow you, they will read the factum to see what you said.

There is nothing wrong with reading selected passages from the factum, and if you have done it properly you have probably said it better there than you will say it in an oral argument. If, therefore, you've got a proposition that is fairly technical, and you have got it in the factum, there is nothing wrong with reading it. But that does not mean that you should read great gobs of the factum. The argument should highlight and supplement the factum. In one case in our court, counsel was reading the factum verbatim. The chief justice said, "Mr. X, we have all read the factum," to which Mr. X replied, "Yes, but with gestures?"

There is a special talent in arguing *Charter* cases. I think counsel who have more of an academic bent do better in *Charter* cases. There's more emphasis on substance and less on form, perhaps because the consequences are often so great. If you strike down a statute, it can affect the whole country. I must admit that counsel who are academically inclined, who have spent a long time teaching or writing, have the edge at the moment. This does not mean that counsel who have not had this experience cannot master the art. However, it requires more in-depth reading and more knowledge of the purpose behind legislation. That is one of the main features in arguing the "law" in a *Charter* case. It is a little more than just citing precedents.

Dos and Don'ts

These are fairly straightforward. Always make certain that the court knows where you are in the argument. It is so simple a proposition, and yet so often violated. The submissions must be firmly tied to the points in issue, and this relationship must always be apparent. If judges are writing, give them time. Do not repeat unless it is apparent that the point was not understood the first time.

Keep the argument as short as possible. To do this, increase the time of preparation. A great American TV evangelist, who is frequently on the lecture circuit, required a month's notice if his speech was to be less than twenty minutes, two weeks if his speech was to be an hour, and no notice at all if he could speak for an unlimited time.

If a time limit is imposed, do not exceed it. Often, counsel find themselves fighting the red light that goes on in our court. To avoid this, organize your argument to stay within the time limit and avoid annoying the court, which has structured its day on the assumption that time limits will be respected.

Do not speak too fast. This is an almost irresistible temptation where there are time limits. In so many arguments in our court, counsel have figured out that they have got five or six points and they are going to argue them all, but three times as fast. The result is that nobody understands anything. Instead, select one or two points that you really think are winners, and argue those as if your time were unlimited.

Some people think that if they throw a bunch of references at the court, the judges will scurry back and read them all. What happens in our court is that right after the oral argument, having spent a lot of time preparing for it, we retire to the conference room. We go around the table and everybody announces their decision. No one is bound by that, but the die is pretty well cast at that point, so all the references that have been thrown at the court, urging it to look at this and look at that, may never be looked at, except when the decision has already been made.

Some of the points I have made are rather general and must be modified in particular cases. However, I hope that I have managed to help you see appellate advocacy "from the other side of the bench."

[This article was first published in the March 1992 issue of *The Advocates' Society Journal*.]

Appellate Advocacy

Justice Sydney L. Robins[*]

[Editors' Note: The lecture that constitutes this article is one of the two David B. Goodman Memorial Lectures delivered by Mr. Justice Robins at the Faculty of Law, University of Toronto, in February 1995.]

John W. Davis, one of the great American masters of courtroom advocacy, once suggested in a lecture on the art of advocacy that this was a subject to be presented by judges. "They, after all," he said, "are the target and trier of the argument. Who," he asked rhetorically, "would listen to a fisherman's weary discourse on fly-casting if the fish himself could be induced to give his views on the effective method of approach?" Today I offer you some reflections of one of those fish.

Let me begin by saying that the importance of advocacy in the appellate process should not be underestimated. True, there are appeals that cannot be lost, and others that cannot be won, regardless of the skill or learning or persuasive powers of counsel. But appellate advocacy can play a substantial, and in some cases a decisive, part in determining the outcome. The argument of appeals should represent an exercise in forensic skill, and counsel should prepare on the principle that it is of high, and often of controlling, importance.

---

*   Mr. Justice Sydney L. Robins, Court of Appeal for Ontario.

Advocacy is said to be an art and not a science, and an art, I am told, is a specific skill in adept performance requiring the exercise of intuitive faculties that cannot be learned solely by study. Advocacy is persuasion, simply the process of trying to convince someone of something, and the form of advocacy to be employed will depend upon the forum in which the advocate is appearing.

When a lawyer negotiates, for example, a contract, or represents a client before an administrative tribunal or at a meeting, or when he or she puts a proposition to a client, the lawyer is engaged in a type of advocacy, in an exercise in persuasion, and the techniques appropriate to one forum may not be appropriate to another.

In an appellate court, the essential question to be asked is how can you, as a co-professional with the judges, best assist the court in the performance of its judicial responsibility, and, more than incidentally, advance your client's position in the matter at issue? In other words, how can you best perform your function as counsel?

The role of the advocate has always had, and continues to have, a fascinating attraction to the public. The drama that often surrounds the advocate's activity, and the human material in which he or she usually deals, are sufficient in themselves to excite public interest. When we recognize that the resolution of disputes by means of advocacy in an adversarial system substitutes persuasion for force or arbitrary action, there is a deeper basis for the interest.

The courts are the instruments by which organized society puts down the controversies that rise up for solution. And it is the advocate's task to determine and shape the materials that call for the court's decision and that provide the foundation for those decisions.

The importance of this role cannot be overstated. As the law comes to deal more and more with economic and social factors, and as governments continue to spread their activity into these realms, the advocate, in presenting individual cases, must deal with the problems and issues that result. Advocacy provides a window through which conflicting social currents and the available choices are put on public display.

The way in which cases are decided necessarily depends on the ability and capacity of counsel to present and fashion the materials that constitute the record. The record must provide a factual underpinning for the legal arguments to be advanced in the appellate court. The bounds of the court's power of decision are obviously set by the record. It is thus the responsibility of the advocate to provide the material upon which the judgment sought can be based — to furnish the court with what Holmes once called "the implements of decision." A fundamental concept of our adversary system is that, with the aid of the advocate on each side of a case, the court will be in the best position to render justice.

How then is counsel to discharge this responsibility?

The best advice on how counsel might prepare an appeal and present argument, both written and oral, is that given by Mr. Davis in the lecture to which I have referred. It is this. Imagine, if you will, changing places with the judge. Bear in mind that courts are not filled with demigods. Some judges are learned, some less so; some are keen and perspicacious, others have more plodding minds. In short, judges are men and women and lawyers, like the counsel before them. That they are honest and impartial, and ready and eager to make a correct decision, you may take for granted. You may rightfully expect, and you should expect, nothing less than fair treatment at their hands.

Yet they know nothing about the matter you are putting before them, and they are not stimulated by any interest or feeling towards anyone concerned. They are simply being called upon to perform their function in their appointed sphere. They are waiting to be supplied with the facts and the law upon which they can properly base a decision — they are waiting for you to show them why they should grant the remedy you seek and, if so, how. In short, they are waiting for "the implements of decision."

If the places were reversed and you sat where they do, think what it is that you would want to know about the case. How and in what order would you want the story — the issues, the facts, the law — related? What would make your approach to the solution easier? These are questions advocates must put to themselves, not only in an appellate court but in every court.

The first thing a judge wants to know is what the case is all about. What are the facts? In your law school studies, your attention is customarily and necessarily focused primarily on analogic techniques that are useful in reconciling what a court did, or at least what it said it did, in one case with what the same or another court did in another case. You study how judges formulate, on the basis of past decisions, tentative generalizations that we call rules or principles of law. You note that these abstractions may not afford a clear or satisfactory guide to decision, that they may be imprecise and equivocal, that often choices must be made between competing rules, and that in the process of choosing, a new rule may be born. You seek to probe the reasons that impel judges to follow or modify or overrule the language used in previous decisions. Little time, however, is spent in studying the facts of a case — they can be reduced to a few introductory paragraphs in a case book. For law school purposes, it is enough that they have been "found" and have been stated in the court's reasons.

Instructive and important though these exercises are, they bear little resemblance to the conduct of oral and written advocacy in the courts. In the courts, the order of priority is reversed. The facts assume transcendant importance as a determining element in the decision of cases. Erwin Griswold, for many years the dean of Harvard Law School and later the solicitor general of the United States, had this point in mind when he once said that perhaps his most famous classroom remark in all his teaching years at Harvard was, "Look at the statute" or "What does the statute say?" He went on to explain that "there is something about students, and some oral advocates too, which leads them to think great thoughts without ever taking the time and care to see just exactly what they are thinking about .... But courts are accustomed to think in terms of concrete, rather specific cases. The oral advocate," he added, "takes a great step in advancing his cause ... if, right at the beginning of his argument ... he tells the court exactly what the case is about. ... If you can get the court moored to the question as you see it, and so that they see it clearly and distinctly, you may be off to a good start towards leading them to decide the case your way."

In similar vein, but in more poetic language, Cardozo once observed in speaking of the difficulty in getting at the facts that "more and more, we lawyers are awakening to a perception of the truth that what divides and distracts us in the solution of legal problems is not so much uncertainty about the law as uncertainty about the facts — the facts which generate the law. Let the facts be known as they are, and the law will sprout from the seed and turn its branches towards the light."

It is perhaps true that in most cases the law itself seldom decides the issue; the facts do. And as contrasted with the ascertainment of the facts, the law is relatively easy to discover. This is why a clear and accurate statement of facts cannot be overemphasized.

In oral argument, there is often little time for a full exposition of the facts. At that stage, you may be able only to highlight the essential facts and must rely on your factum, which the judges will already have read, for the details. The factum is therefore a very important part of your presentation — far more important than most lawyers realize. Indeed, it is an essential component of effective appellate oral advocacy. It introduces the case to the judge, the judge gains his or her first impression of the case from it, and if judgment is reserved, it can assist in the writing of the judgment.

If the facts are outlined in a way that can convince the court of the innate justice of your client's cause, I think it is probably true to say that in many cases the battle is at least half won — the court can usually find a legal theory to support a decision that accords with the equities. Most cases are determined by their facts — the facts perceived and grouped in such a way as to spell justice. The statement of the facts is at the heart of the factum. Counsel should cull from the record, particularly a lengthy record, the significant facts and marshall them in such a fashion that their significance is apparent. This is not a task for the judge.

The statement should be scrupulously accurate and should be presented in a way that lays bare all the pertinent circumstances that have produced the dispute and that may affect the court's decision. It should be restricted to a recital of the material events and transactions involved in the case and not delve into minutiae. It should not be argumentative; the court wants to feel that it is getting the actual facts, not an editorialized version or counsel's comments or contentions. The advocate's objective is achieved when the judge, after reading the factual exposition, can say to himself or herself, "This case does not appear to need much arguing. It seems clear from the facts themselves that this party is in the right."

It is helpful, particularly in a complex case, to commence the factum with a summary that gives a capsular view of the case. The effectiveness of a factum is considerably impaired if the reader must plod through a dozen pages of details before the light begins to dawn as to what is really involved in the case. At the outset, or as soon as possible, you should let the court know what type of case it is, who the parties are, its disposition in the court below, and whether there are any jurisdictional problems, and then provide a quick summary or overview of the case that can form the basis for the detailed statement of facts to follow. It is important to bear in mind that you should communicate in terms as simple and as easily understood as the subject matter permits. In this regard I think of a rather prominent counsel who, when pressed as to why he kept a lawyer on his staff whom everyone regarded as a not too bright fellow, replied, "Well, when I have written a factum or prepared an argument, I have him read it. If he can understand it, I think the judges probably can also."

Underlying a good argument is a carefully-constructed theory of the case — a theory nurtured by a careful presentation of the facts that demonstrates the inherent fairness, as well as the legal validity, of your client's position. The precise form and structure of the argument will depend in large measure on the issues involved. Generally, but not necessarily, the story can best be developed chronologically. But whatever order is followed, there should be some rhyme or reason to it, and it should be told with clarity and candour. You should never misstate any element of the facts; and if there are facts that are adverse to your position, you should frankly put them forth. It will not help to ignore them or try to conceal them, for your opponent, or the court, will surely bring them out. You may be able to blunt their effect and lessen the sting so that they appear less damaging if you present them yourself. Failure to mention them may destroy the court's confidence in your case and, indeed, in you as counsel.

John Robinette is perhaps the best expositor of facts that I ever heard in court. He would spend a good deal of his argument on the facts. He always presented them in a clear and orderly fashion so that the picture came forth very clearly. If he had thin ice to get over, he did not conceal it; but he was over it, and off and away on the other side, before you really realized how thin the ice had been. It was interesting in listening to him to try to figure out where the weaknesses in his case were. It was not easy, for he spoke clearly and strongly, at a steady pace, and even if you thought you saw a hole you were likely to forget about it as he moved on to talk compellingly about some other aspect of the facts in the case. After he concluded, you often wondered why the case got to court in the first place.

One of the first tests of a counsel is the selection of the issues to be argued. It is counsel's job to dispassionately pick the issues that common sense and experience suggest will likely be dispositive. In argument before the court, it is important to begin by stating those issues and then focusing your argument so that the court will be conscious throughout of what specific issue it is that you are addressing. It is easy to spoil an otherwise good argument by arguing too many issues. Indeed, most cases turn on no more than a few. The enthusiasm of counsel, however, can always discover a great number of reasons for urging that the judgment of the court below should be affirmed or reversed, as the case may be. But the argument is stronger if you confine yourself to the major arguments and, difficult as it may sometimes be, let the minor points go. Legal contentions, like currency, depreciate through over-issue. While the mind of an appellate judge is receptive to the suggestion that a lower court committed an error, that receptiveness declines as the number of alleged errors increases. Multiplicity hints at a lack of faith and confidence in your major grounds of appeal and may dilute and weaken a good case and not save a bad one.

In arguing the law, state the applicable principles of law upon which you rely. It should be remembered that judges are less interested in learning what results would follow from analogous extensions of principles stated in cases decided years ago than they are in reaching a result consistent with what is fair and right in the particular circumstances before the court. Judges are more and more concerned with doing justice between litigants and tend to resist appeals premised on purely legalistic grounds. If the recitation of the facts has convinced the court that fairness and justice require the result for which counsel contends, the argument on the law need do little more than set forth a legal basis on which the result may be justified. Often, the best argument on a question of law is to state the question clearly.

It is usually more persuasive if the argument is based on an applicable principle of law rather than a mere recital of precedent. What judges want to know is why this line of cases should apply to these circumstances rather than another line on which your opponent relies with equal certainty.

What is important is that you present the points that form the basis of your appeal and upon which you rely to obtain the relief you seek in a clear and succinct fashion. Where did the court below go wrong, and why? That is more effective than a long-winded presentation. Now, long-windedness perhaps is an occupational disease, one from which judges are hardly free. Perhaps that is why we bear the cross with greater equanimity than most. You may perhaps recall the crushing remark made from the bench by Sir George Jessel while he was presiding in the English Court of Appeal. He had before him a counsel well-known for his verbosity who, after quoting interminably from the testimony at trial, said, "At this point in the trial, My Lords, the trial judge stopped me." "One moment, sir," said Jessel, "it will be a great benefit to me and their lordships if you could explain how this was done."

Counsel should not read the argument. Talk to the court instead, for once you begin to read a written argument the argument loses its spontaneity, and you raise a curtain between yourself and the court. Unlike something prepared for a particular occasion in which the form of every sentence depends on no interruptions, in court, when you are engaged in argument and are subject to instant, insistent interruption, reading just does not go over. An oral argument loses much of its spontaneity if it is written out in advance and read to the court, page by page. This is not to say that counsel should not have notes outlining the argument and listing the points that he or she intends to make. But the notes should serve as a guide and not a text, and they should be referred to only sparingly and when absolutely necessary.

An argument is not a set piece; it is not a monologue. Nor should it be a memorized oration or, at the opposite extreme, an unorganized, rambling discourse, relying on the inspiration of the moment. An argument, no matter how well-prepared, must be adjusted, trimmed, or expanded according to the reaction it evokes. Counsel should prepare accordingly and be sufficiently flexible to vary the argument on the basis of what the court is saying or the reception the argument receives.

Counsel, it seems to me, should welcome questions from the bench. If doing nothing more, questions give the assurance that you have at least awakened some interest. They afford you the only chance to penetrate the mind of the court and to dispel a doubt as soon as it arises. They should be viewed as opportunities to emphasize a favourable point and explain an apparent weakness in your case. Do not evade or postpone, no matter how difficult the question may be or how much it interrupts the thread of your argument. Nothing is perhaps more irritating than to have counsel take refuge behind the familiar evasion, "I'm coming to that," and then have that argument end with the promise unfulfilled. If you are really coming to it, then indicate briefly what your answer will be when it is reached, and never sit down until it is made. If you do not know the answer, then indicate that you do not know and that you would like an opportunity to inquire into it.

Do not think that there is a deliberate design to embarrass counsel by questions. The judge is usually seeking to get to the heart of the matter by testing his or her preliminary views or impressions of the strengths and weaknesses of the case. Sometimes a judge may perhaps be seeking, through the questions, to persuade his or her colleagues one way or the other. If the question is relevant it denotes that the judge is grappling with your contention, even though he or she has not grasped it. The judge knows where his or her doubts lie and on which points he or she wishes to be enlightened. It is, after all, the judge's mind that must be made up. No one can do that for him or her. The judge must take his or her own course of thought to accomplish it, and this means that the judge must sometimes interrupt.

Moreover, a lively, even robust, dialogue may be a swifter and surer vehicle to truth and understanding than a monologue. A wise counsel will embrace the opportunity to put at rest any misconception or doubt that, if the judge waited to raise it in the conference room, counsel would have no opportunity to answer and perhaps no one there would have the information to answer.

Counsel should show some sensitivity to the views of the court. Where the court has indicated, or has made it abundantly clear from its comments and questions, that it is not interested in a particular point, or that it has the point, or that it does not agree with the point, I see little benefit in counsel pursuing the argument on that point. If you have firmly put forth everything that you can and the judges understand the point, then let it go at that. Do not carry on to the extent of tedious repetition and persistence.

An advocate, to be effective, must keep his or her perspective. The advocate is not a party to the case, but an officer of the court, and must deal with the case as it is, warts and all. Although emotion may be a relevant part of advocacy, it must be kept under control. The advocate must not become so emotionally involved in the case as not to see or accept its weaknesses. The strong points on the other side must be recognized and not swept under the rug, lest they loom larger and larger in the eyes of the court. Counsel should dispassionately acknowledge their existence and try to exercise the professional skill necessary to show that they have less substance than would appear or that, though valid, they are not sufficient to outweigh other factors in his or her client's favour.

If I were asked to name the advocate's secret weapon, a weapon that remains a secret to many, I should say that it was a complete knowledge of the record. No lawyer, no matter how able, can afford to argue any case in ignorance of the record. This is another way of stressing the obvious importance of preparation. Whenever a lawyer comes to believe that he or she no longer needs to know the record, no longer needs to adequately prepare, hardening of the forensic arteries has set in. Of course, experience facilitates learning, and an old hand can absorb the essentials of a record far more easily than a novice can. But the lawyer who really knows it is a far more dangerous opponent than the polished veteran who has given the record a glib once-over lightly. I have seen experienced lawyers effectively demolished when they went free-wheeling away from a record that they obviously had not studied and were then caught short by opposing counsel who knew the case inside out. The otherwise gentle visages of appellate judges harden perceptibly when such misstatements are exposed. A lawyer simply has no business getting up to talk about a case he or she does not thoroughly know.

An effective oral advocate must have an appreciation of and an ability to apply the fundamentals of good public speaking. Speak up, speak in sentences and in paragraphs, and not too fast or too slow. Avoid distracting mannerisms, be heard, use proper emphasis and occasional pauses, avoid a monologue, do not mumble. Indistinct speech often appears as the product of indistinct thought, and if a lawyer has not prepared what he or she wants to say, that lawyer is not likely to say it effectively. Oratory is not necessary. An appellate court is not a jury; but the court is not insensible to the average juror's reaction, as witness the timelessness of the observation that hard cases make bad law. Any play on an appellate court's emotions must be subtle and restrained if it is to be effective.

Never express your personal opinion. That, of course, is fundamental but often forgotten. Do not let yourself become personally identified with your client. Remember that you are counsel independent of the case. Do not give evidence yourself, even if you know, unless the matter is undisputed. It is generally of little assistance to the court.

Do not engage in personalities. It is simply not productive. Unfortunately, opposing lawyers not infrequently become antagonistic towards one another. When such personal feelings develop, there is a tendency to resort to invective in referring to the acts or conduct of the other party. It is not helpful to one's case to yield to this temptation. Careless charges of fraud or chicanery or characterizing your opponent's contentions as absurd, ridiculous, nonsensical, and the like are unbecoming. Furthermore, they are unconvincing and ineffectual and are better left unsaid. They distract the court from the real matter at issue. Judges view them with distaste.

A proper mental attitude on the part of the advocate is another factor essential to an effective argument. What should the attitude be? It seems to me that it should be essentially one of respectful discussion between intellectual equals. It does not help the presentation of the case if counsel shows too much respect for the court. By that I mean that counsel must be able to stand up to the judges just as he or she would to a senior member of a law firm or a law professor. If counsel permits himself or herself to be overawed by the court's questions or comments simply because they emanate from judges, or if counsel proceeds on the basis that an off-hand remark from the bench is sacrosanct because of its origin and without regard to it merits, or if counsel is too anxious to agree with the judge, then counsel, and the case, are well on the way to being lost. Counsel must have sufficient confidence in himself or herself and the case to engage in the give and take, the cut and thrust, of courtroom dialogue.

By the same token, counsel should show enough respect for the court. It is not good advocacy to talk down to any court, no matter how much counsel may feel that he or she is more generously endowed with quick perception than the judges he or she happens to be addressing. Sometimes the lawyer's attitude of superiority rests simply upon a keen sense of self-appreciation. On other occasions counsel may, thinking he or she has a particular expertise in a particular subject, feel that the judges, who have not had the same background in that particular field, should be treated as students to whom an expository lecture should be delivered. Whatever the cause, a presentation of that sort is wrong as a matter of protocol and flies in the face of good advocacy. Advocacy is the art of persuasion, and you do not, by talking down to a judge, persuade the judge or, indeed, persuade any person who has the power to decide against you. As I say, the proper attitude is one of respectful intellectual equality.

All in all, the truly effective advocate is one who has the ability to present a case, be it persuasive or dubious, and whether won or lost, in the clearest, most powerful, and most compelling light. If counsel have that ability, they can be of significant assistance to the court, not only in deciding cases correctly, but also in distilling their arguments into decisions that better illuminate the paths of the law marked out by judicial precedent.

Mr. Justice Jackson of the United States Supreme Court, in delivering a lecture on advocacy some years ago, said, "So long as controversies between men have to be settled by judges, proficiency in the art of forensic persuasion will assure one of first rank in our high calling. In the judicial processes practised among English-speaking peoples, the judge and the advocate complement each other for, as Thoreau says, "it takes two to speak the truth — one to speak and another to hear." He went on to express the view that "the most persuasive quality of the advocate is professional sincerity." By that he meant, and I leave you with this thought, that the advocate, as he put it, "must believe that under our adversarial system both sides of every controversy should be worthily presented with vigour ... so that all material for a judgment will be before the court and its judgment will suffer no distortion. He must believe in law as the framework of society, in the independent judicial function as the means for applying the law, and in the nobility of his profession as an aid in the judicial process."

[This article was first published in the October 1997 issue of *The Advocates' Society Journal*.]

Forget the Windup and Make the Pitch: Some Suggestions for Writing More Persuasive Factums

Justice John I. Laskin*

When I began practising law, written advocacy — the factum — was far less important than it is now. Most counsel did not write their own factums. Several did not even read what their juniors or students had written for them.

Although we maintain a strong tradition of oral advocacy in Ontario, you can no longer treat your factum as casually as the bar did a quarter of a century ago. When I practised I worked pretty hard on my own factums. Now that I am on the other side I can say that if I knew then what I know now, I would have worked even harder.

In our court the factum is often far more important than the oral argument. The reasons are not hard to discern:

- Our workload is heavy; to reduce our inventory we have been "over-booking" on both the civil and criminal side and are routinely hearing three or four appeals a day.
- We have limited counsel's time for oral argument.
- Only a few members of the court routinely take pre-hearing bench memoranda, so the factum is the only sure route to the judge's heart and mind before the hearing.

---

*   Mr. Justice John I. Laskin, Court of Appeal for Ontario.

- We decide about 85 to 90 percent of our cases right after argument, by endorsement or by a short judgment.

Before the appeal is heard, you can be sure that each member of the panel will have read the reasons for judgment or the charge to the jury, the appellant's factum, and the respondent's factum. We all would like to read more, and in many appeals we do, but we don't always have the time to read more than the reasons or charge and the factums. Judges cannot help but form an initial impression of your case from your factum. The factum, as former Chief Justice Dubin put it, "whets the appetite of the judge." But often the factum does more than that. It may leave the judge not just with an initial impression of your appeal, but a lasting impression.

In our court we do not have a formal pre-hearing conference to discuss an upcoming appeal. But informal chit-chat is inevitable, so a good or bad factum can take even firmer hold with the panel.

You can overcome a bad factum with good oral argument, but doing so is an uphill struggle. If you write a good factum, you have a great advantage and will enhance your own credibility with the court. Judges like to gossip. We remember the good-factum writers and even come to recognize their styles. In the March 1990 issue of *The Advocates' Society Journal*, the late Justice John Sopinka wrote that in his opinion the quality of advocacy makes a difference to the outcome of 25 percent of appeals in our court. If that is true (and I think it is), the factum is a large part of that 25 percent.

This article offers some suggestions that might improve the clarity and persuasiveness of your factums. These offerings are not inflexible rules; they are just my suggestions. If something else works better for you, then use it.

My theme is readability, and my focus is on the reader. When we write we sometimes forget about the reader. To persuade, you have to consider your reader, your audience. When I write reasons, I try to think of my well-informed next-door neighbour reading my reasons. My neighbour is my audience. The advocate's audience is more limited: opposing counsel and, of course, the judge whom the advocate must persuade.

I firmly believe that although what we say is important, so too is how we say it. You cannot divorce content from language and style. Dull, dense, difficult-to-read prose will detract from what otherwise may be a strong legal point.

Writing well is hard work — at least it is hard work for me. Legal writing is difficult because what we write about usually is complicated. And we all have time constraints — too much to do and too little time to do it in. Writing concisely is harder than writing at length. But taking the time and trouble to write better will make you a much better advocate for your clients and will enhance your reputation with the court.

What is this Appeal All About, and What is the Court Likely to Do With It?

Here I want to make three points, each of which should influence how you write your factum. First, before you write a single word, put yourself in the position of your reader, the judge. This is what the great John Davis of the New York Bar called "the cardinal rule" of advocacy. In your imagination, trade places with the judge. You are immersed in the case, the judge knows nothing of it. What is this appeal all about? What is the key issue on which the appeal turns? Identify and frame this key issue, the issue that will control the outcome of the appeal. Then think about the story that you are going to tell around this key issue. How would you want this story told? What approach will help the court reach the best solution?

Second, appeals generally fall into one of two categories: error-correcting or jurisprudential. Decide into which category your appeal falls. Most appeals are simple error-correcting appeals. Do not make the mistake of trying to turn your error-correcting appeal into the next *Donoghue v. Stevenson*. We have far too much work to do to write a treatise on every case, and generally we do not like opining on more than we have to in order to decide the appeal.

If your appeal is an error-correcting appeal, we will likely decide the appeal by an endorsement. Give us a simple factual or legal basis for your position; do not try to make new law. If you have provided a simple, clear route to the desired result, part of your factum will likely find its way into our endorsement. If the appeal is jurisprudential, then you have to write your factum, especially the law section, differently. You should address social policy or administration of justice concerns, and you should consider the implications of your position for related areas of the law. In other words, you should think, read, and write "around the problem."

If your appeal calls on the court to interpret legislation, we need to understand the legislative scheme, how it works, the rationale for the statutory provisions in question. We don't often get this, even from government lawyers, and we frequently wish we could phone the regulator for a better understanding of the statute.

The third point to consider is whether we are likely to reserve. If you think we are going to reserve, your factum should be more detailed. I often make heavy use of a good factum in writing reasons. But remember the statistics: only about 10 to 15 percent of our decisions are reserved judgments with full reasons.

If the trial judge has written careful or detailed reasons and we are going to reverse, we will likely reserve and write our own reasons. Otherwise, most error-correcting appeals are dealt with by endorsement. Jurisprudential appeals are usually reserved.

The Overview Statement

Jim Raymond, an English professor at Alabama, is the head of the judgment-writing course for federally appointed judges in Canada. He is also the co-author of an excellent book on good legal writing called *Clear Understandings.*[1] The subject of Professor Raymond's lecture at our judgment-writing school is: "The first page says it all." Whether you are writing a factum or a judicial opinion, Raymond recommends that you begin with an overview statement, which tells the reader what the case is about, who did what to whom, the issues, and your position on them — all in no more than a page. Raymond's view reflects a fundamental principle of persuasive factum writing: put context before details. The principle of context before details is also an important theme in a superb book on good legal writing, *Thinking Like a Writer: A Lawyer's Guide to Effective Writing and Editing,* by Stephen Armstrong and Timothy Terrell.

The overview statement has been used for several years by all good counsel arguing criminal appeals in our court, even though it is not

---

1   Ronald Goldfarb & James Raymond, *Clear Understandings: A Guide to Legal Writing* (Tuscaloosa: Goldenray Books, 1982).

required by the criminal appeal rules. The criminal bar has simply adopted the overview statement as a technique of good written advocacy.

Effective 4 January 1999, the Rules Committee amended the factum rules for civil appeals to our court to require an overview statement in Part II of the appellant's factum and in Part I of the respondent's factum.

Although the overview statement is now mandatory, you need to know why it is important. The overview statement is important because it provides a road map for the rest of your factum. It gives the judge the context for your appeal, and with the context the judge can better absorb and understand the details to follow. I consider the overview statement the most important part of the factum. Consider these suggestions for writing effective overview statements:

- In the overview statement, you must begin persuading the court of the rightness of your client's cause. Tell your story in human terms — appeal to the human being in the judge. Forget the legal jargon. Pretend the judge is just your well-informed next-door neighbour. Engage the judge, capture the essence of what the case is all about, and communicate the justness of your position. In other words, solicit the judge's affection for your cause.
- State the key issue or issues on which the appeal turns in your overview statement, but be careful not to state the issue or issues too broadly. If you state an issue too broadly, then your factum will be too long because the amount of detail is tied to how narrowly or broadly you state the issue. Worse, we judges will not know what to look for, what facts are crucial and what facts are background. For example, if you are attacking a municipal bylaw, stating the issue as the validity of the bylaw is too broad. Better to say that the issue is whether the bylaw is invalid because it was passed in bad faith.
- The overview statement should contain just enough facts to give context to the key issue and to preview what is to come. Most counsel do not give enough facts in their overview statements. You should front-load but not overload your overview.

Point-first Writing

Point-first writing, more than anything else, will improve the clarity and persuasiveness of your writing. The best discussion of point-first writing that I have read is in a book by Joseph Williams, a professor of English at the University of Chicago, called *Style: Toward Clarity and Grace*.[2]

Williams delivers the following message: state your point or proposition before you develop or discuss it. Do not write your factum like a mystery novel in which the conclusion is revealed only in the final paragraph, if at all. In other words, give the context before discussing the details. Indeed, point-first writing puts into practice the principle of context before details. Point-first writing should be used throughout your factum, both in the facts part and in the law part, and within those parts, in every section and in every paragraph. Whenever you are about to dump detail on the reader, give the reader the point of the detail first.

We see far too many factums that contain long, meandering paragraphs, in which the point of each paragraph is never stated or, almost as bad, is stated three paragraphs later. This is not reader-friendly advocacy. You can fix this problem in these ways. At the beginning of the paragraph, tell the reader what topic or idea you are going to discuss in the rest of the paragraph. Try to restrict each paragraph to one main idea or topic. Then, in the first sentence or two of each paragraph, articulate the point of the paragraph, usually your conclusion or submission on the issue. The remainder of the paragraph will discuss the submission, elaborate on it, support it, or qualify it. This is point-first writing.

Unfortunately, too many factums contain either point-last writing or no-point-at-all writing. Lawyers seem to resist giving their conclusion up front. They think that readers need to understand how the argument develops, or that readers will not appreciate their point until they are familiar with the relevant facts, or that an anticipated conclusion will make the ultimate conclusion repetitive. As valid as these concerns may be, they do not outweigh the desirability of point-first writing. We absorb and remember information best when we know why it is important and how it is relevant. If we are forced to read a lot of details before we know why they matter, we will skim and skip. Practise point-first writing. The persuasiveness of your factums will increase immeasurably.

Another way to practise point-first writing is to use markers or signals. Tell the reader what is coming next by using headings to separate each issue. Headings are helpful to the court because they give structure or road maps to your factum. They keep the judge on track and empha-

---

2   (Chicago: The University of Chicago Press, 1990).

size the order and organization of your factum. Most good counsel are now using headings. When you write a heading, try using rhetorical language instead of neutral language. Instead of writing "First issue: whether there was a fiduciary relationship," try instead: "First issue: the trial judge erred in finding a fiduciary relationship." The latter formulation is more persuasive.

White Space

The visual impact of your factum plays an important role in its persuasiveness. Most lawyers cram far too much onto each page of their factum, no doubt to meet our court's thirty-page rule. But we will not thank you when we are up late at night reading a dense thirty-page single-spaced factum with no margins. I suggest you ensure that the pages of your factum have enough white space. Generous margins, double-spacing, headings, and lists or tabulations will all improve the visual impact of your factum. These devices will give the appearance of a less-dense document and show that you care about the reader.

The Importance of the Facts

Good advocacy reduces to two simple propositions: first, tell the court why your client should win — capture, in the words of one of my colleagues, the "moral high ground" — then, tell the court how to get there. The first proposition turns on how you present the facts; the second, on how you present the law.

We are powerfully influenced by the equities of the case, by the needs of real people. If we have to, we will bend the law to reach a fair result. Most cases are decided on the judge's view of the facts — certainly in our court, and even in the Supreme Court of Canada.

Because we want to do justice between litigants, we are far less interested than you might think in great pronouncements of law or highly legalistic arguments. If the facts have been persuasively presented, then the law section of the factum should show a simple legal basis for getting to the desired result. The facts, in my opinion, are the hardest part of the factum to write and the part of the factum where we need the most help. We know something about the law. We are far more dependent on counsel to outline the relevant facts.

In the facts section of the factum, counsel must tell a story. Story-telling is persuasive. But counsel must carefully consider what story to tell and how to tell it. You have to tell a story that shows the justice and logic of your position, that persuades the court of the rightness of your client's cause. Lawyers like to tell stories chronologically. This is not always the best method. I suggest that you tell your story, your facts, around a theme that corresponds to the key issue (or issues) in the appeal. You have already identified the key issue in your overview statement. In the facts section, you put flesh on the bones. For example, if the key issue in a criminal appeal is the identification of the accused, acting for the appellant you may want to tell the facts by talking about the frailties in the eyewitness testimony. And you will want to cut out the facts that do not relate to this issue.

Some other suggestions for writing the facts part of the factum more persuasively include: using headings, introducing the facts by giving the context for them, and separating the disputed from the undisputed facts or at least telling the court what facts are not disputed. In some cases, where for example the chronology is long or complicated, a chart can effectively describe the facts for the reader. Also, try referring to the parties by name or by a meaningful term (landlord, tenant, lender, borrower, father, mother, etc.). Especially in cases of multiple parties, do not use "the respondent by cross-appeal" or "the third party."

A frequently asked question is whether you should quote excerpts from the trial transcript in the facts section of your factum. My answer is that on occasion a short excerpt from the transcript, using the witness's own words, can make a point very effectively. But do not overdo this practice. Long transcript excerpts will make your factum too long and may divert the court from your main theme. Preferably the transcript excerpts you rely on should be in your compendium, which is now required in civil appeals and is desirable in most criminal appeals. If you do quote from the transcript, give the context before the quotation. In other words, give the point of the witness's evidence before quoting the evidence itself.

The Importance of Argument

The recent amendments to our factum rules for civil appeals include a requirement for concise argument in the issues and law section.

Although the previous rules did not explicitly provide for argument, they did not preclude it either. Like most of my colleagues, I have always welcomed argument, and most good factums contained argument. I find a succinct and focused argument very helpful, especially in an era of time-limited oral advocacy.

The argument should include three elements for each issue: the controlling law, the pertinent facts, and your conclusion. If you are acting for the appellant, you must address where the trial judge went wrong, why the trial judge went wrong, and the effect of the trial judge's error, because not every error matters or will give you relief. If you are acting for the respondent, you must show why the trial judge was right or, if the trial judge went wrong, why the error was harmless. Sometimes respondents are better to concede the error and then show that it did not affect the result.

For example, in a fiduciary duty case, suppose the trial judge found that the defendant Williams had breached his fiduciary duty to the plaintiff O'Neill. The defendant Williams appeals. The respondent O'Neill seeks to uphold the judgment. The appellant Williams' factum might say the following:

First issue: No fiduciary relationship

Williams submits that the trial judge erred in finding a fiduciary relationship. The elements of a fiduciary relationship are scope for discretion, unilateral exercise of that discretion, and vulnerability. In this case the element of vulnerability is missing because (a), (b), (c), etc.

Or, acting for the respondent O'Neill, you might say:

Second issue: This court should not interfere with the trial judge's finding of a breach of fiduciary duty

The appellant Williams contends that the trial judge erred in finding a breach of fiduciary duty. This finding is a finding of fact. Absent manifest error, this court should not interfere. The following evidence reasonably supports the trial judge's finding: (a), (b), and (c), etc. Therefore, no manifest error exists, and this court should not interfere with the finding.

In the first example, I told the reader early in the paragraph that I attacked the finding of a fiduciary relationship because the element of vulnerability was missing; then I would have discussed the point. Surely this is better than a bland statement such as: "An appeal court can only interfere with findings of fact if the trial judge made a 'palpable and overriding error'" or "the following are the elements of a fiduciary relationship: scope for discretion, unilateral exercise of that discretion, and vulnerability." In the second example, I told the reader up front that the trial judge's finding was a finding of fact and that it was reasonable supported by the evidence. Then I would have listed the supporting evidence. In both examples I used point-first writing.

Your argument should be focused, and if it is focused it will do two other useful things. First, it will avoid the generality problem. One common weakness in the law section of the factum is that statements of law are too general. They are not specific enough to the facts of the case. For example, if the appeal concerns a claim against a real estate agent arising out of a transaction of purchase and sale that went sour, general statements about the duties of real estate agents are not helpful. Focus on the duty or duties that arise on the facts. Second, a focused argument will allow for listing, tabulating, or grouping relevant facts or points in one paragraph — (a), (b), (c), etc. — which can be powerfully persuasive.

Therefore, your factum should contain argument. The level of detail is another matter. For our court, you do not need to be as detailed as for the Supreme Court of Canada. The level of detail depends on the case, the number of key issues, and whether we are likely to reserve.

Standard of Review

The applicable standard of review should be addressed in the law section of the factum. Often it is ignored. This is not just an administrative law point but permeates every appeal to our court. Remember our role: we do not retry cases; instead, we look for error in the trial court. Thus you have to be conscious of the standard of review in the law section of your factum and address it. You must do more than identify where the trial judge went wrong or even why he or she went wrong. You also have to ask yourself whether the Court of Appeal can do anything about it.

You can address the standard of review in the law section of your factum in one of two ways: as a stand-alone section headed "Standard of Review" or as part of the substantive argument on an issue, as I did in my fiduciary duty examples.

If you are acting for an appellant in a criminal case, appealing a decision of a summary conviction appeal court judge, you can only appeal on a question of law. The best factums state up front what the appellant contends is the error of law made by the trial judge. If you are appealing a damage award, you will recognize that the Court of Appeal has a very limited power of review.[3] Write the law section with this limited review power in mind. Tell us why the damage award is reviewable before you get into the detail. If you are reviewing the exercise of a trial judge's discretion, you need to find an error in principle. To do that, you have to know what the error in principle is (for example, failing to take into account relevant factors) and then state it.

Conversely, if you have a finding of fact in your favour, use it. Itemizing or tabulating in a list the evidence that reasonably supports a finding of fact is a persuasive technique for respondents. If you are attacking a finding of fact, you need a major error to persuade our court to interfere. You need "manifest error" or "palpable and overriding error," which is equivalent to review on a standard of unreasonableness. If no such major error exists, then you must argue your appeal by accepting the trial judge's findings of fact.

Remember this, however: though trial judges may not always believe it, we do not go out of our way to overturn them. In colloquial terms, we cut them a fair bit of slack. Even if we do not think that their judgment is perfect, we will strive to uphold it if we think that the result is fair or does justice to the case. The lesson for factum writing is to dispense with highly legalistic or minor errors. You need to identify a major error that affects the justice of the result.

The Respondent's Factum

Most of my suggestions apply both to the appellant's factum and to the respondent's factum. However, here are a few suggestions that apply particularly to the respondent's factum:

- The respondent's factum should be self-contained or free-standing. The judge should be able to read it on its own, without having to refer to the appellant's factum. Therefore, I do not find it helpful when a respondent's factum says, "As to paragraph 11 of the appellant's fac-

---

3   See *Woelk v. Halvorson*, [1980] 2 S.C.R. 430.

tum, it is submitted that ...." Far better to say, "In paragraph 11 of her factum, the appellant Smith contends that the trial judge misinterpreted section 139 of the *Highway Traffic Act.* Jones submits that the trial judge did not misinterpret this section. The trial judge ...." Moreover, cross-referencing to the appellant's factum allows the appellant to control the presentation of the case.

- The respondent can make particularly effective use of the overview statement. For a respondent, the overview avoids the stark and often unpalatable choice of accepting the appellant's statement of the facts or rewriting it. Rewriting often seems petty, but often a respondent does not like the appellant's gloss. The overview statement allows a respondent to give a factual summary of its position. An alternative technique is to outline the facts relevant to an issue in the law section.

- A respondent should not feel limited by the appellant's statement of the issues. It is entirely appropriate to recast the appellant's statement in less antagonistic terms that reflect the respondent's view of the case. "The trial judge erred in admitting inflammatory photographs" can, in the respondent's hands, become "The trial judge did not abuse her broad discretion in concluding that certain photographs were admissible."

- A respondent's factum can make effective use of lists. Frequently a respondent can succeed on an appeal by showing that the trial judge's findings of fact are reasonably supported by the evidence. A submission that says: "The following evidence reasonably supports the trial judge's finding of bad faith: (a), (b), (c) ..." is invariably persuasive.

Candour

A familiar admonition is that candour is an essential ingredient of good advocacy. This is true of both written and oral advocacy. In the factum, candour is essential both in the facts section and in the law section. Candour in written advocacy takes many forms. Let me suggest four ways in which a factum may lack candour:

Being unfair to the record

Because the facts decide the outcome of most appeals, we naturally want to refer only to those facts that help our case. But you must be fair to the record. This is not just an ethical obligation but common sense. Opposing counsel will be sure to point up your misstatements, distortions, or omissions. At the same time, however, you do not need to emphasize facts unfavourable to your position. Unfavourable facts can be dealt with effectively in many ways. For example, you can de-emphasize unfavourable facts by your sentence structure or by referring in the same sentence or paragraph to facts that qualify or explain the evidence against your client.

Overstating your claims

These are examples of overstatement: a defendant's conduct was "egregious," or the trial judge's ruling was "a gross miscarriage of justice," or "three witnesses corroborated every single aspect of the plaintiff's evidence." Overstatement is jarring. Be careful about using this form of advocacy, in which you are really expressing a conclusion in superlatives. If you do use superlatives, then you'd better have the ammunition to back them up. Otherwise, not only will your argument suffer, so too will your credibility with the court. The right noun or the right verb unqualified is far more forceful than the wrong one arrayed in superlatives. In the same vein, restraint or understatement is usually more forceful than exaggeration. Appeal to what you hope is the judge's intelligence.

Facing up to your weakness or difficulties

If your argument has a weakness, not only will your opponent address it, the weakness will concern the court. Far better for you to meet it head-on than to leave it unanswered. Do not fall into the trap of thinking that if you do not address your difficulties, neither will the court.

Demeaning your opponent's case

Do not denigrate your opponent's position either by expressing it weakly or (except in the rare case) by dismissing it as frivolous and without merit. This is a common mistake. You will be far better off to state your opponent's argument fairly — even strongly — and then refute it. Only then will you know that you have a case.

Give the Court Credit for Knowing a Little Law

Many factums do not seem to recognize that there is a core body of legal principles and cases that is well-known by the court. These principles and cases are referred to so frequently that every member of the court is intimately familiar with them. We do not need four paragraphs on the standard of review of a trial judge's finding of fact or five paragraphs on the summary judgment test under rule 20. All of us are a bit weary of seeing the admonition that "the defendant must lead trump," although when one appellant did cite this phrase in a recent factum, the respondent effectively replied that the defendant appellant did not lead trump because he had no trump to lead!

We all know about "palpable and overriding error," about genuine issues for trial, and, in a criminal case, about error in principle as a basis for reviewing a sentence. If you are going to state such well-known principles, one stand-alone paragraph will do. Better still, simply tell us what is the "palpable and overriding" error or genuine issue for trial or error in principle and then discuss it.

A related problem is that many counsel list far too many cases in their factums. The Court of Appeal storage area is filled with casebooks cluttered with cases never referred to by counsel. My guess is that over 90 percent of cases cited in most factums are not referred to in oral argument and are not used in our judgments. Listing too many cases shows that you really have not thought enough about which cases will really help you. In most appeals, you can limit the authorities to the following:

- the most recent case on the subject, either from our court or from the Supreme Court of Canada. For example, for the standard of review of a finding of fact, refer only to one or two cases such as *Schwartz v. Canada*[4] or *Hodgkinson v. Simms*;[5] if the issue is the application of section 24(2) of the *Charter, R. v. Stillman*[6] and *R. v. Feeney*[7] should be enough;
- a case close on the facts;
- a "leading" old case; or
- a case in which the point in issue is fully discussed by a well-respected jurist. We are only human, and we are influenced by who wrote the judgment. The Honourable Arthur Martin's opinion in a criminal case is probably more persuasive to us than are the views of another judge less experienced in the criminal law.

4   [1996] 1 S.C.R. 254.
5   [1994] 3 S.C.R. 377.
6   [1997] 1 S.C.R. 607.
7   [1997] 2 S.C.R. 13.

Of course, if you have a jurisprudential appeal, then you may have to refer to more authorities, both in Canada and in other jurisdictions, to develop your point.

Quotations from Cases and Statutes

Sometimes it is necessary to refer in your factum to the relevant part of a statute, and sometimes it is desirable to quote from a case. If an outside authority can advance your argument in language more convincing than your own, then use it. But long quotations from cases or long extracts from a statute are easy to skim and skip. Try these suggestions:

- Keep the quotation or extract short: refer only to what is essential.
- Give the context for the quotation. In other words, summarize what the judge can expect or at least entice the judge into the quotation by introductory words. Giving the context increases the chance that the judge will actually read what you have cited.
- Unless the quotation is long, do not block or indent it. Instead, put it in the text, which will also improve the odds of it being read.

Writing Concisely

To be persuasive, factums must be concise. Unfortunately, many factums filed in our court are anything but concise. This lack of concision takes many forms.

Often, factums are just too long. Our court's Practice Direction permits a factum of up to thirty pages (and longer with a judge's order). Many counsel think that they have to fill all thirty pages, even in the simplest of error-correcting appeals. They are wrong. With our heavy workload, long factums run the risk that, although they will be read, they may not be read carefully and fully digested. I have never heard a judge complain that a factum was too short. John Robinette, one of the greatest advocates our country has ever produced, wrote factums that were almost always less than fifteen pages. He knew the point he wanted to make, and he wrote simply and concisely. He simply pruned away all the fat.

Why are factums too long? Time and fear are two main culprits. We do not take enough time to write a shorter, more concise factum; and we are afraid of writing too little or of leaving something out. Effective writing requires selection and clear thinking. Conciseness is often a by-product of knowing what your case is about and where you are going.

The facts part of factums often is not written concisely, perhaps because counsel have not clearly framed the controlling issue or issues. Once you have framed the controlling issue, make sure your statement of the facts refers only to those facts necessary for the court to deal with that issue. Cut out the facts that are not needed.

Listing too many issues is another way in which a factum may lack concision. Almost all appeals have only one or two or, at most, three good issues. Yet, even in ordinary error-correcting appeals, we frequently see counsel listing seven, eight, even ten issues for the court to decide. We can never know the case as well as counsel does, and we can spend only a fraction of the time that counsel has spent on it, so you must focus our attention on the one or two issues on which you believe the appeal will turn. Counsel do not always give that question enough thought. Figure out these one or two issues and, in most cases, dispense with the rest. Certainly dispense with legalistic arguments that do not advance the interests of justice, and let the minor points go. As the Honourable Sydney Robins, one of my former colleagues, put it: "Legal contentions, like currency, depreciate through overissue." Multiplicity hints at a lack of faith and confidence in your major grounds of appeal. Multiplicity may weaken a good case and will not save a bad one. The message is: Do not try to make every argument, and do not bury your best argument in the last or second-last paragraph of your factum. Put your best argument up front, unless the logic of your position requires some modest variation.

Counsel frequently write paragraphs that are too long. They like to cram too much into one paragraph. Try to keep each paragraph to one idea or one topic whose point you state clearly at the beginning and then develop in the rest of the paragraph.

Finally, sentences are frequently too long. Counsel want to put too much into one sentence, usually because they worry about absolute statements and wish to qualify or attach conditions to everything they say. Long sentences are not wrong, but they are harder to understand and retain. They do not work as well in legal writing as in, say, fiction. On the other hand, I am not going to tell you that every sentence should be short because good writing has a rhythm that requires variation in sentence length. Indeed, some of the most beautiful sentences in the English language are long sentences, but they are always characterized by a parallel structure for parallel ideas or by some other device that makes them flow. A reasonable working rule is to use only one subordinate clause in every sentence, unless you resort to one of the devices that make a longer sentence coherent.

Language

This topic deserves a paper of its own, preferably by a professional writer instead of a judge. Language and content are intimately connected. Forceful language makes for more persuasive content. Here are some suggestions to help you write factums more forcefully and thus more persuasively. Or, more accurately, this is a "hit list" of what to avoid:

- Avoid using the phrase "it is respectfully submitted" more than twice in your factum. Use it once at the beginning and once at the end of the law section, but not in between. Repeated too often, this phrase disrupts the force and flow of your argument.
- Avoid false intensifiers: for example, "completely wrong," "absolutely unfounded," "very serious error," "clearly," "certainly," "it is important to note that," and "blatant violation." These false intensifiers usually weaken rather than strengthen the force of your argument.
- Romance the verb. Use active verbs; this does not include the verb "to be." Active verbs are forceful and therefore are an important ingredient of persuasive writing. Using active verbs also means avoiding three practices that detract from forceful writing. First, avoid using too many adjectives and adverbs. Second, avoid nominalizations, that is, avoid changing verbs into nouns. Nominalization is a contagious disease among lawyers. Instead of writing "make an argument," write "argue"; instead of "executed a veto," "vetoed"; instead of "gave consideration," "considered"; and instead of "conducted an investigation," "investigated." Third, avoid excessive use of the passive voice. Lawyers are far too enamoured by the passive. Both the passive voice and nominalization have their place in good writing, but limit their use. Nominalization and the passive reflect the lawyer's reluctance to admit that someone is doing something to someone else. Lawyers like to conceal action beneath the surface. We need to correct this.

Nominalization and the passive can be effective and persuasive, but their use should be a conscious choice.

- Avoid the word "not." Unless your tone dictates otherwise, instead of "did not consider," write "ignored"; instead of "did not remember," write "forgot"; instead of "did not allow," write "prevented"; instead of "not very often," write "seldom"; and instead of "did not perform under the contract," write "breached the contract."

- Avoid the "backhanded passive": for example, "it is urged that," "it would seem to appear that," "it is suggested that," "it is observed at the outset that," and "it should be pointed out that." In other words, forget the windup and make the pitch.

- Avoid needless words. Instead of writing "it is imperative that the court consider," write "the court must consider"; instead of writing "this is a case which addresses," write "this case addresses"; instead of writing "may have the effect of increasing," write "may increase"; instead of "on an annual basis," write "annually" or "yearly"; instead of "in the event that," write "if"; and instead of "at this point in time," write "now." On this topic, I highly recommend Bruce Ross-Larson's book, *Edit Yourself.*[8] It contains a long list of what to cut and what to change. I keep this book handy when I am writing reasons.

- Avoid "the fact that" expressions. Instead of writing "the fact that Carter failed to give notice," write "Carter's failure to give notice"; instead of "notwithstanding the fact that," write "although"; instead of "due to the fact that," write "because"; and cut entirely "the fact remains that."

- Avoid the dreaded couplets: null and void, cease and desist, due and payable, free and clear, and force and effect.

- Avoid legal jargon. We do not see too many "hereinafters," "hereins," "*inter alias*," "the said." But counsel still write "prior to" and "subsequent to" instead of "before" and "after"; "the construction of a statute" instead of "the interpretation of a statute"; "mandates" instead of "requires"; "utilize" instead of "use"; "terminate" instead of "end"; "necessitate" instead of "need"; "remuneration" instead of "salary, wages, or pay"; "adjacent to" instead of "next to"; "provided that" instead of "if"; and "pursuant to" instead of "under." Although harder to detect, this is still jargon. I distinguish, however, between

---

8   (New York: W.W. Norton & Company, 1996).

legal jargon and legal terms of art. Parol evidence, summary judgment, and hearsay evidence are terms of art and a necessary part of lawyers' language.

• Avoid "it is," "there is," and "there are" clauses. Instead of writing "it is true that the defendant failed to testify," write "the defendant failed to testify"; instead of "there are many cases that deal with adverse possession of islands," write "many cases deal with adverse possession of islands"; and instead of "there were ten people who witnessed the shooting," write "ten people witnessed the shooting."

Generally, develop a simple, concise style that uses active verbs, avoids excessive use of adjectives and adverbs, limits the use of the passive voice, and puts the subject, verb, and object close to each other.

Sentence Structure

The structure of your sentences has a great impact on the persuasiveness of your writing. Here are a few suggestions:

• Avoid too many "left-handed sentences." Lawyers like to qualify everything they say, so they begin their sentences with a string of dependent clauses beginning with "although," or "if," or "even if." Judges are exhausted by the time they get to the main noun and verb. To avoid the left-handed sentence, either do a flip-flop by putting the dependent clause at the end of the sentence instead of at the beginning, or put the introductory clause into a separate sentence.

• Remember that the two most important parts of the sentence are the beginning and the end. This has important implications for the points in your factum that you wish to emphasize. Your important points should be at the beginning or the end of your sentence, not buried in the middle.

• Conversely, suppose you want to de-emphasize a point or a fact because it is unfavourable to your position. Try putting it in the middle of the sentence or in a dependent clause to subordinate it and give it less prominence, or, dare I say, use the passive voice.

• Use lists — (a), (b), (c), etc. — or even lists within a sentence to make your factums more readable and persuasive.

• Vary the length of your sentences and try using a very short sentence in the midst of longer sentences. Short sentences can provide an

effective contrast. Winston Churchill gives us a wonderful example of
variation in sentence length in this passage from *History of the Second
World War*:

> We must take September 15 as the culminating date. On this date the
> Luftwaffe, after two heavy attacks on the 14th, made its greatest con-
> centrated effort in a resumed attack on London. It was one of the deci-
> sive battles of the war, and, like the Battle of Waterloo, it was on a
> Sunday. I was at Chequers. I had already on several occasions visited
> the headquarters of Number 11 Fighter Group in order to witness the
> conduct of an air battle, when not much happened. However, the
> weather on this day seemed suitable to the enemy and accordingly I
> drove over to Uxbridge and arrived at the Group Headquarters ....

Making the Factum Flow

To make your factum user-friendly you must make it flow smoothly. You
will make it flow smoothly if you make it as easy as possible for the
judge to understand your chain of reasoning. Judges will understand
your chain of reasoning more easily if they see how one sentence con-
nects to the next sentence. A good paragraph, a paragraph that flows
smoothly, will provide effective transitions among its sentences.

Three techniques are particularly useful for making your factum
flow smoothly. The first is to use connecting or transitional words. The
English language is full of them. Words such as "since," "because,"
"thus," and "therefore" express logical relationships. Words such as
"however," "although," "but," and "conversely" show contrast or comparison between what has been written and what is about to be written.
Words such as "also," "next," "in addition," "first," "second," and "finally" show the progression of the discussion. Words such as "still," "nevertheless," and "notwithstanding" indicate a return to the main point
after conceding another point. These transitional words do not always
have to occupy the first word of a sentence, and not every sentence needs
a transition. Judges are smart enough to make some connections themselves. So use transitional words, but do not overuse them.

The second technique is to repeat at or near the beginning of the
sentence some of the content of the preceding sentence, using either the
same words or an easily recognizable substitute. For example, "Section

108 of the *Courts of Justice Act* requires an action for specific performance of a contract to be heard without a jury. This requirement means ...."

The third technique is to organize the information in each sentence so that you put older or familiar information at the beginning of the sentence and new information at the end of the sentence. Williams gives this example:

Original

Some astonishing questions about the nature of the universe have been raised by scientists exploring the nature of black holes in space. The collapse of a dead star into a point perhaps no larger than a marble creates a black hole. So much matter compressed into so little volume changes the fabric of space around it in profoundly puzzling ways.

Revision

Some astonishing questions about the nature of the universe have been raised by scientists exploring the nature of black holes in space. A black hole is created by the collapse of a dead star into a point perhaps no larger than a marble. So much matter compressed into so little volume changes the fabric of space around it in profoundly puzzling ways.

Revising the second sentence of the paragraph makes the entire paragraph flow more smoothly. And you will have noticed that this smooth flow was accomplished by using the passive voice instead of the active voice in the second sentence. Indeed, one of the most important and effective uses of the passive voice is to improve cohesion or sentence flow.

Editing

Many factums are not properly edited. They end up looking like the first draft instead of the final product. Of course, editing runs up against the time pressures of getting your factum out. A decent edit, however, can convert a mediocre factum into a very good factum. I strongly encourage counsel to find time to edit.

- Remember that you can do different kinds of edits and you should not try to do all of them at the same time. What are the different kinds of edits? You can edit for accurate case citations, typing errors, grammar, and punctuation. But you can also edit for tone, for sentence and paragraph length, for proper headings, for clarity and organization, and to eliminate wordiness and jargon. Do not do all of these edits at once. Break them up, or divide and conquer.

- Edit not just what is on the page, also edit what is not there. In other words, edit the white space. Make sure that your factum provides context before details, that it has headings and point-first paragraphs.

- Try one or more of the following:
  a) Use the bottom-drawer technique. Leave your draft factum for a few days and then come back to it. You will have a fresh perspective.
  b) Read your draft aloud to yourself. Your ears are often your best guide to whether your factum is clear and persuasive. If it doesn't sound right it needs fixing.
  c) Have someone else read your draft: a colleague, a friend, your spouse. You are immersed in your factum, and you need a more objective view.

- The most important suggestion of all: always look to cut. "Read with a pencil." No matter how concisely you think you have written, you can always make your factum more concise. So edit, edit, and then edit some more.

Closing

Writing factums puts advocates' reputations and credibility on the line. As I said at the beginning of this article, judges get to know the good factum writers and the bad factum writers and to recognize their styles. And advocates are responsible for the logic and persuasiveness of their reasoning and its implications for the position of their clients. Yet in trying to write decent factums, advocates run up against the pressures of time and of busy practices. One of my main messages is that taking the time to write a decent factum will pay huge dividends. I hope that my suggestions will help you to write better and more persuasive factums.

[This article was first published in the Summer 1999 issue of *The Advocates' Society Journal*.]

What Persuades (or What's Going On inside the Judge's Mind)

Justice John I. Laskin*

[Editors' note: This is an edited version of a talk given on 21 November 2003 at The Advocates' Society Fall Convention in Cancun, Mexico. Justice Laskin would like to thank his law clerk, Leigh Salsberg, for her research, her insights, and her superb editing of this paper.]

I want to thank Wendy Matheson and Sandy Forbes for inviting me to this beautiful resort to speak to you this morning. However, they, not I, should be giving this talk for it is they who persuaded a reluctant judge to speak about persuasion.

My reluctance springs from two sources. One is that this room is filled with many of the finest persuaders our profession has to offer. The other is that some of our finest judges have already given so much valuable advice on this subject. I think of John Arnup's instructive articles,[1] which have withstood the test of time, though written over twenty years ago, when I was a young lawyer; and more recently of Ian Binnie's Sopinka and Dubin lectures, each a *tour de force*.[2] And I think of Horace

---

*   Mr. Justice John I. Laskin, Court of Appeal for Ontario.
1   John D. Arnup, "Advocacy" (David B. Goodman Memorial Lecture) (1979) 13 L. Soc. Gaz. at 27; John D. Arnup, "Advocacy on Appeal" (Bar Admission Course lecture, 1971).
2   Ian Binnie, "A Survivor's Guide to Advocacy in the Supreme Court of Canada" (First John Sopinka Advocacy Lecture) (Summer 1999) *Advocates' Soc. J.*; Ian Bin-

Krever and John Morden, who made persuasion seem so deceptively easy by reducing it to two simple propositions: "make the court want to decide in your favour," then "show it how to do so."[3]

I suppose I can justify this talk in the way any judge can. I am on the receiving end. It is I who must catch what you toss and so perhaps my suggestions will help you throw better pitches. I suppose, as well, what persuades today and will persuade tomorrow differs somewhat from what persuaded in years gone by, in part because judges are busier now and the pace of life is quicker.

Soon after I was appointed the Society kindly invited me to a previous fall convention. My stated topic then was "What I would have done differently if I knew then what I know now."[4] My sub-text, however, was the catalogue of errors that I had made as an appellate counsel. A central theme of my talk was that as an advocate I had greatly underestimated the importance of the factum.

Well, seven years later I am certainly older and more experienced, and I hope a little bit wiser. Though I do not resile from my views about the factum's importance, I have come to appreciate more and more the complementary importance of oral argument. We have so much to read that often the nuances of each side's position are not apparent to us before the hearing. Sometimes it takes the oral hearing to find out what the case is really all about, what the real debate is. Every judge, of course, goes into the hearing of an appeal with some leaning about the case, sometimes strongly held, more often tentatively held. Yet — and though I have no hard data to back it up — I think it a fair anecdotal estimate to say that oral argument has changed my mind in as many as 25 percent of the appeals I have heard. It is oral argument I would like to focus on this morning. So here are six aspects of oral persuasion that have influenced me and that I would like to share with you.

1. Credibility
2. Conviction
3. Cognitive Clarity: How We Listen

---

nie, "In Praise of Oral Advocacy" (Third Charles Dubin Lecture on Advocacy) (Spring 2003) *Advocates' Soc. J.*

3   John W. Morden, "The Partnership of Bench and Bar" (David B. Goodman Memorial Lecture) (1982) 16 *L. Soc. Gaz.* 46 at 72.

4   (Spring 1998) *Advocates' Soc. J.*

4. Persuasive Burden = Distance x Resistance
5. Appeals to Emotion and Leeways
6. Concreteness

I hope that when I have finished discussing these topics you will not feel like the New York State trial judge, who in a recent autobiography of his years on the bench, had this to say about his own appellate court: "When the Court of Appeal speaks we are all in danger."

1. Credibility

Persuasion starts with your credibility as an advocate. In saying so, I am doing nothing more than affirming what the greatest of all rhetoricians, Aristotle, said over two thousand years ago by making *ethos* one of the three modes of persuasive discourse.[5] Your credibility is a hidden persuader. It is not overt but it permeates your entire presentation. Gerry Spence, the well-known American lawyer, put it this way: "One can stand as the greatest orator the world has known, possess the quickest mind, employ the cleverest psychology, and have mastered all the technical devices of argument, but if one is not credible one might just as well preach to the pelicans."[6]

Credibility translates into this: are you someone we think can help us find a sensible, reasonable, workable solution to the real-life problem we must resolve? And credibility is built on two pillars: trust and expertise. Hence, my simple equation:[7]

trust + expertise = credibility

First, a word about trust. I tend to trust lawyers who do three things: they come to court prepared, they do not oversell, and they acknowledge weaknesses in their position, even making a concession where appropriate.

---

5   Edward P.J. Corbett, *Classical Rhetoric for the Modern Student*, 3rd ed. (Oxford: Oxford University Press, 1990) at 22–24, 37. Aristotle's other two means of persuasion are *logos* (reason) and *pathos* (emotion). I deal with the appeal to emotion later in this paper.

6   Gerry Spence, *How to Argue and Win Every Time* (St. Martin's Press, 1995) at 4; quoted in Harry Mills, *Artful Persuasion* (New York: AMA Publications, 2000) at 14.

7   This equation is taken from Mills, *ibid.* at 14.

Sitting on the other side we can instantly spot an advocate who does not know the record, no matter how senior or experienced that advocate may be. At the risk of embarrassing him, let me say that one reason Earl Cherniak has such great credibility with our court is that as busy as he is, he always comes to the oral hearing superbly prepared.

Nothing weakens trust more than overselling. Understatement works far better. Conversely nothing instills trust more than facing up to your weaknesses. Better to come from you than from your opponent.[8] The right concession not only enhances your credibility, it is itself a persuasive technique and, I may say, an underused technique. A well-timed concession does not merely narrow the focus of the appeal, which judges like, but also makes your strong arguments seem even stronger. A brilliant and highly successful example of this technique is the advertisement for Buckley's cough mixture: it tastes awful but it works great.

The other half of my credibility equation is expertise. More and more we are being called on to consider areas of law, especially regulatory schemes, with which we have little familiarity. We can read the cases and the statutes. But reading does not always give us a feel for how the scheme really works, how it all fits together. We yearn to talk to the regulator. You have to fill that role for us. Demonstrated expertise over the subject matter carries great influence with a judge. I think of recent cases on the federal gun legislation, on the province's effort to regulate flying truck wheels and on the inspection provisions of the *Occupational Health and Safety Act* where counsel's mastery of how the legislation was meant to work changed my understanding of the case.

2. Conviction

In his elegantly written biography of Lyndon Johnson, *Master of the Senate*, Robert Caro describes why Johnson persuaded his colleagues to pass the *Civil Rights Act*: he came to believe — with unwavering conviction — that it was the right thing to do. In Johnson's own words: "What convinces is conviction. You simply have to believe in the argument you are

---

8   In his Goodman Memorial Lecture on "Advocacy" at 34, Arnup quotes Chief Justice Cartwright's advice on facing up to your difficulties: "Nail it up on the side of the barn for everyone to see. Then proceed to show that it is neither as large nor as immoveable as it first appeared."

advancing; if you don't you are as good as dead. The other person will sense that something isn't there."[9]

How can you show us your conviction? In oral, unlike written advocacy, judges can see and hear you. In the courtroom, judges process persuasive messages not just by scrutinizing their content, but as well by absorbing the way that content is delivered.[10] Words matter but so do your tone, your pace,[11] your posture, your hands and face, and even your eyes — perhaps more so than one might suppose. A recent study of persuasive elements in an information-heavy context (similar to a courtroom) suggested that the impact of words was 53 percent, body language 32 percent, and tone 15 percent.[12] One might quarrel with the percentages a little bit but the point remains.

Alan Lenczner is a great advocate in part because of the energy, passion, and confidence he brings to every argument he makes, and because of his firm but never shrill delivery. When asked a tough question he and other great advocates don't grimace or fidget; they look composed and confident, like they are trying to help us.

Word choice, of course, plays a role in delivering a convincing message.[13] Romance forceful, active verbs; use affirmative language; and avoid fillers, too many adjectives and adverbs, and the dreaded false intensifiers such as "certainly," "clearly," and "absolutely," which weaken rather than strengthen your point. Above all, use plain language and

---

9   Robert A. Caro, *The Years of Lyndon Johnson: Master of the Senate* (New York: Alfred A. Knopf, 2002) at 887. My friend Paul Pape told me about this quotation. Paul — an excellent advocate — always argues with great conviction.

10   See Peter F. Jorgenson, "Affect, Persuasion, and Communication Processes" in Peter A. Anderson & Laura K. Guerrero, eds., *Handbook of Communication and Emotion: Research, Theory, Applications and Context* (San Diego: Academic Press, 1998) at 405ff; see also Robert B. Cialdini, *Influence: The Psychology of Persuasion* (New York: Quill/ William Morrow, 1993).

11   Mills, *supra* note 6 at 89 says that most speakers average 120–180 words per minute. He suggests that most listeners prefer a slightly faster than average speaking rate to a slower than average rate. But don't go too fast: a rapid-fire delivery is a judicial turn off. The right pace? Slow enough to follow; quick enough to be interesting.

12   *Ibid.* at 41–43, 59. See also Andrew Ellis & Geoffrey Beattie, *The Psychology of Language and Communication* (New York: Guilford Press, 1986); Jorgenson, *supra* note 10 at 416. Jorgenson says that facial expression and tone are the most important parts of appeals to emotion.

13   Word order matters, too. Compare "Socrates was old, but wise" and "Socrates was wise, but old."

avoid convoluted sentences. Pretend you are speaking to your well-informed next-door neighbours, who talk about their cars, not their motor vehicles; where they work, not where they are employed; and using their savings to build a cottage, not utilizing the proceeds of their remuneration to construct a summer dwelling-place.

The occasional use of effective repetition also helps. Winston Churchill, one of the greatest persuaders of all time, was a master of wise repetition. Witness his tribute to the Royal Air Force: "Never in the field of human conflict was so much owed by so many to so few." What makes this line memorable is the repeated use of the little word "so" and the little-understood fact that information delivered in chunks of three has a magical effect on people.[14] We remember it. Other examples of the so-called rule of three permeate our history: Lincoln's "Government of the people, by the people, for the people" and Julius Caesar's "I came, I saw, I conquered" to name but two.

3. Cognitive Clarity: How We Listen

From law school onward we have been trained to worry about clarity, but we have been trained to do so from a substantive point of view. Another kind of clarity is equally important: cognitive clarity. This has to do with how people receive, absorb, and retain information.[15] Cognitive psychologists can teach us a lot about what persuades. Here are a few points about how we listen and what it means for how you should make your arguments.

First, judges absorb and remember new information better when they know it's significant as soon as they hear it, when they know why it matters and how it relates to your overall point. In a word, they understand information better when they have a context for it. Judges do not listen passively; they are always looking to make sense of what they are hearing. As advocates you have to give them the context. So before you throw a lot of information and a lot of detail at a judge, begin with the point of the detail, the context for it, even your conclusion, not the other way around.

---

14   Mills, *supra* note 6 at 102, 135.

15   Stephen V. Armstrong & Timothy Terrell, *Thinking Like a Writer*, 2nd ed. (New York City: Practising Law Institute, 2003), c. 2.

Point-first advocacy, as I call it, important in the factum, is perhaps even more important in oral argument where we hear your speech only once. The judge is always asking you — notionally or actually: "Why are you telling me all this?" So begin your argument by telling us what the case is all about and why you should win.[16] But don't stop there. Continue giving us the context all the way through your argument. Not surprisingly, teachers of effective communication stress the value of continuous introductions throughout an argument.[17]

In the same way, judges like structure; they like to know where you are going; they like a map. So give them a map. Ensure that the form of your argument matches its substance.

Second, remember that judges, like everyone else, can only absorb so much information and for so long. We too live in our current accelerated culture of sound bites, limited attention spans and a quicker pace of life. We have or think we have a lot to do, with many competing demands on our time. And, of course, in our court we have time limits on oral argument.

Thus, we constantly want answers to two questions: can you help us, and how fast?[18] What this means for advocates is: do not overwhelm us with unimportant arguments. Do not inundate us with unimportant details. Do not drown us in a sea of words. In brief, do not tax our absorptive capacities.[19] And get to us quickly.

Do not be afraid to choose one argument to emphasize. When you choose fewer arguments you reduce the risk that we will filter out the points you want us to remember. So have faith and confidence in your choices, and have the courage to be selective. Less is invariably more. The rule of three is a good working rule here: in most appeals no more than three main points.

What this also means is that you need to uncomplicate your argument for us. People like to reduce big problems into simple sub-problems. Judges are no different. Research on how expert chess players play

---

16   And if you can, try to do so in a way that sparks our interest. We appreciate counsel who make their arguments interesting.

17   Armstrong & Terrell, *supra*, note 15, c.3; Jonathan Baron, *Thinking and Deciding*, 2nd ed. (Cambridge: Cambridge University Press, 1994) at 102–103.

18   Armstrong & Terrell, *ibid*, 5.

19   Remember Shakespeare's line: "It is better to be brief than tedious." *King Richard III*, Act I, Scene 4.

against the computer, for example, shows that although the computer considers all possible moves, humans consider only a few moves, but invariably the right few.[20]

I don't mean that you should oversimplify your argument. I mean that you should scale down the complexity you have to deal with. We cannot absorb too much complexity because we hear your oral argument only once. You therefore need to keep your message simpler than you do in writing. This is a sophisticated form of simplicity I am talking about, out of which comes cognitive clarity.[21]

Finally, what all this means is that you should be concise. Concision is a relative term and depends on the nature of the case. But look at concision or brevity as a persuasive strategy, a strategy that adds to your credibility.

Third, in addition to giving context and telling us only what we need to remember, you can persuade by saying the right things at the right times. Research shows that where you position your message affects its influence. Psychologists call these primary and recency effects. We are more likely to absorb and retain what you say first and last.[22] This translates into these suggestions: begin by showing why your client should win, not why the other side should lose. Do not throw away your openings or your closings. Use reply effectively. Most advocates close poorly because they don't save any time for their ending. And many follow the advice of my former principal: "The best place for reply is on the seat of your pants."[23] But a closing that makes your point in a pithy new way, or a reply that effectively answers the main argument against you, can be devastating.

4. Persuasive Burden = Distance x Resistance

Here I have borrowed from Richard Posner because he has succinctly captured how most appellate judges go about their decision making. In

---

20   Alan J. Parkin, *Essential Cognitive Psychology* (East Sussex: Psychology Press, 2000) at 282–86; Baron, *supra* note 17 at 102–3.

21   Steven D. Stark, *Writing to Win* (New York: Doubleday, 2000) at 194–95; Armstrong & Terrell, *supra* note 15.

22   Mills, *supra* note 6 at 137–38.

23   I was fortunate to article and junior for Walter B. Williston, in his day a legendary counsel.

his book, *Overcoming Law*, he gives this simple piece of advice to litigators: the best arguments are those that reduce the costs of persuasion.[24] I have reduced his advice to this equation:[25]

persuasive burden = distance x resistance

Minimize the legal distance we must travel to agree with you and minimize our resistance to being moved. In practical terms this equation translates into making the court as comfortable as you can with your position. Aim for a reasonable solution to the dispute. Give the court narrow, not adventuresome, grounds to decide in your favour, and narrower, not broader, rules to adopt.

Individual and institutional reasons underlie this advice. As Cardozo reminds us in his famous lectures on "The Nature of the Judicial Process,"[26] each of us has our own philosophy of life, and try as we may to see things objectively we can never see them with any eyes but our own. Many unseen forces guide our thoughts and actions — our likes and dislikes, our moods, instincts, emotions, habits, and convictions.[27] All these forces make judges resist radical change to their beliefs. Judges look for consistency between their existing beliefs and any new information presented to them. The less they have to travel to agree with you and the smoother the journey to get there, the more likely you are to persuade them.

Virtually every provincial appellate judge I know is a judicial minimalist, to use the phrase coined by the Harvard Law professor Cass Sunstein in his influential book on decision making in the United States Supreme Court, *One Case At A Time*.[28] Judges like to resolve the dispute in front of them and they don't mind leaving many things undecided. They prefer to say as little as possible to justify a result.[29]

---

24   Richard A. Posner, *Overcoming Law* (Cambridge: Harvard University Press, 1995) c. 24, "Rhetoric, Legal Advocacy and Legal Reasoning" at 500–1. Posner relies on Akira Yokoyama, "An Economic Theory of Persuasion" (1991) 71 Public Choice 101.
25   See Armstrong & Terrell, *supra* note 15, c. 12, "The Art of Persuasion," at 274–75.
26   Benjamin N. Cardozo, "The Nature of the Judicial Process," *The Storr Lectures* (New Haven: Yale University Press, 1921).
27   *Ibid.* at 11–13.
28   Cass R. Sunstein, *One Case at a Time: Judicial Minimalism on the Supreme Court* (Cambridge: Harvard University Press, 1999).
29   *Ibid.* at ix–x, 3–4.

Why do judges like to say less rather than more? Because they are alert to the problem of unanticipated consequences of their decisions.[30] Because they live in a world of collegial decision making and they wish to make it easier for their panel members to agree with them. Because they wish to make few judicial errors and those they do make less damaging. All judges have had the experience of reading one of their reported cases and recoiling in horror at having said too much.

And finally, judges are minimalists because they do not want to close off options for their colleagues in future cases. My colleagues are among my most important readers. The prospect of having a colleague ask me why I had to say something four times when I could have decided the case by saying it two times is not a pleasant one.

For all these reasons judges say less instead of more. So in *Falkiner*,[31] where a group of single mothers challenged the Ontario Government's "spouse in the house" rule, we accepted the applicants' argument under section 15 of the *Charter*, and declined to deal with their alternative argument under section 7, leaving the important issues raised by that argument to a case in which their determination was central to the outcome. In *R. v. Dhillon*[32] we overturned the appellant's conviction for first-degree murder on narrow grounds and did not decide the broader question raised by the appellant: when, if ever, the defence should be permitted to introduce investigative hearsay evidence to support an allegation that the police's investigation of other leads was inadequate. And in *Maple Valley Acres Limited v. CIBC*[33] we dismissed the bank's appeal by upholding the trial judge's key factual finding, but stopped short of determining the reach of the trial judge's alternative basis of liability for unjust enrichment. All these examples show judicial minimalism at work.

5. Appeals to Emotion and Leeways

I start with this quotation: "Ninety percent of any decision is emotional. The rational part of us supplies the reasons for supporting our predilections." These are not the words of some starry-eyed junior judge, but of

---

30   *Ibid.* at 259–63.
31   *Falkiner v. Ontario (Director, Income Maintenance Branch)* (2002), 212 D.L.R. (4th) 633 (Ont. C.A.).
32   (2002), 166 C.C.C. (3d) 362 (Ont. C.A.).
33   Unreported, 21 Nov. 2003 (Ont. C.A.).

Charles Evan Hughes, the former Chief Justice of the United States Supreme Court and echoed (in his autobiography) by Justice William O. Douglas.[34]

There is undoubtedly some hyperbole in the quote. But, as Aristotle said in speaking of *pathos*, appeal to emotion plays a role in persuasion and I can say that it does even on the Ontario Court of Appeal.[35] Emotion has the power to move hearts and minds, even the hearts and minds of judges.[36] The trick, however, is not to make it appear obvious. Persuasion works best when it is invisible.[37] Beginning your argument by telling the court that you are going to appeal to its emotions is not likely a winning strategy. The skill comes in evoking emotion indirectly, not in invoking it directly.

How do you do that? By a persuasive presentation of the facts. Judges strive to do justice between the litigants and almost always the facts show where justice lies. I call this the paradox of appellate advocacy. Despite "patently unreasonable," despite *Housen*,[38] and despite deference to discretionary decisions, the facts matter far more than the law in most appeals.[39] Even those facts that are the subject of findings at trial

---

34 William O. Douglas, *The Court Years, 1939–1975* (New York: Random House, 1980) at 8, 33.

35 Aristotle, *On Rhetoric: A Theory of Civil Discourse*, trans. G.A. Kennedy (New York: Oxford University Press, 1991). Many rhetoricians have emphasized the important role of emotional appeals in persuasion. See e.g. Corbett, *supra* note 5 at 86–94, citing the eighteenth century Scottish rhetorician George Campbell's treatise *Philosophy of Rhetoric*, Book I at c. 7: "So far, therefore, is it from being an unfair method of persuasion to move the passions, that there is no persuasion without moving them." Mills, *supra* note 6 at 106, put it more simply: "[I]n most persuasive situations, people buy on emotion and justify with fact." In our profession Paul Perell has done a marvellous job of telling us what rhetoricians — ancient and modern — can teach us about advocacy. See e.g., Paul M. Perell, "Aristotle's Advice to Advocates" (January 2000) [unpublished]; Paul M. Perell, "Written Advocacy" (1993) 27 *L. Soc. Gaz.* 5.

36 Corbett, *ibid.* at 86–94.

37 Armstrong & Terrell, *supra* note 15, c. 12, at 273–74.

38 *Housen v. Nikolaisen*, [2002] 2 S.C.R. 235, where the Supreme Court amplifies the meaning of "palpable and overriding error," the very stringent standard of review of fact and credibility findings.

39 The great American attorney John Davis had this to say about the importance of the facts in the argument of an appeal: "[I]n an appellate court the statement of the facts is not merely a part of the argument, it is more often than not the argument itself ... [I]n many, probably in most, cases when the facts are clear there is

can be put in a different light on appeal. The best advocates are the ones who can best spin the facts, who are the best storytellers.[40] And every story needs a theme, often unstated, and usually about the justice or fairness of your cause. A law suit is really a clash of competing stories and competing underlying themes. So think of yourself first as an expert storyteller rather than an expert litigator.

The last case I argued in our court before being appointed was *Adler,*[41] where I sought government funding for Jewish day schools in Ontario, equivalent to the funding of Roman Catholic schools. I had a good story and a good theme: after 1982 the freedom of religion and equality rights of my clients made our position seem eminently fair. But my opponents had a better story: it was only right and just that we respect the bargain made in 1867, a bargain that constitutionalized Catholic funding and immunized it from a *Charter* challenge. So I lost.

In emphasizing the decisiveness of the facts I do not suggest that judges ignore the law. Appellate judges feel a duty to the law as well as a duty to justice. And we will do our utmost to satisfy both wherever possible. But the truth is few cases demand that we reach a legal result that seems unjust. Karl Llewellyn — one of the great legal realists — explained this in a path-breaking book about how appellate courts really decide cases. The book, called *Deciding Appeals*, was written in 1960, but Llewellyn's insights remain true today.[42]

---

not great trouble with the law." John W. Davis, "The Argument of an Appeal" (1940) 26 A.B.A. J. 895 at 896.

    My father similarly believed that the facts drove the result in most appeals. In reflecting on his years on the Ontario Court of Appeal in a 1975 speech to the Lawyers' Club he said:

> The cases coming before us were open-ended, with the ultimate decisions being very much at large. What my short experience at that time suggested, and what my longer experience since then has confirmed, is the degree to which appellate adjudication provides a choice of result, even if not as often a choice of legal principle.

Bora Laskin, "The Common Law is Alive and Well ... and, Well?" (Lawyers' Club of Toronto, 20 February 1975). See also Karl N. Llewellyn, *The Common Law Tradition: Deciding Appeals* (Boston: Little, Brown, 1960).

40   For the importance of storytelling in written advocacy, see Stark, *supra* note 21 at 80.

41   *Adler v. Ontario* (1997), 140 D.L.R. (4th) 385 (S.C.C.); (1994), 116 D.L.R. (4th) 1 (Ont. C.A.).

42   See Llewellyn, *supra* note 39 at 62–120, 219–22.

In his book Llewellyn stressed that precedent is malleable; many standards are framed in general terms; and many cases fall between precedents. The law guides, suggests, even pressures, but it does not control the result. The law allows judges a lot of scope to emphasize the facts because of what Llewellyn called the leeways of precedent. Appellate judges have a great deal of leeway to do what they perceive is the right thing. In other words, there is a lot of play in the joints.

6. Concreteness

Law is replete with abstract words, terms, and expressions that cannot quite be grasped, that cannot be perceived, such as "a free and democratic society," "the administration of justice," "the reasonable person," and many, many others. We cannot avoid using some of these in our discourse. But try not to stay too long on these high levels of abstraction. Where you can, use examples, analogies, even the occasional metaphor to translate your argument into more concrete, more familiar, and thus more persuasive terms.[43]

Activate the judges' senses. Paint word pictures that judges can see, hear, and feel.[44] Do not talk about the effect of a legal rule in the abstract, but about what a person may or may not do. A memorable example is Holmes' sentence showing that the right of free speech is not an absolute right: "The most stringent protection of free speech would not protect a man in falsely shouting fire in a crowded theater and causing

---

43   See Mills, *supra* note 6 at 111, 123. Martin Luther King was a master of the use of metaphor. Here is a brilliant example from his famous "I Have a Dream" speech delivered on 23 August 1963 at the Lincoln Memorial in Washington, D.C.:

> I have a dream that one day on the red hills of Georgia, the sons of former slaves and the sons of former slave owners will be able to sit down together at the table of brotherhood.
>
> I have a dream that one day, even the state of Mississippi, a desert state sweltering with the heat of injustice and prejudice will be transformed into an oasis of freedom and justice.

Quoted in William Safire, ed., *Lend Me Your Ears: Great Speeches in History* (New York: W.W. Norton, 1992) at 499.

44   The same advice applies to written advocacy. See Stark, *supra* note 21 at 83–86; Thomas S. Kane, *The Oxford Essential Guide to Writing* (Oxford: Oxford University Press, 2003) at 262–66.

panic."[45] Less memorable but still effective is this simple metaphor in answer to an argument in favour of public funding of parochial schools: "Government funding of religious schools is a bramble patch."[46]

In a related vein, avoid generalities. Generalizations seldom persuade. It is the details, the specifics that persuade, that allow judges to cross the legal path to your position.[47] Of course, you must target the right amount of specificity. Too much detail can turn off your listeners. But the operative message is: "Show, don't tell."

Do not talk about the general duties of a real estate agent but about those duties that apply to your case. Do not say "she felt sad" when you can say "she had tears streaming down her face." Do not say "Carter tried to mitigate his losses but could not find other employment" when you can say "Carter applied for eight other jobs but did not get a single interview." One effective way of "showing" is to read a compelling excerpt of a witness's testimony so that the court can see and hear the evidence in the witness's own words.

I have come to the end of my talk. I close with a vignette that my dad used to tell about two members of the legislature who sat outside Queen's Park. One said to the other: "You weren't in your seat today." "No," his friend replied. "I couldn't be there, but what went on?" "Oh," said the other. "I listened to Jones speak vigorously for about an hour." "Well, what did he talk about?" The reply came: "I don't know, he didn't say."

I hope that I have done a little better than Mr. Jones this morning. I thank you again for inviting me to speak to you and I thank you for your patience and attention in listening to me.

[This article was first published in the Summer 2004 issue of *The Advocates' Society Journal*.]

---

45   *Schenck v. United States*, 249 U.S. 47 (1919).
46   This metaphor is taken from Corbett, *supra* note 5 at 444.
47   See Stark, *supra* note 21 at 87; Mills, *supra* note 6 at 135–36.

A Survivor's Guide to Advocacy in the Supreme Court of Canada

Justice W. Ian Binnie[*]

[Editors' Note: The following is an edited text of the first John Sopinka Advocacy Lecture presented to the Criminal Lawyers' Association at Toronto, 27 November 1998.]

John Sopinka died almost exactly a year ago this week, and it is very fitting for the Criminal Lawyers' Association to inaugurate this series of lectures to perpetuate and to honour his great talent. It is a double honour to have John's daughter Melanie here. She not only shares her dad's feistiness but is, as her opponents have come to appreciate, a very considerable advocate in her own right.

It seems somewhat less fitting that I should be called on to give the first of these lectures. John Sopinka fit neatly into the long line of heroic counsel reaching back to Edward Blake, and descending through W.N. Tilley to John Robinette and others, including Bert MacKinnon and John's contemporary, Ian Scott, in our own day. The most I can claim is that I am a survivor, but in this room we are all survivors. What I have to say today should therefore be seen as a survivor's guide to advocacy in the Supreme Court of Canada.

---

[*]   Mr. Justice W. Ian Binnie, Supreme Court of Canada.

The first point I want to make about John Sopinka is that he was a man with an attitude — only in extreme circumstances would he tug his forelock or use the phrase "May it please the court." He liked to win cases. He didn't think it was his job necessarily to give pleasure to the court. And he never knew when he was beaten. The last occasion we worked together was at the Sinclair Stevens inquiry the year before John's appointment to the Supreme Court. He was representing Mr. Stevens in his personal capacity, and I did so in his government capacity. Of course, the hearing in the end was, unfortunately, an overall disaster for "Sinc." It was said that the only difference between the sinking of "Sinc" and the sinking of the Titanic is that when the Titanic sank, there was a band playing. John exhibited his usual defiance and resilience as the icebergs closed in. In one of the numerous motions to exclude evidence, which were invariably lost, John began by saying, "I have three arguments, one is hopeless, the other is arguable, and the third is unanswerable." The commissioner, somewhat impatient, said, "Well, why don't you just give me your best argument." John said, "Oh, I am not going to tell you which is which."

The Mother of All Juries

Another of John's great strengths as an advocate was his ability to adapt his personality and strategy, depending on what court or tribunal he was addressing. I only saw him once argue a case in the Supreme Court of Canada. Instead of the usual "in your face" style that he preferred before trial courts, he adopted an altogether more conciliatory approach, pitching his case one way to one judge and another way to another judge as he looked back and forth around the semi-circle of wintry faces from end to end of the bench. Unlike some counsel, he didn't focus all of his argument at the middle of the bench, where experience is deepest but the votes carry no more weight. Like the experienced violinist that he was, he played to every corner of the auditorium. It struck me then, as he challenged each judge in turn, sensing who was leaning this way or that, that his argument before the Supreme Court of Canada was very much in the style of a jury address. An address, if you will, to the mother of all juries. It is a style that works well at the Supreme Court. In some ways, the criminal bar, with its constant exposure to jury work, is probably better adapted to arguing an appeal before a court of nine judges than is the civil litigation bar.

But — I have to say this — there are some important differences between an everyday jury and the mother of all juries. Some lawyers seem to think they're talking to a group of nine people who have been randomly picked off the street. This is carrying the jury analogy too far. Let me list some of the differences.

First of all, you're not looking just to hang the jury, you're trying actually to persuade a majority to your point of view. You can't afford to give up on any of the nine votes until it's all over. You don't know who is on your side until the judgment issues. John didn't abandon his deck chair on the Titanic until the band played.

Second, don't be too rigid in your conception of the argument. Unlike the case with a normal, everyday jury, you didn't select the jurors; they selected you and your case because there are issues in it they want to address. If you're a good advocate, you won't necessarily talk about what you want to talk about, you'll talk about what they want to talk about. You may think they've misread the "real point." If so, that's their problem. Your problem is to win the case.

Third, this jury has a relatively short attention span for secondary arguments. The present foreman joined the court eighteen years ago. If at times he thinks he's heard it all before, it's maybe because he has. Collectively, the present members of the court have been sitting there for over seventy-five years.[1] A lot of your argument probably consists of rehashing their old judgments. They likely remember more or less what they decided. You too could move quickly if your old opinions were the subject matter of the debate. There is really no need to recite once again the facts in *Regina v. Oakes*.[2] Get quickly to your real point, and hit it with a two-by-four.

1	Lamer C.J., appointed 28 March 1980	10 yrs. 3 mos.
	appointed Chief Justice 1 July 1990	8 yrs. 5 mos.
	L'Heureux-Dubé J., appointed 15 April 1987	11 yrs. 7 mos.
	Gonthier J., appointed 1 February 1989	9 yrs. 10 mos.
	Cory J., appointed 1 February 1989	9 yrs. 10 mos.
	McLachlin J., appointed 30 March 1989	9 yrs. 8 mos.
	Iacobucci J., appointed 7 January 1991	7 yrs. 11 mos.
	Major J., appointed 13 November 1992	6 yrs.
	Bastarache J., appointed 30 September 1997	1 yr. 2 mos.
	Binnie J., appointed 8 January 1998	11 mos.
	Total:	**75 yrs. 7 mos.**
2	[1986] 1 S.C.R. 103.	

The Sundown Rule

Fourth, keep in mind that in most cases the Supreme Court operates on what I would call the "sundown rule." When you start your submission at 9:45 in the morning, remember that the judges are probably going to want to reach a tentative decision on the appeal before the sun goes down. This procedure is driven, I think, by the logistics of operating panels of up to nine judges and seems to be a practice shared by other final appellate courts.[3] Courts of this size require the judges to prepare and think in advance of the hearing. Once oral argument is heard, the court wants to capitalize on some of the adrenaline pumping around the courtroom to, as Justice Estey used to say, "get this baby airborne." The "sundown rule" is a good thing from the lawyers' perspective. It allows your advocacy real impact by giving you a voice in the decision-making process at the moment it counts most.[4] The only difference between the lawyers and the judges on the day of the hearing is that you don't get to vote, and you have to leave our discussion when it's only half over.

I used to be concerned as a lawyer that if the court heard fifteen to twenty appeals over a two-week period, the facts and arguments would be a jumble before the judges really focused on my case. I didn't appreciate the "sundown rule." My anxiety was aggravated by the length of time between the hearing and the ultimate rendering of the court's decision, which at one point in the mid-1980s occasionally stretched to a year and a half or more. My mistake was not to distinguish between the initial decision-making process and the more leisurely reasons-writing process. In the months following the hearing there is a lot of writing and rewriting,[5] and there is debate among the judges who sat on the case

---

3   The United States Supreme Court holds Friday conferences to deal with appeals heard during the week, plus literally hundreds of *certiorari* applications, or so say the law clerks: see Bob Woodward and Scott Armstrong, *The Brethren* (1976); and Edward Lazarus, *Closed Chambers* (1998). I was recently told by a retired law lord that the practice in our Supreme Court is comparable to that followed by the House of Lords and the High Court of Australia.

4   *The Brethren, ibid.* at 167: the rule of thumb in the U.S. Supreme Court is that advocacy at oral hearings sometimes loses appeals but seldom wins them. I don't think this is true of the Supreme Court of Canada. Oral advocacy can move the court both ways.

5   Judges want to know the views of colleagues before starting to write. The view attributed to Frankfurter J. is quoted in Lazarus, *Closed Chambers*, at 323:

about how propositions should be formulated and what should be put in and what should be left out; there is supplementary research done on points of difficulty, and the air is filled with memoranda to and fro among the judges. Opinions are modified. Minds are changed. If the court is closely divided on a particular appeal, the outcome could shift. But all of this is not your responsibility. As a practising lawyer I never cared much about why I won or lost. What counted to the client was the result. Getting "this baby airborne" in the right direction as soon as practicable after your submission is what the "sundown rule" is all about.

The Court Conference

If you understand a few things about the court conference that takes place after the hearing, it should help you structure your approach to oral argument, to our collective benefit. The dynamic of the court conference is probably a function of its size. You have up to nine opinionated people trying to persuade each other about the correct legal result. The advocacy never stops, it just becomes more blunt. The court conference is a little bit like a family dinner where the arguments continue after the guests have left and the gloves come off.

From the judges' perspective, the appeal has gone through a process of ever-increasing distillation and concentration. At the time of the initial preparation, an enormous amount of paper is flowing around. Bench memos are written, the facta are gone through, the leading cases are looked at, and the judges come to terms with what the appeal is all about. The oral hearing is still more focused. When the argument moves back into the conference room, it is distilled down to its most critical essentials. Thus, oral submissions should narrow, not broaden, the area of controversy. Judges at the oral hearing do not really need to be harangued in generalities as if they were bystanders at a public meeting.

When you have to have at least five people to agree on something, they can't have that comprehensive completeness of candour which is open to a single judge giving his own reasons untrammelled by what anybody else may do or not do. *Brown v. Board of Education* is an outstanding example where Warren determined that the court would give a unanimous decision without separate concurrences and in a rhetorical style calculated not to give unnecessary offences to the South. As a result, *Brown* is a short, flat and almost unexplained opinion.

As a respondent, I used to like starting my submissions by saying, "Let me take a few minutes to set out where my friend and I agree and where we disagree." I would then do a tally of where we stood on the issues. I thought this opening created the illusion of a responsible individual open to reason and ready to focus on the issues ultimately in dispute. That is how I saw myself. The judges apparently saw me differently. I am told that when I was appointed, Justice Major said to the Chief Justice, "Tell Binnie he won't have to shout at us any more."

At court conferences the judges speak in reverse order of appointment.[6] The junior judge goes first. This is unlike the Supreme Court of the United States, where the Chief Justice speaks first.[7] In a recent book on that court,[8] Edward Lazarus argues that the two great prerogatives of the Chief Justice of the United States in relation to his colleagues are, first of all, the right to speak first (because, of course, then he or she gets the opportunity to define the issues and to give an indication of how a decision should be written, whether narrowly or broadly, what kind of issues have to be resolved, and so on). The second great prerogative, it is said, is the assignment of the writing of the opinion, which, Lazarus claims, can become manipulative.[9] In an earlier book, *The Brethren*, it was said for example that Chief Justice Warren Burger was careful to stay away from Douglas, Brennan, or Marshall when it came to writing a decision under the First Amendment or the Due Process clause. Chief Justice Burger preferred to give the assignment to his more conservative colleagues.[10] It will be clear to you that in our court, by contrast, there is no insurmountable inhibition on any of the judges picking up a pen, or at what length. The Chief Justice allocates the writing of the principal

---

6   This seems to have been the English tradition since Tudor times. In *The Lion and The Throne, The Life and Times of Sir Edward Coke*, Catherine Drinker Bowen writes of the Star Chamber at p. 109: "Judgment was delivered seriatim, as in a jury, with the least important man speaking first and so on up to the Lord Keeper."

7   Apparently the Chief Justice also had to keep the minutes. See *The Brethren*, above note 3 at 64. The following thought is attributed to Chief Justice Burger: "It was hard to participate fully in the arguments, lead the discussions, and at the same time keep precise track of the Justices' votes and positions. Since no one other than the Justices was allowed in the conference room, he had to do it alone."

8   *Closed Chambers*, above note 3.

9   *Ibid.* at 354.

10   *Ibid.*

opinions, but apart from seniority where insisted upon, the exercise is generally open and largely consensual.

In our court conferences there is a fair degree of discussion about the points that have been made as well as points that may not have been made in the oral argument. Chief Justice Rehnquist, in a television interview with Charlie Rose about Rehnquist's newly published book, certainly came across as a "no nonsense" type of character. In his view, according to the recent study,[11] little importance is attached to the discussion at the court conference. He thinks the judges are sufficiently opinionated and independent that they are not going to change their minds based just on what their colleagues think. He says to his judges, why don't you just tell us where you are at, which way you are going to vote, and then we'll get on into the writing phase and "the details will emerge in the writing." The Canadian style is more discursive. Parts of the oral and written submissions are frequently referred to around the conference table. What you say, or fail to say, does make a difference.

There is nothing new about this description of the court conference. What is surprising, I think, is how few counsel, myself included, really put their minds to how to use an understanding of the process in the design of their written and oral arguments.

Oral Advocacy

John Sopinka's extensive writings on appellate advocacy[12] provide a pretty good insight into how to conduct an appeal in the Supreme Court of Canada. John tells you how to write a factum and construct a winning argument. I don't want to go over ground which he and others like Jus-

---

11   *Ibid.* at 285: "Rehnquist actively discourages discussion or debate at conference. In his assessment, the Justices' views were determined beforehand and a lot of talk wasn't going to change anybody's mind. As Scalia admitted with a note of disapproval, 'To call our discussion of a case a conference is really something of a misnomer. It's much more a statement of the views of each of the nine Justices.' Rehnquist was fond of saying that once the Justices voted, the details of any particular ruling 'would come out in the writing'."

12   "The Many Faces of Advocacy," *Advocates' Soc. J.*, Hilary Term, March 1990, vol. 9, no. 1; "The Conduct of an Appeal from the Perspective of Counsel and Judge," *Advocates' Soc. J.*, Hilary Term, March 1992, vol. 11, no. 1; "Advocacy in the Top Court," *The National*, May 1995, vol. 4, no. 4; Sopinka and Gelowitz, *The Conduct of an Appeal*, 1993 (Markham: Butterworths, 1993).

tice John Arnup[13] have already covered so well. In a forum like this, to paraphrase Professor Albert Abel,[14] you have to choose between tedious particularity and overarching generality; I am going to stick to "overarching generalities." I want to suggest a few dos and don'ts that may help you to survive your next hearing in the Supreme Court and live to docket another day.

The Key to Advocacy is Focus

A wonderful metaphor was used by an American lawyer by the name of John Davis, who used to argue regularly before the Supreme Court of the United States. He drew an analogy between the appellate advocate and a fly fisherman: "In the argument of an appeal, the advocate is angling, consciously and deliberately angling, for the judicial mind. Whatever tends to attract judicial favour to the advocate's plea is useful. Whatever repels it is useless or worse. The whole art of the advocate consists in choosing the one and avoiding the other."[15] This piscatory metaphor was formulated with the U.S. equivalent of the "sundown rule" in mind, but it applies equally to our Supreme Court, and is as concise a definition as one can find of the kind of focus that was characteristic of John Sopinka's arguments.

Look at Your Appeal from the Judges' Perspective

You might be surprised at how many practitioners apparently fail to reflect on why leave was granted in an appeal that is not as of right. In my short time on the court, there have already been occasions when the legal issue that the court expected to be argued in a criminal case was ignored by the appellant. If the respondent saw the issue, he or she wasn't about to volunteer it. Perhaps the court's practice not to give reasons in disposing of leave applications contributes to this problem, but most Rumpole-like survivors spend at least some quality time thinking about

---

13   The Law Society of Upper Canada Gazette (1979), at 27. Justice Arnup's article is an excellent source of wisdom about advocacy as well as plenty of entertaining anecdotes.

14   15 U. of T. L.J., at 102.

15   John Davis, "The Argument of an Appeal" (1940), 26 A.B.A.J. 895, quoted in Arnup, supra, note 13.

the appeal from the court's perspective. Everybody knows — or should know — that leave isn't usually given to sort out the facts. There may be all kinds of cases that appear to you to be wrongly decided on the facts that appellate courts can do little about. The Supreme Court has neither the mandate nor the capacity to retry the case. If leave was granted, there must be more to your appeal than your overwhelming sense of grievance at the courts below and your desire for vengeance in what we used to call the "Big House." The "mother of all juries" has a heart of gold, but submissions that ignore the limits of appellate review will get short shrift at a court conference.

Don't Assume Everyone Agrees About What the Issue Is

A related point: some counsel operate on the assumption that everybody will ultimately agree on what the argument is about. This is a mistake. A key to success to advocacy in the Supreme Court of Canada is the ability to set the agenda; in other words, to define the issue or issues raised by the appeal in a way that the judges find attractive and that will motivate them to want to write in your favour.[16] It helps, of course, if your argument also lays out a path by which the writing part can be accomplished.

Some trial lawyers think appellate advocacy is about supplying answers to questions that arise naturally and inevitably out of their fact situation. My experience, such as it was, demonstrated, sometimes unhappily, that there is nothing inevitable about the issues on which an appeal ultimately turns. It is possible in some cases to define issues on which there is general agreement. I illustrate my point by a recent case called *Cuerrier*.[17] This was a criminal case in which the accused was charged with sexual assault for having unprotected sex with two complainants, one of whom he had actively misled as to his HIV status, while to the other he deliberately failed to disclose his HIV status. The lower courts acquitted on the basis that the women had ultimately consented to sex, and therefore no assault occurred. The Supreme Court unanimously allowed the appeal, holding that as a matter of law it would be open on the facts to convict the accused of sexual assault, and ordered a retrial.

---

16 Counsel writing leave applications, in particular, need to keep this in mind.

17 *R. v. Cuerrier*, [1998] 2 S.C.R. 371.

Three judgments concurred in the result. This offended at least one editorial writer, who argued that the fact Mr. Cuerrier may wilfully have endangered others is certainly the sort of behaviour the criminal law must punish, and severely. And the court unanimously agreed that Mr. Cuerrier should stand trial for assault. But how they got to that result is even more vital than whether or not Mr. Cuerrier is eventually convicted. In this single decision, the court gave three opinions that ran the gamut from feminist radicalism to traditional common law conservatism.[18]

I have learned over the past year the truth of the saying that it is unwise to argue with people who buy printer's ink by the ton. Nevertheless I have to tell you that the editorial writer missed the point when she complained that the judgments confused matters by providing different answers to the same question. The point is that the judges were focusing on different questions. At the risk of oversimplification, let me illustrate my point. Those judges who stood accused of "traditional common law conservatism" looked at the 1983 amendments to the *Criminal Code,* the introduction of the word "fraud" into the list of factors in section 265 of the *Code* capable of vitiating consent to an assault, and interpreted the "fraud" amendment as introducing a more flexible test that nevertheless takes its colour from the context of a physical assault. They thought the dishonesty of an accused has to be such as to expose the victim to a significant risk of serious physical harm. Here, the duty to disclose increased with the potential gravity of the health consequences from unprotected sex, and AIDS stood at the head of the line.

What the editorial writer considered "feminist radicalism" was a set of reasons that in fact turned on a different interpretation of what the case was really all about. In this view, the intent of the 1983 amendments was to recognize and affirm the physical integrity and individual autonomy mainly of women, but also of men, and the question was how to give effect to this broad purpose. Having posed the question in this way, it easily followed that autonomy and bodily integrity should not be violated as a result of fraud of any description. The deception was not limited to physical harm. The vitiating deception would extend to almost any "dishonest act" that induced the consent. The premise was that Parliament considered the common law to be too narrow and intended to draw entirely new boundaries.

---

18   *Ottawa Citizen*, editorial, 10 September 1998.

The third concurring judgment thought that in 1983 Parliament intended to somewhat modify but not to throw out the traditional limits of the old law. The question was how far could the court push the interpretation without exceeding Parliament's limited expectations. In effect, from this perspective, the question was where to draw the line on judicial activism. The court should be conscious of its policy limitations. Proceeding incrementally, the notion of fraud could legitimately be expanded to include deceit about the risk of infection of a venereal disease, including AIDS. More radical expansion would put in question the respective constitutional roles of Parliament and the courts. A different framing of the question begat a different solution.

Running through all three judgments was yet a fourth question: "Should the criminal law be messing about in what is fundamentally a public health issue? Could criminalization of some aspects of unprotected sex chill compliance with reporting requirements and undermine the ability of the public health authorities to deal with a very serious health problem?"

Three judgments. Three quite different perspectives on how to characterize the real issues underlying the appeal. My point is that your role as the advocate is to do your utmost to get all members of the court on the same page, asking a question to which the only reasonable answer favours your client. Beyond that, *Cuerrier* shows that in a particular case there may be many routes to victory, and you should not overlook any of them.

Nailing the Jelly to the Wall

The same issue can be presented differently in different appeals. The outcome may depend on how successful you are at nailing the forensic jelly to the wall in a particular case. Take, for example, the third potential question in *Cuerrier;* namely, the respective constitutional role of Parliament and the courts. The issue is full of ambiguities and surfaced in different ways in at least three other appeals that I survived before the court over the past fifteen years, one for the government,[19] one against the government,[20] and one for the Speaker of the Senate.[21]

---

19 *Operation Dismantle,* [1985] 1 S.C.R. 441.
20 *Thomson Newspapers Co. v. Canada (Attorney General),* [1998] 1 S.C.R. 877.
21 *New Brunswick Broadcasting Co. v. Nova Scotia (Speaker of the House of Assembly),* [1993] 1 S.C.R. 319.

In the *Thomson Newspapers* case, we attacked an amendment to the *Canada Elections Act* that banned the publication of polls seventy-two hours before a federal election. Some of you may remember John Crosbie's reaction to the decision of the court striking down the publication ban. He saw it entirely as a constitutional issue. He said the judges had become the Godzillas of government, and the legislature and the executive had become the Mickey Mouses. The question, he thought, was whether non-elected, appointed judges should be telling elected people how to run an election. On the other hand, my clients, the Thomson and Southam newspaper chains, argued that the "question" was whether freedom of expression, a right entrenched in section 2(b) of the *Charter*, could be limited by politicians in what was contended to be their own self-interest. Our question was why Parliament should be allowed to single out opinion polls from all of the other potentially misleading bits of information swirling about in the dying days of a general election. There was nothing wrong with "strategic" voting based on last minute polls. So far as we were concerned, voters should be free to cast a vote based on the candidate's haircut, if that was their preferred criterion. On that appeal, on a razor-thin 5 to 3 vote, the court defined the issue as freedom of expression, not the appropriate role of the various constitutional players. If one vote had shifted, the court would have divided evenly, and the result would have been to preserve the decision of the Ontario Court of Appeal, which had unanimously upheld the ban.

It was otherwise in the *Nova Scotia Legislative Assembly* case, where the challenge was whether CBC cameras should be allowed into the House of Assembly against the opposition of the elected members. The CBC argued its section 2(b) point. In response, the various legislative bodies across the country, including the Senate of Canada, for whom I acted, raised the barricade of parliamentary privilege and said, "Look, parliamentary privilege is as much part of the Constitution of Canada as is freedom of expression under 2(b) of the *Charter*. You can't have one value in the Constitution trumping another. The exercise of privileges by Parliament and the provincial legislature is not subject to judicial review." Our subliminal message was that if the media has a *Charter* right to introduce cameras into the legislature over the members' opposition, the media should have the same *Charter* right to introduce cameras in trial courts over the opposition of the trial judges. Soon after that point was grasped, the media goose was cooked, and manifestly seen to be cooked. Once again, it all depended on how you defined the question.

The earliest of the three cases is *Operation Dismantle*, where a coalition of disarmament groups sought to halt the testing of Cruise missiles on the basis that such tests increased the possibility of nuclear war. I argued for the federal government that the court should not involve itself in political questions relating to national security. We relied on a number of cases in the United States Supreme Court which held that in the nature of things, judges lack the expertise, background, and information to determine defence policy.[22] Our Supreme Court disagreed. While it dismissed the appeal of *Operation Dismantle* on the basis of non-justiciability, Madam Justice Wilson said that *Charter* rights trump defence policy and national security. "I think we should focus our attention on whether the courts should or must rather than on whether they can deal with such matters," she said.[23] In short, in these examples, where the court was persuaded that human rights was the issue, the decision went one way. Where the court was persuaded that the issue was judicial restraint and a recognition of the proper constitutional order, the decision went the other way. Which way the question on any appeal gets to be formulated is, I think, a key function of appellate advocacy.

Obviously the question that you say governs the appeal will normally drive the answer that you want. It if were otherwise, you would not be advocating that particular question. On a practical level, you can often get better mileage arguing concepts in your hour before the Supreme Court than you can by trudging through pages of black letter law. If you persuade the judges about the right question, they will generally figure out how to get to the answer, even if it means circumnavigating some difficult precedents. The beauty of the "sundown rule" is that it gives you the chance to motivate the judges at a critical stage, when their views about the correct characterization of the appeal are crystallizing.

Don't Overlook in Oral Argument Any Point Essential to Your Success

Oral argument should be complete and self-contained. Don't overlook any point essential to your success. A wise practice for counsel in the

---

22   *The Brethren*, above note 3 at 126: "The Court had ceded to the President and the military virtual autonomy in war-related matters. 'You can't fight a war with the Courts in control,' Black had said."

23   *Operation Dismantle*, at 467 [emphasis is in the original].

Supreme Court is to hand to the judges a book of extracts or "condensed book" at the beginning of the oral argument. Most lawyers include the key extracts of evidence and passages from the case law. This avoids wasting time while waiting for the judges to shuffle through a mountain of paper, looking for the particular document you want to refer them to. Having handed in the Book of Extracts, however, many lawyers don't take the time to go through it. They'll say, "Well, Tab 37 — that's the contract. I won't take time to go to it now. I know you are going to read it in due course. I just want you to know that it is there." Bad mistake! If a particular extract of testimony contained in the middle of a dozen or more volumes of transcripts is essential to your success, or if you think everything turns on a particular provision in the contract buried in five volumes of exhibits, stop and read the extract to the court. This is "must have" information for the court conference that is to follow; the "sundown rule" teaches that the time to make your point is now. The great old advocates in the heroic tradition figured out the necessity of doing that a lot faster than I did. Mr. Justice John Arnup[24] tells the story of W.N. Tilley, who was grinding through a contract case in the Supreme Court years ago. The judges became worried that he was going to read the whole document to them. The Chief Justice stopped him and said: "You don't need to do that, we'll read the evidence." Tilley responded, innocently: "Will all your Lordships read the evidence?" "Yes." "Will all your Lordships read all the evidence?" "Yes, of course." "Then," said Mr. Tilley, "let's read it together!" And he carried on.

Questions From the Bench: Listen Before You Leap

The last thing I want to touch on in terms of the oral hearing is the matter of questions from the bench. Of course, everybody who talks about advocacy at any level of the courts will emphasize the need to face up to questions. If something is bothering the judges, better that it be out on the table than concealed in the recesses of their minds, only to pop out later at the court conference, when you are no longer around to deal with it. Some lawyers complain that a problem in the Supreme Court is that often the hearings consist of little else but questions. This is an unfair criticism. We didn't interrupt you when you were preparing your factum. Now it's our turn.

---

24   Arnup, above note 13 at 27.

You are confronted with nine judges who are going to have to deliver at least their preliminary views of what this appeal is all about shortly after the conclusion of oral argument. If something is in the back of my head and I am not sure what the answer would be from one side or the other, I'm going to ask it. You may have spent the previous night in a hotel room mapping out each minute of your argument. I am sorry if my interruption disrupts your game plan and burns valuable time. I need the answer to my question because it helps me to do my job, even though it may make your job a whole lot messier. As the expression goes, *sauve qui peut.*

Having said that, there are many different kinds of questions, and you should respond to different types of questions in different ways. I will try to illustrate this point by dividing questions into what I think are seven useful categories, then give a hint about how I think you should handle them.

The first type of question is the genuine inquiry for enlightenment. It may be something as simple as clarifying a point of fact, or a question like "Well, you are resting your argument on the *Charter*, but is it not really a division of powers case?" or "How would you say our decision in *Re The Sliding Door Company* applies to this situation?" This category consists of straightforward questions that you likely anticipated in preparing the appeal. Your reaction should be extremely helpful and solicitous.

The second category is slightly more confrontational and has to do with the fact that some members of the court are more linear in their thinking and others prefer a more dialectical approach. An example of the second category question is, "The appellant says this, and you say that, but I don't see how your point answers her point. Could you elaborate?" This category is slightly more confrontational in that it brings into collision the opposing views. I think your posture should be one of mild surprise that it is not evident what your position is, but nevertheless you are happy to oblige with a short elaboration.

The third category of question is where the court goes further than asking you to elaborate, and a judge purports to state your position. Justice Cory is expert at this. He says something like: "I suppose your position is that the presumption of innocence is a golden thread that goes through the warp and woof of the criminal law, do I have your point?" You can adopt his formulation, but you have to realize that you are before the mother of all juries, and, while he is being helpful in terms of his own thinking, your impetuous adoption of his formulation could potentially inflame colleagues of a contrary view at the other end of the bench. I call this category the "friendly fire" kind of question because although it comes from a supportive source it may wind up fatally wounding your argument when the other eight votes are counted.

The fourth category of question is overtly hostile fire. The *Rose*[25] case included a good example of "hostile fire." That case involved an attack on the constitutionality of requiring a defence counsel who calls evidence to forfeit the right to be the last to address the jury. The obvious hostile question to the appellant was, "Are you saying, counsel, that every jury trial where the accused called evidence since 1892 has violated fundamental principles of justice?" It's at moments like this that you should close your eyes and think of John Sopinka standing on the deck as the icebergs gathered at the Sinclair Stevens inquiry. Don't try to please the questioner at the expense of weakening your argument. You don't know at that stage how many of the judges are silently agreeing with you. Sometimes hostile fire questions provoke counter-fire from other judges, in which case, agreeably from your perspective, the hostile questioner may be engulfed in back-fire.

How can you tell what is friendly fire and what is hostile fire? I had my own rule of thumb as an advocate before the court: if Peter Cory asked the question it was probably friendly; if anybody else asked it, it was probably hostile.

The fifth category of question should probably be called collateral fire. That occurs where you are proceeding happily along one train of argument and then, suddenly, a question seems to come off the wall. I remember years ago listening to Michael Goldie arguing the *Canadian Arctic Gas* case.[26] He was taking the court through minutes of a key meeting when, suddenly, Justice Pigeon threw down his pencil and said, "Now, are you going to read this over and over and over again?" Well, the fact was, neither Mr. Goldie nor anyone else had previously referred to it. Nevertheless Mr. Goldie, the agile warrior that he was (and is), recognized the question as totally collateral to the flow of his argument. He

---

25   *R. v. Rose* (S.C.C., 25448: judgment released 26 November 1998, unreported).
26   *Committee of Justice & Liberty v. Canada*, [1978] 1 S.C.R. 369. Michael Goldie, now Goldie J.A. of the British Columbia Court of Appeal, acted for the Canadian Arctic Gas Consortium.

adroitly backed off, apologized, circled around, and eventually came back to the extract he needed to refer to and carried on without interruption. I would say that the proper posture for an advocate experiencing collateral fire is submission! By definition, if it's collateral it can't hurt you and therefore there is no point in making an issue of it.

The sixth category of question is cross-fire. This is where you become an innocent bystander. The *Borowski* case[27] a few years ago was about whether a high-profile anti-abortion crusader, Joe Borowski, could get public-interest standing to attack the constitutionality of the abortion law, section 251 of the *Criminal Code*. Chief Justice Laskin, who had pioneered the concept of public-interest standing in *Thorson v. Attorney General*[28] and *Nova Scotia Board of Censors v. McNeil*,[29] was opposed to giving standing to a political crusader who, as he saw it, was merely experiencing "an emotional response" to the abortion legislation. Justice Martland took a different view and wanted to use Chief Justice Laskin's earlier decisions to put the skids under some of the remaining barriers to public-interest status. I was there opposing Borowski and was caught in a cross-fire between Chief Justice Laskin and Justice Martland, who both regarded my submission as essentially irrelevant to their debate. My advice in a category six situation is to mumble inaudibly and let the titans slug it out.

The seventh and last category of question is what used to be called the "Martland question." Justice Martland, during the 1970s and early '80s, was not inclined to ask many questions, but he would sit and fret and fool around with his papers and look quizzical and scratch an ear and call for books to be sent in, and talk to his neighbours, but at some point in the proceeding there would be a kind of chilly silence and Martland would clear his throat and out would come the question, trailing wisps of smoke behind it. There wasn't anybody in the courtroom who didn't realize that the moment of truth had arrived. If you were able to deal with the Martland question the case was as good as won, and you felt yourself galloping toward the sunlit uplands of victory. If you failed, a kind of a death watch set in. The questioning from other members of

---

27   *Minister of Justice v. Borowski*, [1981] 2 S.C.R. 575.

28   *Thorson v. Attorney General of Canada*, [1975] 1 S.C.R. 138.

29   *Nova Scotia Board of Censors v. McNeil*, [1976] 2 S.C.R. 265.

the bench dried up. The judges began to make their notes for the court conference. Nowadays, mercifully, the red light goes on.

Attitude

Finally, I want to go back and pick up my first point about John Sopinka's attitude. Attitude is everything in advocacy. No matter how disastrously you think the hearing is unfolding, be steadfast and defiant. Don't crumple. Don't take up the posture of a whipped cur, signalling by your body language that you wish you were somewhere else. You don't know who your friends are on the bench or how many they are in number. If you let yourself down, you let them down as well, and above all you let down your client. If at the conclusion of an apparently disastrous hearing you can walk out of there with flags flying and your chin up, then you can say that you are an advocate worthy of the John Sopinka tradition.

[This article was first published in the Summer 1999 issue of *The Advocates' Society Journal*.]

Appellate Advocacy in an Abbreviated Setting

Justice George D. Finlayson*

This brief article is designed to give some insights into what is required of an advocate in the new regime, where the court has imposed mandatory time limits on the argument of counsel. I anticipate that the reader, upon reflecting on what I have to say, will recognize that my suggestions propose nothing radical and, indeed, set out no more than my observations as to the way successful counsel have presented argument in the Court of Appeal, certainly from the outset of my experience.

It is trite to observe that advocacy is the art of persuasion. In the modern setting of the Court of Appeal, that means making effective use of your greater knowledge of the specific case on the court's docket to assist the panel of judges to arrive at a proper result: your result. Unfortunately, too many counsel regard their role as that of verbal gladiator and that of the court as an informed audience. Consequently they resent any intrusion on their performance, not recognizing that their client's case is not being judged on form but on substance. However, the reality is that the court is committed to time limits on oral advocacy, and, subject to seeking adjustment to the time allotments in the particular case, counsel must learn to live with them and indeed exploit them to their client's advantage.

---

* Mr. Justice George D. Finlayson, Court of Appeal for Ontario.

I start with a quotation from *The Conduct of an Appeal,* by Sopinka and Gelowitz:

> In order to argue effectively in the face of a time limit, the argument must be prepared having regard to this factor. Unfortunately, some counsel do not plan at all, and find that they have frittered away the time available on preliminaries or non-essentials. Others decide to argue the appeal as if time is unrestricted; they just argue it twice as fast. The result, usually, is that the benefits of oral argument are seriously compromised.[1]

I agree with this overview of the problem and hope to give counsel some guidance as to how they can make the most effective use of the time allotted to them. The first and most obvious tool in the effective presentation of your appeal is the factum. It is as if you were permitted to write a letter to your judges which they can read at home in their studies. Take full advantage of the opportunity. My colleague Justice Laskin has prepared a paper on the content of this document, and I do not intend to encroach on his subject. My comments are limited to the use of the factum in the course of your argument.

A second useful tool is a compendium of extracts from exhibits, transcripts, and authorities that you propose to rely upon. This is not only useful in complex cases, it is essential if you are to avoid the waste of time and loss of focus that inevitably accompanies the search by panel members for the document, transcript, or authority to which you intend to refer. The court has encouraged the use of such compendiums.[2] Oddly enough, although a number of counsel have realized the value of such a compendium, they then dissipate its usefulness by not handing it up until the opening of argument. The panel members can hardly read it and do justice to your oral submissions at the same time. If it is worth looking at during argument, how much more useful it would be to have it in advance.

Again, and on the same theme, where it is not practical to use a compendium or the compendium does not contain everything that

---

1   (Toronto: Butterworths, 1993) at 216.

2   See Dubin C.J.O.'s Practice Direction Concerning New Scheduling Procedures for Civil Appeals, dated 18 December 1995, at s. VII.4: "In a complex case, counsel are encouraged to file an extract book for the use of the panel hearing the appeal. The extract book should contain relevant extracts from the appeal book and transcripts of evidence and relevant case references."

counsel wishes to rely upon, ask the registrar to select the material that you will be referring to and set it out beside the individual judges. The assistance of the registrar will be of particular assistance to counsel for the respondent, who will not be sure of what he or she will be relying upon until the completion of the appellant's argument. This assistance can usually be sought during a recess, but if there is no convenient time and the court is sitting, do not hesitate to ask the panel to set aside the material you are relying on before commencing your submissions. The panel will not consider that a waste of time.

Finally, as part of your preparation, do not make the mistake of needlessly replicating your opponent's material in your Book of Authorities. As a practical matter, this advice is directed to the respondent's counsel. In almost every case, the number of directly relevant authorities is limited. If they are important cases, they can be found in different law reports. There is no reason for duplication. There is definitely no need to have reports from different reporting services. The panel members usually mark up their copies or make notes in the margins, and it is obviously helpful to have all these notations in the same place. I have sat on cases that lasted a week in which the appellant, the respondent, and a number of intervenors have referred over and over again to the same cases and insisted that the court look at the photocopy of the case that is in their Book of Authorities "because I have marked in my copy the passages I am relying upon." Counsel must be flexible. Do not unnecessarily tax this ability in your judges.

Now to the oral presentation. First and foremost, believe the president of the panel when he tells you that the members of the panel have read the facta of the parties and the judgment on appeal or the relevant portions of the charge to the jury, as the case may be. Assume that the panel is familiar with the facts and is aware of the legal principles involved. Counsel should be prepared to proceed directly to the argument. I can assure you that the members of the panel are well-prepared before going into court. Each has his or her own standard of preparation, just as counsel have, but do not think for a moment that they have not prepared themselves sufficiently so that counsel can proceed to develop any point in the argument without being concerned that it will not be understood.

Just as the court will not insult counsel by questioning counsel's readiness, and thus competence, do not offend the panel by proceeding on the assumption that its members do not know their responsibilities under the new regime. Their state of preparedness will usually become evident as the argument proceeds and individual members ask for amplification or clarification of the facts and issues. These interjections will help counsel to understand what matters are of concern to the court, and they should be answered fully and directly. By responding knowledgeably and immediately, counsel can demonstrate familiarity with his or her brief and start to establish a comfortable rapport with the panel.

Your opening should establish which points in your factum you intend to argue orally, which ones you are abandoning, and which ones you feel that you have developed sufficiently in your factum that you do not need deal to with in oral argument. Make it clear, however, that you are still relying upon the written material in your factum as part of your argument.

This opening is critical and gives counsel the opportunity to exercise some much-needed judgment as to what are the most significant issues in the appeal. It also sets the agenda for the appeal itself. Your opponent and the court will be responding to your presentation. In any given case, the most significant issues cannot number more than three. As an *aide memoire* to be attached to every counsel's brief, permit me to state unequivocally that no judge in a single trial has made more than three reversible errors. Counsel may think the judge has made many more, and the panel members may have their own thoughts, but that is an impermissible thought process for the true advocate. Three is the outside number for judicial purposes. Look at it this way: the appellant needs to establish only one reversible error to succeed, and the "rule of three" gives counsel three chances to achieve that result. If counsel proceeds to argue that there are more errors than that, counsel is acknowledging failure with respect to the first three.

Limiting the number of issues to be argued is just good clock management. Counsel should concentrate on the issues that are likely to carry the court and leave in the factum others that, while superficially appealing, are not going to result in overturning the judgment below. Some, such as suggestions as to costs, will not come into play unless you win the appeal, and you lose nothing by relying on your written treatment in your factum. The same applies in reverse in criminal cases when the sentence appeal is premised on losing the conviction appeal. Unless the true focus of the appeal is sentence, or counsel is relying upon fresh evidence, counsel can usually leave the sentence appeal to be decided on the basis of written argument.

I have emphasized the importance of your factum. Assuming it is first class, leave it alone in oral argument. While you should not ignore it, under no circumstances should you read from it. In stating the points that you have decided to argue orally, simply indicate to the court where the issues are set out in your factum. The oral argument must be prepared separately from the written argument and should complement, not repeat it. Proceed orally, but follow the pattern of your factum — a brief overview, and then to the first and strongest argument. It is in the argument that you commence dealing with the detail of the facts, but only in relation to the legal principle that you are advancing. Any effective counsel has developed the art of co-mingling the facts and the law to present a seamless argument that puts the client's position in the most favourable light.

Remember always that this is your argument, not the respondent's. Do not make the mistake of commencing your argument by responding to points made by the respondent in its factum. First of all, this is an acknowledgement that your factum is incomplete, or worse, has misstated the facts or the issues. If there is some deficiency in your factum that has been exposed in the respondent's factum, rest assured that some member of the court will ask you about it. This gives you your best opportunity to respond to the problem. Failing a question from the bench, the substance of the point or points raised by the respondent can be dealt with affirmatively in your own argument. Remember that if you start out by referring to the respondent's factum, a lot of things can go wrong. First of all, you may be accused of misstating the point raised by your opponent and waste valuable time trying to explain what your opponent is saying while at the same time trying to convince the court that it is wrong. Second, you are using up your allotted time on the defensive instead of attacking the errors in the judgment or verdict on appeal. Third, you have foreclosed your ability to reply to the respondent on the particular issue.

As to the merits of the argument, in my experience the most consistent mistake made by appellants' counsel is in failing to recognize the limited jurisdiction of the Court of Appeal. We are not a trial court, and we do not conduct trials *de novo*. We are a court that reviews the record of the trial or other proceedings in a lower court or tribunal. We must be persuaded that the court or tribunal below made an error and that it is an error of sufficient magnitude that we cannot allow the decision under appeal to stand. While we are a statutory court with jurisdiction over fact, we are restricted severely as to what we can do with findings of fact. Either there must be no facts to support the finding or the finding must be subject to palpable and overriding error.[3] I am aware that language has been used by appellate courts that is more appellant-friendly, such as the trial judge "misapprehended the evidence"[4] or "failed to give proper weight to the evidence,"[5] but I can tell you that the practical hurdle in our court is to establish that there is no evidence to support a finding or that the finding reflects palpable and overriding error. Our appellate court will only resort to the lower threshold of factual overview in the course of discussing a judgment that, over all, it is satisfied is wrong. It is very difficult to argue that the trial judge has misconceived the facts to the point that the judgment cannot stand. A more effective strategy is to make use of uncontroverted facts in the framework of a legal argument directed to exposing flaws in the judgment.

Accordingly, in dealing with facts on appeal, it is most unwise to attack the trial judge's findings directly unless you are confident that you can establish the higher threshold of appellate intervention. Unfortunately, some counsel, forgetting that the court has read the material, attempt to embark upon an analysis of the evidence under the guise of a submission that they can demonstrate that there is no factual basis for the findings of the trial judge or that the findings disclose palpable or overriding error. While they have no expectation of accomplishing their stated objective, they hope that a review of the evidence will persuade the court to substitute its opinion of the facts for that of the trial judge. They want to review the evidence in the hope that they can persuade the court to arrive at a different conclusion than that of the trial judge. In other words, they want to retry the case in the Court of Appeal — something we will not permit. By obtaining permission to embark on a detailed examination of the facts on a false premise, counsel loses credibility with the court, not only on the instant case but for the future as well. No case is worth it.

My earnest suggestion is that when there is evidence that supports findings of fact that are adverse to your position, you should state that you are accepting the express findings of fact of the trial judge and are

---

3   *Stein v. The Ship "Kathy K,"* [1976] 2 S.C.R. 802.

4   *R. v. Baranski* (1994), 71 O.A.C. 157 at 158 (C.A.).

5   *Nemeth Estate v. McGuffin Estate,* [1978] O.J. No. 553 (C.A.) at para. 5.

aware that his findings of credibility have taken away arguments that you relied upon at trial. You should then proceed upon the trial judge's account of what the evidence revealed, supplemented by additional uncontroverted facts or ones that, while contentious, were not the subject of express adverse findings. This most favourable and sustainable version of the evidence will, it is to be hoped, give you a sound enough factual base that you can relate your version of events to the law and demonstrate that in the final result, the trial judge was in error.

Like most articles on appellate advocacy, the focus of my remarks has been upon the presentation by the appellant. However, my advice to the respondent is very much the same. I emphasize once again the importance of the factum; if anything, it is probably more important. If it has been done properly, you will notice that questions from the bench have their genesis in your written material. However, do not make the mistake of reading what it is obvious the court has already read.

Last, but by no means least, I come to what is potentially the most effective, but regrettably the most misused, tool of advocacy: the reply. This is counsel's opportunity to get in the last word, and unfortunately, in too many cases, that last word does not always assist. Your first consideration is: should I say anything? Believe me when I tell you that saying nothing is never a mistake. Silence may not advance your case, but it most assuredly will not hurt it. Many counsel feel that if they do not say anything, the court will assume that they have nothing to say in response to the respondent's argument. So rather than leave the court in doubt on the matter, they remove that doubt by standing up and repeating what they have said in their argument in chief.

If you do decide to reply, be sure to invoke the rule of three: write down all the points to which you wanted to reply, and throw away all but three — the best three. Once again, the immutable rule of advocacy is that the fourth point in reply never won a case and, in many cases, convinced the appellate court that there really was nothing in the appeal after all. This was a good rule before the introduction of time limits. It is a better rule now. Remember that your reply was part of your original time allocation as the appellant. The chances are that you did not reserve any time to reply. Limitations on reply are rarely enforced as such, but if they are, you know that your reply has been ineffective.

On the other hand, a good reply can be devastatingly effective if you can score but one point. If the respondent has raised an argument against you that you did not anticipate in your argument in chief and that point appears to have caught the attention of the court and you can refer the court briefly to a portion of the evidence or an authority that has not already been addressed and your reference does provide an answer to the court's concern, then by all means reply. Note that there are three conjunctions in the last sentence. Again, be reasonably certain that your friend has made a point that appears to have raised a concern with at least one member of the panel. If your opening argument has been well-received, do not encourage the court to become interested in a matter that it has not focused upon. You can usually determine the extent of the court's interest in your opponent's argument by questions from the bench and sometimes by the lack of them. If your assessment is wrong, the court will usually ask you about the matter in issue.

A proper reply should not require an extended introduction. If you have to introduce your point by restating your opponent's point at length, you run the risk of having a member of the court correct you or indicate that you have quoted it out of context. Never give a judge an opportunity to articulate your opponent's position. He is likely to embrace it as his own. Similarly, do not be in a hurry to embrace a suggestion made by a member of the panel during your opponent's argument and attempt to make it your own. The judge who made the suggestion is unlikely to be impressed, and the other judges might think it was a very bad idea.

Lectures and articles on advocacy usually contain more "don'ts" than "dos," which causes your audience to wonder if you have anything useful to offer. However, reply is for experts. If your factum is sound and your presentation appears to have been well-received, you can be sure that each of the individual panel members has probably arrived at least at a tentative view of how he or she intends to vote. Learn to leave well enough alone.

I turn briefly to the matter of answering questions from the bench. My advice is that you answer them briefly and immediately. Leave out the old chestnut: "I will be developing my response to that question later on in my argument." Chances are you will not have a "later on."

As to the type of question that you can expect, I can do no better than to refer you to the article by the Honourable Mr. Justice Ian Binnie which appears in this issue of the *Journal*. The article is authoritative and reflects Justice Binnie's irreverent sense of humour. I strongly recommend the section entitled "Questions from the bench: Listen before you leap." His analysis of the types of questions counsel may expect from the panel is witty and insightful. I cannot improve upon it.

Fielding questions can be difficult. My only contribution will be examples of some very bad answers.

1.   I was not counsel at trial.
2.   I did not prepare my factum.
3.   That isn't in my friend's factum.
4.   I did not understand my friend to have said that.
5.   My friend would have the court believe ...
6.   The trial judge did not deal with that.
7.   I will be coming to that later in my argument.
8.   My colleague will address that point.

Some of my readers may have expected this article to contain a more detailed road map to success in the Court of Appeal, but over the course of what has become a lengthy exposure to the appellate process both as counsel and as judge, I have come to realize that appellate advocacy is the most difficult of forensic art forms. The heart of what counsel must contend with is to be found in the nature of a review process that limits significantly the control counsel has over the proceedings. Unlike trial work, where the judge is captive to counsel and must wait for them to lead the witnesses and build the evidentiary record, in our court the record is set and an adjudication on that record has already been made. Consequently, the control counsel had at trial over the flow of the proceedings has disappeared. Counsel must now anticipate the concerns of an informed panel of judges and is not in a position to proceed on a predetermined course of advocacy. Accordingly, there is no set-piece structure for an appellant's argument. All counsel can do is analyse the judgment or verdict on appeal and direct his or her forensic skills to what counsel perceives to be the areas most vulnerable to attack.

If you can proceed without significant interruption, you are on the right track. If interruptions occur, you must respond to them and then try to return to your original plan of attack. It is not an easy task, but it can be an immeasurably rewarding one, for you and your client.

[This article first appeared in the Summer 1999 issue of *The Advocates' Society Journal*.]

Advocacy in Jurisprudential Appeals

Justice Rosalie Silberman Abella*

[Editors' note: This article is the edited text of the keynote address given at The Advocates' Society Fall Convention in Montego Bay, Jamaica, on 15–18 November 2001.]

The theme of this article about appellate advocacy in jurisprudential appeals is a simple proposition: it is not just what you say, it is also how you are heard.

This article is a direct descendant of all the advocacy articles whose collected wisdom urges advocates to write, speak, and think clearly; be prepared; weave the story together with interesting threads; and make the punchline seem irresistible. I agree with all of this advice. With one caveat.

Most of the articles I read on appellate advocacy adopted the metaphor first cast in a 1940 article on appellate advocacy by an American lawyer, John W. Davis.[1] He said appellate advocacy is like fly-fishing. Lawyers were the fishers and judges were the fishees. I confess that this metaphor bewildered me. I knew from the movie *A River Runs Through It* that in fly-fishing, you stand in the water for hours hoping to catch a fish. This, I said to myself, is not going to fly in an appeal court like

---

*   Madam Justice Rosalie Silberman Abella, Supreme Court of Canada.
1   John W. Davis, "The Argument of an Appeal" (1940), 26 A.B.A.J. 895.

mine, where we have time limits. One of my colleagues told me that his father and brother have been fly-fishing for salmon for ten years and have yet to catch one. We judges cannot wait ten years to be caught.

There must be something more to this, I said to myself. So I called my friend Jack, who fly-fishes, and asked him how it works. He said you take a nine-foot pole and aim it where you think the fish are. Then you jerk the pole around in different directions to try your luck in a variety of spots. Then you give up and change ponds.

"What lures do you use, Jack?" I asked. "Are they bright and shimmery?"

"Some are, some aren't. Some are wriggly, some aren't. Fish tend to be bottom-feeders, so you have to use a lure you think will bring them to the surface," he responded.

I am astounded that we have tolerated this metaphor for over sixty years. First of all, if you cast your rod towards where you think the fish are, you are just guessing. Guessing is not a good advocacy technique. Second, if you have to jerk your rod around to get results, you are being haphazard. Haphazardness is also not a good advocacy technique. Third, if you give up and change ponds, you are being impatient. Impatience is most certainly not a good advocacy technique.

And if lures are arguments, I never saw a wriggly one I liked. Do I even have to mention how unhelpful it is for judges to know advocates think of them as bottom-feeders?

So what advice would I give an appellate advocate who is asking the court to consider conflicting authorities, overturn previous lines of authority, and make new law? I will not attempt to offer the kind of taxonomy of guidelines usually found in articles on advocacy since, in jurisprudential appeals, different strategies work in different cases at different times and in different ways before different judges. All the skills the skilled advocate already has at his or her disposal will undoubtedly continue to enhance the chances of success, but so too will a great deal of luck and timing.

My advice, distilled to its purest form, would be this: it depends on the panel.

This is the article on advocacy that says it is not always about you the advocate. So much depends on how receptive the particular judges you are appearing before are to the idea that their proper role includes drawing new maps for uncharted legal territory or redrawing the boundaries on old ones.

Far from intending to impugn either the integrity, rigour, or independence of Canada's judiciary, it is more to acknowledge that there is a philosophical continuum on which judges may find themselves, a continuum that may make them more or less receptive to judicial lawmaking. So, rather than make any false promises that my prescriptions will ensure a successful outcome, I will make a real promise that an advocate who follows my observations about the institutional environment in which the jurisprudential case is being argued will at least take it less personally when he or she loses.

It should be no shock to experienced appellate advocates that often the result depends on who is hearing the appeal. But to put the observation in a principled context, I will try to explain why and how this unspoken reality can factor into an advocate's ability successfully either to urge — or resist — the making of new law.

This was an exotic topic to research, because I had never seen a discussion of what appears to persuade judges to make new or change old law. That, I think, is in part because so few judges comfortably admit they are doing it. And that, in turn, is because of the classic debate between those who say only legislatures, not judges, should make law and those who say making law is a normal part of what judges do. Inside each of those Russian dolls — the one that says lawmaking is judicial trespass and the one that says lawmaking is authorized judicial territory — are several smaller ones. They are the layers that either reject or confirm the judicial consideration of public policy, reject or confirm the judicial application of social values, or reject or confirm the potential threats to judicial impartiality from the use of policy or values.

I confess to being somewhat confused by judges who assert that their role is immune from the duty to consider public policy or social values, or that they are institutionally prohibited from making law. Judges have always had a close relationship with public policy and values and have always made law. To pretend otherwise is fiction worthy of the Giller Literary Prize.

In particular, judges have always reached legal conclusions based on their understanding of, sympathy for, or antipathy for current social values.[2] The judge who in 1983 said "the paramount destiny and mis-

---

2   See Rosalie Silberman Abella, "Public Policy and the Judicial Role" (1989), 34 McGill L.J. 1021.

sion of women are to fulfill the noble and benign offices of wife and mother";[3] the judge who in 1915 thought admitting women to the legal profession would be a "manifest violation of the law of ... public decency";[4] the judge who said in 1905 that fault-based support laws were desirable because wives "ought to be preserved from imminent temptation";[5] the House of Lords who said in 1959 that privative clauses ousting the jurisdiction of the courts were to be disregarded;[6] the court that said in 1975 that property rights take precedence over peaceful picketing;[7] the courts that said in 1949 that sanctity of the contract and restrictive covenants took precedence over the rights of Jews to purchase property;[8] the court that said in 1939 that freedom of commerce took precedence over the rights of blacks to be served beer;[9] and the court that said in 1959 that the premier of Quebec, Maurice Duplessis, had overstepped the boundaries of permissible political behaviour[10] were all invoking or articulating their view of what public policy either required, prevented, or permitted.

Insofar as the sifting of legal choices is the sifting of policy values, judges, in interpreting law, do consider and always have considered, in addition to logic and precedent, the values or policy implications their legal conclusions represent. But because judges tended to be wary about appearing to make policy judgments that some thought were more acceptably made in a political forum, they historically used anodyne terminology to shield the exercise of policy choice from conspicuous view. Policy-laden words like "reasonable," "arbitrary," "due process," "good faith," "unjustified," or "discretion" are what Learned Hand called a "protective veil of adjectives"[11] for insulating judicial policy-making from

3   Bradwell v. Illinois, 83 U.S. (16 Wall.) 130 at 141 (1873).
4   Langstaff v. Bar of the Province of Quebec (1915), 47 S.C. 131 at 139 (C.A.), affirming (1915), 25 C.B.R. 11.
5   Squire v. Squire, [1905] P. 4 at 8.
6   Anisminic Ltd. v. Foreign Compensation Commission, [1969] 2 A.C. 147.
7   Harrison v. Carswell, [1975] 2 S.C.R. 200, 62 D.L.R. (3d) 68, reversing Chief Justice Freedman of the Manitoba Court of Appeal, whose balancing list yielded the opposite result, as did Chief Justice Laskin's in his dissent.
8   Re Noble and Wolf (1949), 4 D.L.R. 375.
9   Christie v. York, [1940] S.C.R. 139.
10 Roncarelli v. Duplessis, [1959] S.C.R. 121.
11 Learned Hand, The Bill of Rights (Cambridge, MA: Harvard University Press, 1958) at 70.

censure for perceived policy-making. When judges interpret terms of art like "best interests," "discrimination," "unfair labour practice," or "responsibility for damage caused by his fault," they are making policy judgments. The areas of family law, especially custody and support, sentencing, damages in tort, and contractual interpretation, not to mention the entire history of common law, represent processes whereby judges evaluated which values or policies ought to be operational at the time. This reality check is important when formulating arguments about the proper judicial role.

What then, I wondered, appeared to work for advocates trying to induce a court to apply new legal norms? What could I learn by reading the tea leaves of judicial reform that I could usefully offer by way of suggested tactics?

I will not concentrate on how to argue for preserving the status quo, because that, it seems to me, is easy and self-evident: just argue the resulting chaos, unpredictability, shattered expectations, and, most importantly, argue the Darth Vader of judicial law reform — that it is the legislature's job to decide if the public is ready for a new law, not the court's. Talk about how uncertain the impact of the change is, how there is no evidence that the change is necessary, or about how expensive its ramifications might be. And a court will be putty in your hands.

The real challenge is how to persuade the court that, despite the resulting uncertainty, expense, unpredictability, or expectations, it has a duty to make the change.

In preparing this article, I read a great deal of academic and judicial writing about the court's institutional responsibility, right up to Cass Sunstein's recent plea for judicial minimalism[12] and Ronald Dworkin's for judicial philosophers.[13] I read some factums in a few Supreme Court of Canada jurisprudential groundbreakers, and I read a couple of books, including James Patterson's book[14] on the 1954 case of *Brown v. Board of*

---

12   Cass Sunstein, ed., *Behavioral Law and Economics* (New York: Cambridge University Press, 2000).

13   Ronald Dworkin, "Must Our Judges Be Philosophers? *Can* They Be Philosophers?" (Scholar of the Year Lecture, New York Council for the Humanities, 11 October 2000) [unpublished].

14   James T. Patterson, *Brown v. Board of Education: A Civil Rights Milestone and Its Troubled Legacy* (New York: Oxford University Press, 2001).

Education,[15] the most seismic jurisprudential shift in the United States until *Bush v. Gore.*[16]

And from that reading I learned that this debate is almost as old as this country. In a brilliant new book published by The Osgoode Society, Canadian historian John Saywell traces the history of how the Judicial Committee of the Privy Council and the Supreme Court of Canada interpreted federalism under the Constitution.[17] Professor Saywell observed that during the first fifty years of the *British North America Act,* when many of its members were too old to either see or hear counsel, the Privy Council engaged in technical interpretations and narrow constructions.

This was an era when the formalism of Dicey prevailed, and when the restraining — and conservative — instincts of the judiciary so frustrated England's then prime minister Lord Salisbury, who found his social and labour legislation consistently declawed by the literal interpretations of the Law Lords, that he rebuked Lord Halsbury with the warning:

> The judicial salad requires both legal oil and political vinegar, but disastrous effects will follow if due proportion is not observed.[18]

Change came with the arrival of Lord Sankey in the 1920s. After a conversation in the late 1920s with Lord Sankey a year before he was appointed Lord Chancellor, the iconoclastic political philosopher Harold Laski approvingly attributed to Lord Sankey "the obvious and sensible view that judges inevitably legislate."[19] Laski welcomed Sankey's refreshing interest in endeavouring to make a case emit "a big, working principle,"[20] an interest evident in Lord Sankey's first decision in 1929 in *Edwards,*[21] where he declared, generously, that despite the Supreme Court of Canada's unanimous decision to the contrary a year earlier, "Persons" in the *British North America Act* included women. And then

15   *Brown v. Board of Education of Topeka,* 347 U.S. 483 (1954).
16   531 U.S. 98 (2000); 121 S. Ct. 525.
17   John T. Saywell, *The Lawmakers: Judicial Power and the Shaping of Canadian Federalism* (Toronto: University of Toronto Press, 2002).
18   Cited in G. Jones, "Should Judges Be Politicians? The English Experience" (1982) 57 Ind. L.J. 211 at 213.
19   *Supra* note 17 at 154.
20   *Ibid.*
21   *Edwards v. A.G. Canada,* [1930] A.C. 124 (P.C.).

he articulated perhaps his most famous constitutional dictum for Canadian lawyers and judges when he said:

> The *British North America Act* planted in Canada a living tree capable of growth and expansion within its natural limits. Their Lordships do not conceive it to be [their duty or desire] to cut down the provisions of the Act by a narrow and technical construction, but rather to give it a large and liberal interpretation.[22]

The decision in the "Persons Case" was, observed Professor Saywell, an abrupt departure from previous Judicial Committee jurisprudence. Arthur Berriedale Keith, an eminent British authority at the time, described it as "unfortunate," and one that even the Judicial Committee's "admirers have found difficult to reconcile with their conception of the judicial function."[23]

The Supreme Court of Canada became untethered from the Privy Council in 1949. Incrementally, it distanced itself from the policies of the Judicial Committee and, as Professor Saywell noted, recognized precedent and doctrine when absolutely necessary or desirable, but distinguished or ignored them when necessary or convenient. History, text, doctrine, and structure were conveniently reworked and blended as the court invented a body of law.[24]

The 1960s, when it consistently reined itself in, was a quieter decade for the court, until the magic combination of Bora Laskin and Brian Dickson in the 1970s, and then Bertha Wilson in the 1980s, completely rechoreographed the court.

Consider, for example, the expanded reliance on scholarly studies. In 1957, there were ten references to secondary literature in sixty decisions.[25] From 1991 to 1996 there were 2,817 academic citations in 680 decisions.[26] "I can assure you," Chief Justice Lamer said in 1992, "that good scholarship plays an important role in shaping the legal principles that evolve through the judicial process."[27]

---

22. *Ibid.* at 136.
23   *Supra* note 17 at 192.
24   *Ibid.*, introduction at xx.
25   *Ibid.* at 243.
26   *Ibid.*
27   *Ibid.* at 244.

The court relied increasingly on extrinsic and contextual evidence. The "major breakthrough," said Chief Justice Dickson, was the *Anti-Inflation Reference*,[28] when counsel presented extensive statistical evidence in support of their respective socioeconomic arguments.[29]

Four years later, Chief Justice Dickson observed that "extrinsic evidence has been admitted to assist in the task of interpretation. Decisions no longer need be rendered in a vacuum — currents in social, economic, and political thought can now assist in the resolution of constitutional disputes." "Justice," he added, "must not be blind to the purposes of Parliament," and resort to legislative history, "including Hansard, committee minutes and White Papers ... might well be considered to be admissible, subject always to the Court's determination of relevance and weight."[30]

But interestingly, despite the patently revised judicial approach, the ambivalence about the judicial role and the limits on judicial law reform appeared nonetheless to be deep-seated, as some of the Supreme Court's cases in the 1970s and '80s revealed.

In *Rathwell v. Rathwell*[31] in 1978, in which Justice Dickson overhauled one hundred years of matrimonial property law by imposing the remedy of constructive trust first suggested in Chief Justice Laskin's dissent in *Murdoch v. Murdoch*[32] three years earlier, the factums consisted of a total of 108 pages. Only two of those pages were devoted to the remedy of a constructive trust. No academic writing was cited, only British and Canadian cases.

Notwithstanding the absence of advocacy on the point, Justice Dickson changed the law. His words resonate with the spirit of Lord Sankey fifty years earlier, when he said:

> Many factors, legal and non-legal, have emerged to modify the position of earlier days. Among these factors are a more enlightened attitude toward the status of women, altered life-styles, dynamic socio-economic changes. Increasingly, the work of a woman in the

---

28   *Reference re Anti-Inflation Act*, [1976] 2 S.C.R. 373.
29   *Supra* note 17 at 244.
30   *Ibid.* See generally *R. v. Morgentaler*, [1993] 3 S.C.R. 463 at paras. 27–30 regarding extrinsic materials and at paras. 30–33 regarding evidence about the practical effect of legislation.
31   [1978] 2 S.C.R. 436.
32   [1975] 1 S.C.R. 423.

management of the home and rearing of the children, as wife and mother, is recognized as an economic contribution to the family unit.[33]

He then observed that the inconsistency of prior court decisions and the number of successful appeals revealed an uncertain and unstable state of law which, he said, was inevitable in a fluid area like family law. Anticipating the argument that further reform would create further uncertainty, he concluded:

> The need for certainty in matrimonial property disputes is unquestionable, but it is a certainty of legal principle hedging in a judicial discretion capable of redressing injustice and relieving oppression.[34]

One can only wonder how provocative a comment like that would be today.

On the other hand, in the same case, Justice Martland was the voice of judicial restraint, writing, in dissent, that the court did not have a wide discretion to do what is "just and equitable." The proposed reform of introducing the constructive trust to matrimonial matters, he held, "should be determined, as a matter of public policy, by legislation."[35]

These two streams of judicial thought also found expression eleven years later in *Andrews*,[36] when the Supreme Court of Canada, in its first decision designing the contours of equality under section 15 of the *Charter of Rights and Freedoms*, rejected the arguments set out in both the appellant's and the respondent's factums — and in every Canadian appellate judgment to date interpreting section 15 — that equality meant treating likes alike, the similarly situated test. Instead, the Supreme Court relied on the arguments of the intervenor, which argued that equality meant acknowledging and accommodating differences to protect individuals from discrimination.[37]

This bold new test was articulated by Justice McIntyre, who surveyed a myriad of statutes, academic articles, and American and Canadian cases before drawing a new map for equality seekers in this case

---

33   *Supra* note 31 at 443.

34   *Ibid.* at 448.

35   *Ibid.* at 474.

36   *Law Society of British Columbia v. Andrews*, [1989] 1 S.C.R. 143.

37   The court adopted the definition of discrimination and equality from the *Report of the Commission on Equality in Employment* (Ottawa: Minister of Supply and Services Canada, 1984).

about a challenge to the citizenship requirement for admission to the Bar. Ironically, this boldness did not extend to his section 1 analysis, and he concluded, in dissent on this point, that a citizenship requirement for lawyers was not an unreasonable limit in a free and democratic society. Echoing those like Justice Martland before him who favoured judicial deference to legislative choice, he said:

> Public policy, of which the citizenship requirement in the *Barristers and Solicitors Act* is an element, is for the Legislature to establish. The role of the *Charter*, as applied by the courts, is to ensure that in applying public policy the Legislature does not adopt measures which are not sustainable under the *Charter*. It is not, however, for the courts to legislate or to substitute their views on public policy for those of the Legislature.[38]

Justice LaForest, on the other hand, echoing Dickson *et al.* felt, as did the majority, that deference should not trump justice.

> I would conclude that although the governmental objectives ... may be defensible, it is simply misplaced *vis-à-vis* the legal profession as a whole. However, even accepting the legitimacy and importance of the legislative objectives, the legislation exacts too high a price on persons wishing to practice law in that it may deprive them, albeit perhaps temporarily, of the "right" to pursue their calling.[39]

Different judges, different approaches, sometimes even different approaches from the same judges.

By the time we get to *Watkins v. Olafson*[40] in 1989, we have the future chief justice, Beverley McLachlin, describing the boundaries as follows:

> This branch of the case, viewed thus, raises starkly the question of the limits on the power of the judiciary to change the law. Generally speaking, the judiciary is bound to apply the rules of law found in the legislation and in the precedents. Over time, the law in any given area may change; but the *process of change is a slow and incremental one*, based largely on the mechanism of extending an existing principle to new circumstances. While it may be that some judges are more activist than others, the courts have generally declined to introduce major and far-

38   *Supra* note 36 at 190.
39   *Ibid.* at 204.
40   [1989] 2 S.C.R. 750.

reaching changes in the rules hitherto accepted as governing the situation before them.[41] [Emphasis added]

...

Finally, and perhaps most importantly, there is the long-established principle that in a constitutional democracy it is the legislature, as the elected branch of government, which should assume the major responsibility for law reform.[42]

And in *R. v. Salituro*,[43] Justice Iacobucci, defining the contours of judicial law reform, explained that laws get changed when the court thinks the law needs incremental changes to "bring legal rules into step with a changing society."[44] In other words, judges make law reluctantly and infrequently; legislatures do it for a living.

This I think, is how most judges feel.[45]

It is important to know, however, that this expressed reluctance from the Supreme Court of Canada to make dramatic changes in the law, has nonetheless resulted in new hearsay rules in *Khan*,[46] new matrimonial property laws in *Rathwell*,[47] new human rights laws in *Alberta Dairy Pool*,[48] new discovery rules in *O'Connor*,[49] new support laws in *Pelech*,[50] and new laws of judicial review in *CUPE v. New Brunswick Liquor.*[51]

As evidence that the judicial process is fluid and ongoing to reflect a constantly "changing society," it is worth noting that the changes kept right on going: *Khan*[52] was revisited in *Smith*[53] and restricted in *Parrott*;[54]

---

41   *Ibid.* at 760.
42   *Ibid.* at 760–61.
43   [1991] 3 S.C.R. 654.
44   *Ibid.* at 666.
45   See *R. v. Vetrovec*, [1982] 1 S.C.R. 811; *R. v. Jobidon*, [1991] 2 S.C.R. 714; *R. v. Robinson*, [1996] 1 S.C.R. 683; *Bow Valley Husky (Bermuda) Ltd. v. Saint John Shipbuilding Ltd.*, [1997] 3 S.C.R. 1210; and *MacAskill v. The King*, [1931] S.C.R. 330.
46   *R. v. Khan*, [1990] 2 S.C.R. 531.
47   *Supra* note 31.
48   *Central Alberta Dairy Pool v. Alberta (Human Rights Commission)*, [1990] 2 S.C.R. 489.
49   *R. v. O'Connor*, [1995] 4 S.C.R. 411.
50   *Pelech v. Pelech*, [1987] 1 S.C.R. 801.
51   *Canadian Union of Public Employees, Local 693 v. New Brunswick Liquor Corp.*, [1979] 2 S.C.R. 227 (hereinafter *CUPE*).
52   *Supra* note 46.
53   *R. v. Smith*, [1992] 2 S.C.R. 915.
54   *R. v. Parrott*, [2001] 1 S.C.R. 178.

Rathwell morphed into *Pettkus v. Becker*,[55] which sired *Peter v. Beblow*;[56] *Alberta Dairy Pool* expanded into *Action Travail*,[57] then collapsed into *Mossop*;[58] *O'Connor* was chastened by the legislature into *Mills*;[59] *Pelech* begat *Moge*,[60] which begat *Bracklow*,[61] which begat *Miglin*;[62] and the "patently unreasonableness" standard of *CUPE*[63] had to endure the revisionism of *Bibeault*[64] and the jurisdictional triumph of *Pushpanathan*.[65] And all this without the benefit of the *Charter*.

And so, when reading, as one does, that the Supreme Court feels itself restricted to making only those "incremental changes necessary to keep step with the dynamic and evolving fabric of our society," the guiding adjective appears to lean more towards "dynamic" than "incremental." There appears, in other words, to be a gap between the rhetoric of judicial restraint and the reality of judicial activity, a gap wide enough for any intrepid reform-minded advocate to push his or her submissions through.

It comes down to how the times, the constitution of the court, and serendipitous circumstances conspire to make judges accept or reject the advocacy, no matter how eloquent. Consider with me, by way of concluding example, the cautionary tale of *Brown v. Board of Education*.[66]

By 1950, the American Supreme Court had, with *Sweatt v. Painter*,[67] begun to move away from segregation. The advocate Thurgood Marshall and his colleagues had carefully and courageously mounted a series of litigious assaults on segregation, culminating in a direct attack on the

55   [1980] 2 S.C.R. 834.
56   [1993] 1 S.C.R. 980.
57   *C.N.R. v. Canada (Canadian Human Rights Commission)*, [1987] 1 S.C.R. 1114 (better known as *Action Travail des Femmes*)
58   *Canada (Attorney General) v. Mossop*, [1993] 1 S.C.R. 554.
59   *R. v. Mills*, [1999] 3 S.C.R. 668.
60   *Moge v. Moge*, [1992] 3 S.C.R. 813.
61   *Bracklow v. Bracklow*, [1999] 1 S.C.R. 420.
62   *Miglin v. Miglin* (2001), 198 D.L.R. 4th 385 (Ont. C.A.), leave to appeal to S.C.C. granted [2001] S.C.C.A. No. 328, appeal inscribed for hearing during the session commencing 30 September 2002.
63   *Supra* note 51.
64   *Union des employés de service, Local 298 v. Bibeault*, [1988] 2 S.C.R. 1048.
65   *Pushpanathan v. Canada (Minister of Citizenship and Immigration)*, [1998] 1 S.C.R. 982.
66   *Supra* note 15.
67   339 U.S. 629 (1950).

1896 decision in *Plessy v. Ferguson*,[68] which had declared separate railway cars for blacks in Louisiana to be constitutional.

In the early 1950s, with *Brown v. Board of Education*, the frontal attack finally came to the U.S. Supreme Court, where Chief Justice Vinson worried about how momentous the issue was. "We face," he said, "the complete abolition of the public school system." As a delaying tactic, Felix Frankfurter suggested rehearing the arguments because he foresaw a 5–4 decision, which would clearly affect implementation. In September 1953, three months before the scheduled rehearing, Chief Justice Vinson died suddenly of a heart attack.

Eisenhower picked as the new Chief Justice, Earl Warren, the Governor of California, who was coming to the end of his third term. Warren immediately concluded that the court had to overturn *Plessy*.

However, he was anxious to avoid unnecessarily dividing the country and wanted to try to make the decision unanimous, particularly given the climate and the vulnerability of the court as an instrument of social policy. As Justice Tom Clark had pointed out: "We don't have money at the court for an army and we can't take ads in the newspapers, and we don't want to go out on a picket line in our robes. We have to convince the nation by force of our opinions."

While the court was considering its decision, Eisenhower invited Warren to a dinner at the White House and seated him beside John W. Davis, the lead counsel opposing school desegregation (and the same John W. Davis who authored the fly-fishing metaphor). Eisenhower praised Davis to Warren as a "great American" and explained that the southern whites "are not bad people. All they are concerned about is to see that their sweet little girls are not required to sit in school alongside some big overgrown Negro."[69]

---

68   163 U.S. 537 (1896).

69   Patterson, *supra* note 14 at 81. Citing quotes in Stephen Ambrose, *Eisenhower: Soldier and President* (New York: Simon & Schuster, 1990) at 367–68; and Emmet John Hughes, *The Ordeal of Power: A Political Memoir of the Eisenhower Years* (New York: Atheneum, 1963) at 2001, Patterson noted that after the decision was released, Eisenhower, while publicly committed to obeying the court's decision, privately told a speechwriter (at 81–82):

> I am convinced that the Supreme Court decision set back progress in the South at least fifteen years .... It's all very well to talk about school integration — if you remember that you may also be talking about social disinte-

Justice Robert Jackson was scornful of the briefs of the NAACP, thinking them to be sociology, not law. But he was gradually won over in conferences. While he accepted the political purpose of the decision, his dilemma was how to turn what he saw as a political conclusion into a judicial decision. Nonetheless, he wanted to write his own concurring opinion, but a major heart attack on 30 March ended that undertaking.

That left Justice Stanley Reed, a Southerner, who had his clerks start working on a dissent in December. As late as the following April, Reed was still holding out. Warren's tactic was to have lunch with him regularly, often including Justices Burton and Minton, Truman appointees who were closer to Reed than the others. In the end, Reed gave his concurrence in exchange for dismantling segregation gradually, not as an immediate process.

And so, based on this confluence of timing, personalities, and the times, on 17 May 1954, Earl Warren read a unanimous six-page opinion of the Supreme Court ending segregation with the words: "We conclude that in the field of public opinion the doctrine of 'separate but equal' has no place. Separate educational facilities are inherently unequal."[70]

This was lawmaking of the most dramatic kind. Times changed, the judges changed, and both were ignited by Thurgood Marshall's relentless persuasive advocacy.

And so, back to Canada, where the receptivity to judicial law reform this generation has been high. Based on effective advocacy, Law Reform Commission and Royal Commission reports, international law and jurisprudence, academic writing, media reports and articles, parliamentary debates, and collegial influence, appeal courts have often willingly acknowledged that the benefits of reform outweigh the benefits of tradition, or, put another way, that the law's stability does not necessarily argue for its stagnation.

It is important to remember, however, that above all, judges do not want to be seen to be irresponsible. A case has to be made that the times and the public interest are ripe and that, while change unsettles expec-

gration. Feelings are deep on this, especially where children are involved .... We can't demand perfection in these moral things. All we can do is keep working toward a goal and keep it high. And the fellow who tries to tell me that you can do these things by FORCE is just plain NUTS.

70   *Supra* note 15 at 495.

tations predicated on the status quo, there is the reassurance, learned from past experience, that while transitions may create disrupted expectations, the dislocation will be temporary and the public will, as it always does, adjust. Better and more responsible to have the short-term uncertainty of new and fairer norms than the long-term certainty of old and unjust ones.

My final advice to advocates arguing jurisprudential appeals? Use any lure you think will work, in any direction you think it will work, and, if it doesn't work, change ponds.

Just like fly-fishing ...

[This article first appeared in the March 2003 issue of *The Advocates' Society Journal*.]

The Wrong Stuff:[1] How to Lose Appeals in the Court of Appeal

Justice Marvin Catzman[*]

[Editors' Note: For maximum enjoyment, read the notes with the text.]

I used to teach appellate advocacy. There were very few of us in the field then. I cannot remember whether we taught it well or badly, but it didn't matter, because we were the only game in town.

These days, however, it seems as if everyone and her[2] sister[3] is teaching appellate advocacy. People write books and give speeches and run seminars about it. *The Advocates' Society Journal* even dedicated a whole issue to it.[4] So the area is no longer my private preserve: it has been taken over by other, and better, teachers.

---

[*]   Mr. Justice Marvin Catzman, Court of Appeal for Ontario.

[1]   I wish I could say that this title originated with me, but I can't. It was the title that Alex Kozinski of the Ninth Circuit Court of Appeals gave to a paper he delivered to a meeting of the State Bar of Montana in 1997. But it was such a great name that I decided to steal it and pass it off as my own.

[2]   This is a gender-sensitive paper. If "her" offends you, read "his."

[3]   Or, if you prefer, "brother": see note 2.

[4]   Summer Issue, August 1999, vol. 18, no. 2. The issue contained articles by Finlayson J.A. and Laskin J.A., who are members of the Ontario Court of Appeal, and by Binnie J. and Blair J., who aren't, but who apparently know a little about advocacy. They all got their pictures on the cover. That's more than I got for this piece. [Editors' note: All of these fine pieces are reprinted in this volume.]

Then, recently, I had a good idea.[5] People were so busy teaching lawyers how to win appeals that they were completely neglecting the art of losing appeals.[6] And so I have decided to exploit that vast, untapped market.

In this article, I propose to share with you seven helpful tips designed to ensure that you lose your next appeal in the Court of Appeal.[7] Using about two or three of these helpful tips should be enough to do the job; using more will guarantee a loss, no matter how good your case. Please do not try to be creative and dream up tips of your own. Deviate from this list at your own risk: if you do, and if by some accident you win, don't blame me.

Tip 1: Always File an Incomprehensible Factum

The *Rules of Civil Procedure* contain a number of provisions governing the form and content of factums. Ignore them.[8] Every other lawyer ignores them; why shouldn't you?

Let the court know right off the bat that you have a rotten case by filing a lengthy factum[9] filled with gobs of conflicting evidence and lengthy quotes from irrelevant cases. And, while you are ignoring things, ignore the rule[10] that requires double-spacing, left-hand margins of forty millimetres, characters of at least twelve point or ten pitch size,

---

5   This sentence is not true. See note 1.

6   I'm not exactly sure why lawyers would want to lose appeals, but there are so many of them trying to do it that there must be a good reason. It probably has something to do with tax write-offs, which are beyond the scope of this paper, not to mention the expertise of the author.

7   While I am in a confessing mood, I should also acknowledge that, while most of the suggestions in this paper are mine, a couple of them were also stolen from Judge Kozinski. But I don't feel all that badly about it. Cribbing the product of other people's labour and publishing it under your own name is what appellate judges do for a living.

8   For example, Rules 61.11 and 61.12 use the word "concise" (as in "concise overview," "concise summary," and "concise argument") a total of six times. It is widely rumoured that "concise" was a typographical error and that the word that Legislative Counsel intended to use was "verbose." I have been unable to find anyone who is prepared to confirm that mistake for the record.

9   There is a practice direction that limits factums to thirty pages. Ignore that, too.

10 Rule 4.01, if you must know. Rule 4.01 was the winner in 1998 and 1999 of the prize awarded for "The Least Well-Known and Most-Contravened Rule of Civil Procedure." It is said to be strongly in the running for the current year's title as well.

and good-quality paper 216 x 279 millimetres in size. Make repeated random changes in type size, letter spacing, and margin widths. Keep the content confusing and disorganized. Convey the message that your argument is not even remotely capable of presentation in a simple, direct fashion. Simple arguments are usually winning arguments and therefore are to be scrupulously avoided.

Counsel who are familiar with foreign languages[11] have a great advantage in the preparation of factums. Emulate, if possible, those languages that drive the reader to distraction waiting for the verb that is never disclosed until the conclusion of the sentence or, better still, the paragraph. Learn to write sentences that go on endlessly, sentences that are filled with dashes and with subordinate clauses that are — by the time the sentence is done — hopelessly unrelated to anything at the beginning.[12] Write your factum out in longhand, then strike out all the periods and substitute conjunctions[13] so that the factum becomes one long, undivided sentence. Now insert, in completely inappropriate places, punctuation marks such as commas, colons, and semicolons, sprinkled in such a way as to make your factum completely incoherent.[14]

Tip 2: Never Begin at the Beginning

One of the most common mistakes in appellate advocacy, made usually by young counsel, is to argue their appeal by beginning at the beginning. This immediately signals to the court that it is dealing with a novice. Do as senior counsel do. Plunge into your argument roughly two-thirds of the way through the facts and the law you want the court to think about.

To master this skill, try the following experiment. Go home tonight and read a nursery tale to your favourite child or grandchild.[15] Don't

---

11   Other than Latin. Latin is not a foreign language. Judges of the Court of Appeal speak it for hours and hours on a daily basis.

12   This sentence is a good illustration of what I mean.

13   Alternating between "and" and "but" several times in each sentence is a useful method of attaining the desired effect.

14   As originally written, this sentence read: "Now: insert in, completely, inappropriate places punctuation marks such as commas; colons; and semi-colons: sprinkled in such a way as, to make your factum completely: incoherent." See footnote 12.

15   This experiment is best performed with children between the ages of five and seven, who are said, generally speaking, to approximate most closely the level of sophistication and mental acuity of the average appellate court judge.

begin at the beginning. Begin well past the middle. Take, for example, "Little Red Riding Hood." Begin at the point where the Wolf is lying in bed in Grandmother's cottage, all dressed up to look like Granny, and Little Red is skipping up the front path with her basket of goodies. Or, if you prefer, begin at "Oh, Granny, what big eyes you have." Observe your subject's eyes carefully. If you have a stopwatch available, record how long it takes before her eyes glaze over in mystified incomprehension; then total confusion; and then, finally, resigned indifference. Now think back quickly to the last time you lost in the Court of Appeal. Remember the very same looks of incomprehension, confusion, and indifference you saw then?[16] Now you know you are on the right track.

Tip 3: Never Start With your Strongest Point

There is usually a fair lapse of time between the time you appeal from a trial judgment and the time your appeal is heard.[17] If, during that period, you have been following the development of the law carefully by noting all of the helpful suggestions made by colleagues, friends, and the janitorial staff in your office building with whom you have discussed your case, you will have boiled your argument down to about fifteen or twenty well-honed points. At this stage, you should write all of the points down and assign numbers to them in the order that you assess the strength of each point. It does not matter whether they are numbered in ascending order of importance or in descending order of importance. The key is to remember to bury your strongest point approximately halfway between your first point (which should usually be your weakest) and your last point (which should usually be your second-strongest). When photocopying your factum in preparation for filing with the court, make sure that, when your photocopier reaches the page on which your

---

16   Piaget, Jean, "Why Little Kids Are Smarter Than Most Judges" (1994), 25 *Can. Jo. Child Psych.* 436, suggests that many judges move directly from mystified incomprehension to resigned indifference, bypassing the stage of total confusion. It doesn't matter, really, so long as the ultimate objective of indifference, resigned or otherwise, is achieved.

17   The Court of Appeal keeps trumpeting that it is reducing the time lag to some laughingly short period measured in months, not years. This totally overlooks the fact that most counsel need a minimum of two or three years in order to refresh their retainer, figure out what the case is all about, and unleash an army of juniors to research every case decided from Genesis to the present day in the vain hope that they will find some peripheral proposition, however irrelevant, for insertion in the factum.

strongest point appears, it is almost completely out of toner and that the glass reflector has been scratched repeatedly with a letter opener, thus leaving the page so faint as to be barely readable and streaked with annoying, distracting lines.[18]

Tip 4: Never Say the Magic Words

Suppose your entire appeal turns on the language of a section of a statute or a paragraph of a contract. And suppose there is a distinct danger that, if you let the court know what precisely those words are, you will win your appeal hands down. What should you do? This one is a no-brainer. Keep those words away from the court's view at all costs. Do not quote them. Do not set them out in your factum. Do not set them out in a schedule to your factum. Do not even say them out loud.

Instead, talk policy. Judges love policy, because it makes them feel important. They can talk policy forever. Keep their minds away from the crucial words on which your appeal turns by talking instead about the need to adopt "a purposive approach" to whatever area of law you are discussing. That will effectively focus their attention where it belongs, and will almost certainly ensure defeat.

Tip 5: Always Make a Speech for the Jury

Judges are people, too.[19] They don't like dry, boring legal arguments. They hunger for something to enliven their day. Help meet this judicial need by making at least one passionate speech to the jury every time you appear before an appellate court. Invite your client and her[20] entire family to observe your performance. Instruct them carefully how to nod

---

18   While on the subject of copying factums, you might wish to consider following the lead of some eminent counsel who give to opposing counsel a different draft of their factum (earlier or later, it doesn't matter which) than the draft filed with the court. This makes it impossible for opposing counsel to follow your argument, and their repeated objections cannot fail to arouse the court's sympathy for them and animosity toward you.

19   Though there is a strong body of opinion to the contrary. See the paper "Machines Would Be Better," appearing in Proceedings of Annual Symposium on Judicial Reasoning, University of Toronto Faculty of Law (Toronto: University of Toronto Press, 1998).

20   Or "his," if your client is male: see note 2. In the interests of gender sensitivity, I have assumed throughout that all clients are women.

enthusiastically, whistle, and cheer in support of your submissions. Endeavour to whip the court into an emotional frenzy that leaves them thirsting for the scalp of your opponent. Overstate your case. Excoriate opposing counsel. Pound the desk. Sprinkle your argument with such phrases as "travesty of justice," "abuse of process," and "wisdom of Solomon."[21] (This last phrase should be addressed, with a sly wink, to whichever judge you think has been least receptive to your submissions.)

The more hysterical your argument, the more likely it is that one of the judges will then ask you a question about the weakest aspect of your case.[22] Then another judge will join in, and another. Soon, they all will be parading dozens of flaws in your argument, each more egregious than the next. Press your advantage. Turn the judges into advocates for the other side. You now have them exactly where you want them.

Tip 6: Never Answer a Question Directly or, Better Still, at All

Once in a while, despite your best efforts to discourage any interest at all in your argument, some judge is going to ask you a question. Questions must be handled with great care.[23] Remember your objective. Your goal must be to turn that flickering spark of interest into a firestorm that reduces your argument to ashes.

There are a number of ways to accomplish this. One is to wait until the judge is halfway through her question, raise your hand disdainfully and say, in a loud, clear voice, "Now, look, I still have a few more submissions to make and, when I'm good and finished, then I will entertain your question." This clever tactic enables the judge to dwell upon her question, let it roll around in her mind a bit and brood about it. Meanwhile, you should ramble on about how airtight your case is and how foolish it is even to be arguing about it. See whether she has the gall to return to her question after you are through.

---

21   Generally speaking, Solomon was a pretty good judge, although that business about cutting the baby in half would probably not play well today with the Office of the Children's Lawyer. But that's another story. (For the other story, see Solomon (King) in 1 Kings 3:16–28.)

22   But be careful. There is a right way and a wrong way to deal with questions. Never choose the right way: see Tip 6.

23   See note 22. Didn't I tell you?

But be warned. The judge may realize that you are just trying to talk out the clock and will wait, sharkishly,[24] to renew the attack. Time your next move carefully. When you perceive that the judge is just about to fly into a rage, turn to her, smile sweetly and say, "Oh, yes, did Your Ladyship have a question?"

Whatever the question is, avoid at all costs giving a clear, straightforward answer. Stonewall, stonewall, stonewall. Some helpful methods of stonewalling are as follows:

- talking over, under, and around the question. This might be a useful occasion to say some more nice words about policy;
- saying, "The answer to that question is found in the evidence of the witness X"[25] and proceeding to read three or four lengthy passages from the transcript that have nothing whatever to do with the subject under discussion;
- rephrasing the question in a manner more to your liking ("I gather that what Your Ladyship is really asking me is ...") and then proceeding to answer that question,[26]

and, perhaps most effective of all,

- making fun of the question. Look as if you are doing everything in your power to keep from bursting out with laughter. Cast at the judges who didn't ask the question a knowing look that says: "I really feel for you two; it must be tough to sit up there day after day and listen to all these ridiculous questions." Then glance condescendingly at the judge who did ask you the question, blurt out the first thing that comes into your mind and move on quickly, before he thinks of something else to ask you.[27]

---

24   My guess is that many of you think I made this word up, but I didn't. I got it out of *Roget's International Thesaurus*, and it's a real word: see *The New Shorter Oxford English Dictionary* (Oxford: Clarendon Press, 1993), vol. 2, p. 2814 (between "sharker" and "sharky").

25   Choose a witness whom the trial judge expressly disbelieved and whose evidence she utterly rejected.

26   But remember: the answer should have nothing to do with the original question.

27   Those of you who are keeping track will note that I have switched genders at this point but, having regard to the context (stupid questions), it seemed the politic thing to do.

Tip 7: Never Keep Your Promises

Never, never, make a promise that you intend to keep. As noted,[28] if a judge asks you a particularly incisive question, say calmly, "That is a very interesting question, My Lady. I shall answer it presently." Then forget all about it.

Other promises you may make but should under no circumstances keep include the following:

- "There is a case directly on point that answers that question, and I will get the name and citation over the lunch hour";
- "The court has noted that I raised fifteen separate grounds of appeal in my factum, but of course I do not propose to argue all of them in my oral submissions";
- "I will not weary the court by repeating what I said at the outset";
- "I will just read a short passage from the leading case on this subject";[29] and
- "I have only a brief reply."

Conclusion

I hope that you will find these tips helpful in significantly lowering your batting average in the Court of Appeal. If they do, console yourself by remembering that winning isn't everything.[30]

---

28   We've done this already (see Tip 6). Weren't you paying attention?

29   Reading is an important skill. Be guided by the aphorism "Reading maketh a full man" (Bacon, Francis: *Essays*. "Of Studies," 1624). (This is an inappropriate aphorism in a gender-sensitive paper (see note 2), but that's Bacon's fault, not mine.) Try to read at least five paragraphs from your factum and five pages from your authorities on every appeal. Pretend you are appearing before a court whose members don't know how to read. Brook no interruption. If a judge tries to stop you, put your finger down at the point where you were interrupted, glare menacingly at the offender, and then continue reading as if nothing had happened.

30   I disagree with Knute Rockne, who said (rather unkindly, in my view), "Show me a good and gracious loser and I'll show you a failure" (Rockne, Knute, Remark to Wisconsin Basketball Coach Walter Meanwell, 1926). But then again, he also said, "Win this one for the Gipper," and you all remember what happened to the guy who played George Gipp in the movie (Knute Rockne: *All-American*, Warner Bros. Pictures, 1940, B&W; 96 min.).

This concludes my remarks. Even if you find them of no assistance whatsoever, I hope you will be reassured by my promise that I will never write on this subject again.[31]

[This article first appeared in the Summer 2000 issue of *The Advocates' Society Journal*.]

---

31   But see Tip 7.

The Wrong Stuff: Tip # 8

Justice Marvin Catzman

Modesty[1] prevents me from saying that accolades have been pouring in since the publication of my article in the Summer 2000 issue of this *Journal*. In the months that followed, I received hundreds of dozens of seven very complimentary letters from completely unbiased readers.[2] What I also got, however, were a lot of angry complaints from lawyers across the province who used three, four, or, in one case, all seven Tips on Losing but who still won their appeals.

I have been compelled to go back to the drawing board. In doing so, I have realized that my earlier list of seven tips was incomplete. The problem is that, unlike the original seven, which struck me all at once,

---

*   Mr. Justice Marvin Catzman, Court of Appeal for Ontario.

1   Well, not "modesty" exactly. "Honesty" would be more accurate. See the sentence that follows in the text.

2   To be completely truthful, there was something fishy about the letters, too. I submitted them to a handwriting expert, whose opinion was that, although they purported to be written by different people, the signatures on all seven were in the same handwriting. Worse yet, the handwriting was identical to that of one of my kids who always used to write notes in my name to her high school teachers asking to be excused from class because she had a dentist appointment. When she wrote those notes, she didn't really have a dentist appointment. Come to think of it, when she wrote those notes, she didn't even have a dentist. But I digress.

294 Ethos, Pathos, and Logos

the new tips keep striking me one at a time.[3] So I will have to pass them on the way I get them, one at a time. Herewith Tip # 8.

Tip # 8: Always Overstate Your Case

In all but a few instances, the Court of Appeal is the last court in which you will have an opportunity to argue your client's case.[4] That is why it is so important to grab the court's attention early and to focus on the weakness of your client's position.

One very helpful way to do this is the following:

Overstate. Take liberties. Exaggerate. Tell lies.

Nothing is more likely to turn the court irreparably against you than catching you in a whopping misstatement. Impress them with the fact that the injustice wreaked upon your client is the greatest outrage in legal history and that the decision at trial is the most execrable in recorded memory. If, for example, your client was caught red-handed making a withdrawal at gunpoint from a financial instruction, witnessed by twelve sharp-eyed bank security guards all holding high-resolution colour video cameras, expound sneeringly about the frailties of eyewitness identification and deprecate video recording as an untested technological fad that is notoriously unreliable. If you act for a wife whose husband regularly refused to let her watch "Survivor" whenever a hockey game was on, tell them that this is the most egregious act of matrimonial cruelty since Abraham banished Hagar and Ishmael into the wilderness of Beersheba.[5]

If all else fails, refer to some case, statute, or regulation that does not exist. Tell the court, for example, that your argument finds strong support in the provisions of rule 78.04 of the *Rules of Civil Procedure*. Never mind that there are only 77 Rules of Civil Procedure; they will think that a new one was recently added, and will be too embarrassed to challenge

3   Thinking up tips on losing is very much like what Stephen Leacock said about writing: "Writing is no trouble: you just jot down ideas as they occur to you. The jotting is simplicity itself — it is the occurring which is difficult."
4   Indeed, if you follow this tip, it may be your last opportunity to appear in court on behalf of this client, period. For that matter, if you follow more than one or two of these tips, it may be your last opportunity to appear in court on behalf of *anybody*.
5   Genesis 21: 9–14. The Bible is always a terrific source for this type of hyperbole.

you. By the time your opponent realizes your duplicity, the court — fascinated by still more of your losing gambits — will have moved on and won't care anymore. You get the idea. (Please see the Appendix.)

Appendix: A Letter from Justice Côté

I was pleased, and greatly surprised, to receive recently a letter of testimonial from someone who is *not* a member of my family.[6] As a matter of fact, it came from a distinguished member of the Court of Appeal of Alberta. It is reproduced below. It also contains some useful tips on losing that I think you may find helpful. But please don't write the Editor telling him how much more you like Justice Côté's tips than you like mine. If you do, the Editor will ask him to write guest editorials instead of me, and then what will I do during my judgment weeks?

Honourable J. E. Côté
Court of Appeal of Alberta
The Law Courts
Edmonton T5J 0R2
Fax: 427-5507

September 5, 2002

The Honourable Mr. Justice M.A. Catzman
Court of Appeal for Ontario
Osgoode Hall, 130 Queen St. W.
Toronto, Ontario M5H 2N5

Dear Marvin:

I have read with profit and enjoyment your paper on "How to Lose Appeals in the Court of Appeal," but I feel it my duty to point out a corollary which may necessitate a sequel.

Omissions from the factum no longer suffice. Now that the judges have hired lots of help to do their work for them, those staff sometimes go looking at things in the appeal books not cited by either counsel, even the key contractual clause governing the matter at hand. And they are persistent. They will go through all the drafts of the contract in the

---

6   See note 2.

appeal book, all the ten or twenty similar contracts governing other parties against whom the plaintiff has discontinued, and all the similar contracts (except for the clause in question) from fiscal years which are not in issue, and find the one version which is relevant.

So back-up measures in the appeal book are necessary. Bad photo-statting is very good: shrunk (legal size onto letter size) and fourth generation. Best of all is a fax of a fax *after* shrinking. Even if everyone is all in the same city; only old, pedantic folks use mail or couriers.

And the prudent lawyer will forestall anyone nosing about in the trial court's files for originals, by marking only such derivative faxes as trial exhibits. Or better still, a looseleaf binder of hundreds of them as a single trial exhibit. Oversized three-hole punches can then be used to remove key phrases from the key clause.

Yours very truly,

Jean E. Côté

Losing Tip # 9: Make Your Factum Read Like War and Peace

Justice Marvin Catzman[*]

Leo Tolstoy would have been one of the greatest factum writers in history. At least, I think he would have,[1] though he was a little before my time.[2] He is clearly the model for most factum writers today, because they do everything they can to emulate his style.

Take, for example, *War and Peace*. Tolstoy wrote this novel in instalments that were published between 1865 and 1869.[3] In the original Russian (a language not known for its economy of style), it took up 1,436 pages from beginning to end.[4] In addition to being known for its length, the novel is distinguished by its incomprehensibility. It depicts the story of five families and their friends, all with impossibly long and unpro-

---

*   Mr. Justice Marvin Catzman, Court of Appeal for Ontario.

1   Tolstoy was born on 9 September 1828, and died (depending on whom you believe) on 10 or 17 November 1910. For present purposes, it doesn't matter whom you believe; both 10 November 1910 and 17 November 1910 are before my time.

2   See note 1. There is a pernicious rumour going the rounds that Tolstoy and I were classmates in high school. That is not true. He and I did not go to the same high school. As a matter of fact, I'm not sure that Tolstoy even *went* to high school. Which would explain why he is famous and I am not.

3   Just like factums. Factums, too, are frequently written in instalments. Which explains why, like *War and Peace*, different parts of the same factum look as if they were written by different people, none of whom was on speaking terms with any of the others.

4   Qualifying it for inclusion in the *Guinness Book of World Records*.

nounceable names, against the backdrop of Napoleon's invasion of Russia in 1812.[5] To add to the disorder, twelve of the characters are named Andrei, seven are named Boris, and there are four Natashas. Worse yet, all of the Natashas look identical. By the time the reader finishes Chapter 4, she[6] is hopelessly confused about who is who, which villain is doing what, why he[7] is doing it, and whether he has got the right victim.

Very much like the modern factum.

The moral is this: be like Tolstoy. Ignore the Rule of Civil Procedure that would have you give "a concise summary of the facts relevant to the issues on the appeal."[8] The rule is far too constricting. Why limit yourself to relevant facts? For that matter, why limit yourself to this appeal? Feel free to wander far afield. Include facts that are irrelevant to the issues on the appeal. And include facts that are relevant to three other appeals in which you are currently preparing factums. Surely, somewhere in all those facts, there will be *something* that will catch a judge's eye.

Put a little mystery in your factum. A good technique for doing this is to refer to the parties by different names in different places, never twice in the same way. For example, if the appellant is the plaintiff, Leo Tolstoy, refer to him as "the plaintiff" on page 1, "Tolstoy" on page 3, "the appellant" on page 7, and "Leo" on page 10. Another way to add mystery is to introduce new characters, at random, in unexpected places throughout your factum. Be sure to conceal whether your new character

---

5   Tolstoy got his buddy, Pyotr Ilyich Tchaikovsky, to write an overture about this. An informal survey of the judges of the Court of Appeal revealed that most thought that the *1812 Overture* was written in memory of Major General Isaac Brock and the Battle of Queenston Heights. Unsettling, isn't it?

6   We have been through this before. In all of these Tips, intelligent, thoughtful persons are referred to as "she" while dolts and villains are always "he." I should have thought that this enlightened approach would win me an award from some national women's organization, but it hasn't — yet.

7   Dolts and villains are always "he": see note 6.

8   Rule 61.11(1)(c). While you're at it, ignore every Rule of Civil Procedure you can. On this subject, see Justice John Morden, "Rules Are Made to Be Broken" (1984), 5 *Advocates' Quarterly* 259. This is the seminal article on the *Rules of Civil Procedure* introduced in 1985. "Seminal article" is a particularly apt expression. Mr. Justice Morden has frequently been called "the father of the 1985 Rules." He has never admitted paternity, but samples have been sent to the Centre for Forensic Studies for DNA analysis, and the results are expected shortly.

is a party, a witness, the trial judge or your daughter's Grade 4 teacher. Dazzle the court with your footwork. Keeping the judges off balance will only serve to heighten their interest.

And conclude your factum as you would a Russian novel. Leave the court guessing whether, where, and how it ends. Never disclose who should win, who should lose, or what should happen and to whom. Who cares? So you lose this appeal. Big deal. It's the future that counts. Remember that, like *War and Peace*, there will always[9] be a sequel, an *Anna Karenina* waiting just around the corner, in which you can again trot out all your new-found skills and imbue yet another court with complete indifference to the merits of your appeal.

[This article first appeared in the Autumn 2002 issue of *The Advocates' Society Journal*.]

---

9   Well, maybe not *always*. Depending how fast and how far your reputation as a skilled loser gets around, there is always the possibility that you might not be back.

Losing Tip # 10: When the Law is Dead Against You

Justice Marvin Catzman*

What should you do when faced with a recent decision of the Supreme Court of Canada, on facts identical to those of your case, that is dead against your position?

To experienced losing counsel, this situation presents no real challenge.

First, just in case your opponent is unaware of this authority, be sure to refer to it, early and prominently, in your factum. Remember to add citations to all of the twenty or thirty law reports in which Supreme Court of Canada cases are currently reported.[1]

Second, show your disdain for this case by noting an unreported decision,[2] directly on point, of a master of the Alberta Court of Queen's

---

*   Mr. Justice Marvin Catzman, Court of Appeal for Ontario.

1   This is critical. For all you know, budgetary restraints may have compelled your judge's law library to drop its subscriptions to the *Supreme Court Reports*. But it undoubtedly will have maintained its subscriptions to such essential topical reports as the Left-Turns-on-an-Orange-Light Reports (the "L.T.O.L.R.s") and the Cases-Decided-on-a-Tuesday Reports (the "C.D.T.R.s"). You just never know for sure.

2   Unreported decisions are getting harder and harder to come by. These days, *everything* is reported. The electronic reporting services are crammed with reports of every word that dropped from the judge's lips, including the order she gave to the waiter at the restaurant around the corner from the courthouse when the trial she was conducting broke for lunch.

Bench[3] that holds precisely the opposite. Never mind that the master's decision was rendered ten years ago and was expressly overruled in the recent judgment of the Supreme Court. Authorities are fungible: a case is a case, and every case is as good as every other case.

Third, when opposing counsel refers to the Supreme Court decision in her oral argument, break into sudden uncontrolled laughter, all the while sneering disdainfully, so that your court is left in no doubt about the significance of the authority being cited to it. This will highlight the case's importance and underline the sense of utter panic that it engenders in you.

When all else fails, there is a tip of last resort. But it should be used with caution, and never more than once. It is this. If you are *absolutely sure* that the law is completely against you, consider referring the court to some case that doesn't exist. In other words, make one up. This will show great initiative on your part.

If challenged, you can offer the defence of necessity. Necessity is, after all, the mother of invention.[4] Anyway, your ruse will probably go undetected.[5] There are now so many law reports that judges register no surprise when confronted with an unfamiliar citation, and counsel are now citing fictitious cases all the time.[6] If, however, you do make up a

---

3   But see "Schedule A: Citing Masters of the Alberta Court of Queen's Bench."
4   The earliest record of the aphorism "Necessity is the mother of invention" is found in Plato's *The Republic*, Book II (Socrates/Adeimantus). In modern times, it is generally attributed to Jonathan Swift: *Gulliver's Travels*, Part Four, "A Voyage to the Country of the Houyhnhnms," Chapter Ten, paragraph 1.
5   Care should be taken, however, not to confuse "Necessity is the mother of invention" with other maxims about necessity. During the 1930s, my father shared space with a lawyer whose nickname was "Necessity." My father assumed that the nickname derived from the lawyer's inventive nature. It didn't. It derived instead from the ancient Latin maxim *necessitas legem non habet*: "Necessity knows no law." Neither did this lawyer. To be fair, my father didn't know that when he entered into the space-sharing arrangement. But I digress.
6   We recently had an example of this. A counsel, whose initials are Harvey Strosberg, argued and won an appeal in which he referred the court to three cases appearing in consecutive volumes of the "S.F.R.s (Third Series)." After judgment had been pronounced in his favour, he burst out laughing and told the chagrined members of the court that S.F.R. stood for "Strosberg's Fabricated Reports." He thought that was a great joke. He forgot, however, that (1) the only joke a judge likes is the one that he or she tells, and (2) a judge has a memory like an elephant. Stay tuned for further developments on this one.

phoney citation, try very, *very* hard not to get caught; the results may be most unfortunate.[7]

Schedule A

Citing Masters of the Alberta Court of Queen's Bench

Be careful. The most frequently cited master of the Alberta Court of Queen's Bench, Master Michael Funduk, tends, on occasion, to be a little irreverent. For example, in a builder's lien case in which he declined counsel's invitation to follow an Ontario decision instead of an Alberta trial judgment, he had this to say about the "pecking order" created by *stare decisis*:

> Any legal system which has a judicial appeals process inherently creates a pecking order for the judiciary regarding where judicial decisions stand on the legal ladder.
>
> I am bound by decisions of Queen's Bench judges, by decisions of the Alberta Court of Appeal and by decisions of the Supreme Court of Canada. Very simply, Masters in Chambers of a superior trial court occupy the bottom rung of the superior courts judicial ladder.
>
> I do not overrule decisions of a judge of this Court. The judicial pecking order does not permit little peckers to overrule big peckers. It is the other way around.

I kid you not. He really wrote that: *South Side Woodwork (1979) Ltd. v. R.C. Contracting Ltd.* (1989), 95 A.R. 161, 33 C.L.R. 43, 23 C.D.T.R. 143. You could look it up.[8]

Even counsel desperate to lose should think twice about reading this passage to the Court of Appeal. Or, for that matter, to any judge. Depending how robust the sense of humour of your judge or judges, the ramifications on your continued entitlement to practice law could be rather startling.

[This article first appeared in the Winter 2002 issue of *The Advocates' Society Journal*.]

---

7   See the last two sentences of note 6.

8   If you really do look it up, do not spend too much time trying to find the third of these citations: see note 1.

Losing Tip # 11: Distinguishing the Indistinguishable (and a Note on Alphabet Soup)

Justice Marvin Catzman[*]

Following the publication of "Losing Tip No. 10: When the Law is Dead Against You," I received some fan mail from the Law Society of Upper Canada.[1] In response, I have gone back to the drawing board and now offer the following easier and less drastic method of dealing with this thorny problem.

Remember our example: your appeal raises an issue of law that has recently been conclusively decided against you by the Supreme Court of Canada. Remember, too, that the wrong way to deal with this situation is to tell the court, flat out, the name of the blockbuster case, lower your eyes to the ground, assume a defeated posture, and wait for the sword to slide ineluctably between your shoulder blades. This is the hallmark of a bad loser. It will only serve to embarrass your opponent, whose client will wonder why she has to pay good money to her dumb lawyer, who missed this devastating precedent.

---

*   Mr. Justice Marvin Catzman, Court of Appeal for Ontario.

1   Well, not "fan mail," exactly. It was a letter from Senior Discipline Counsel, threatening to report me to the Canadian Judicial Council unless I came up with some suggestion, short of making up fictitious cases, for dealing with the situation.

The right way to meet this adversity is to be generous.[2] By all means, draw the attention of the court to the fatal authority. Then solidly cement it into the judicial consciousness by pretending to distinguish it on a basis that is patently unsupportable.

How can this be accomplished? Cases involving cars, trucks, and motorcycles should be distinguished on the basis that the vehicles involved were different makes and models than those involved in your appeal.[3] Breach of contract cases, though slightly more difficult, should be distinguished on the ground that the contract in the earlier decision was entered into on a different day of the week than your client's contract. If, by some unfortunate coincidence, your client's contract was executed on the same day of the week, explore with the court whether, on the day the contracts were signed, the place of execution was governed by Standard Time or Daylight Saving Time.[4] If the time argument is untenable, examine the contracts in question to see whether one was signed with a fountain pen and the other with a ballpoint pen. Make a great show of fumbling through the Appeal Book and the original exhibits in a vain attempt to locate the contract on which the entire appeal turns. Remember the objective: to fix firmly in the minds of the judges that your case is so completely and hopelessly ravaged by the catastrophic Supreme Court precedent that your appeal cannot possibly succeed.

Finally, if all else fails, confront the problem head on. Read in a loud, clear voice a particularly catastrophic paragraph from the judgment against you. While doing so, make a wry face and spit out the name of the authoring judge with disdain and a withering look that says, "And we all know what we think of her judgments, don't we?" Spare no

2   This generosity is not altogether altruistic. The next time around, your opposing counsel might be appellant and *you* might be the guy who blew it. (*Note:* the expression "guy" in the preceding sentence is perfectly consistent with my announced philosophy of gender neutrality. In these Tips, all good counsel are presumed to be female; all dumb counsel are presumed to be guys.)

3   If, by some misfortune, your case involves the same make and model, try to establish that the vehicle in the earlier authority was a different colour. If the colours are the same, argue that one had power steering and the other didn't. If, after all that, both vehicles had, or didn't have, power steering, you are on your own.

4   This is a particularly useful tack to take in cases involving contracts signed in Saskatchewan. As everyone knows, Saskatchewan never goes on Daylight Saving Time, and the apparent plausibility of this distinction therefore increases by 50 percent.

effort to inflame the passions of the members of your court, so that they will be falling all over one another to skewer your appeal and you along with it.

A Note on Alphabet Soup

At the risk of inflaming the Law Society,[5] I forgot to pass on, in "Losing Tip No. 10," a piece of advice about the most fertile source of fabrication in modern advocacy: the "alphabet soup" cases.

In recent years, it has become common to identify the parties not by name but by initials. This is done in order to protect children, victims of crime, young offenders, and nearly everybody else. The Supreme Court of Canada appears to be particularly enamoured of this practice. Hardly a week goes by when that court doesn't release a judgment that abounds with references to "a W.(D.) instruction"[6] or an "F.F.B. warning"[7] or a "K.G.B. application."[8 & 9] So many cases are now cited by initials instead of names that no judge will ever challenge you if you make the initials up.

However, I warn you that, if you *are* going to make the initials up, you should try to do it in a way that will avoid antagonizing the court. In a recent appeal, defence counsel insisted on characterizing the trial judge's Crown-oriented instructions to the jury as an "*S.(O.B.)* charge." He lost. We weren't born yesterday, you know.

[This article first appeared in the Spring 2003 issue of *The Advocates' Society Journal*.]

---

5   See note 1.

6   Named for *R. v. W.(D.)*, [1991] 1 S.C.R. 742.

7   Named for *R. v. F.F.B.*, [1993] 1 S.C.R. 697.

8   Named for *R. v. K.G.B.*, [1993] 1 S.C.R. 740.

9   You really have to be a little careful about throwing these initials around. We recently had a case where, in a trial involving an accused of Russian extraction, the Crown announced that it would be making a *K.G.B.* application the next morning. The accused fled from custody on the way back to the Don Jail after court, and has not been seen since.

Losing Tip # 13: Never Discard a Hopeless Argument

Justice Marvin Catzman[*]

Here is the scenario.

Your client was arrested while driving up the on-ramp on the Windsor side of the Ambassador Bridge during an intense thunderstorm. He[1] came to the attention of the local constabulary because his convertible top was down, he was shirtless, he was wearing a red fireman's hat on his head at a rakish angle, and he was belting out, at the top of his lungs, his impression of Gene Kelly doing "Singin' in the Rain."[2] When the police officer asked him to step out of the car, he responded by picking up a tire iron and swinging it wildly, missing the police officer by a country mile[3] but opening a three-inch gash[4] over his left eye that took twen-

---

[*]   Mr. Justice Marvin Catzman, Court of Appeal for Ontario.

1   I think we have done this before. "She" and "her" are reserved for smart judges, smart lawyers, and smart clients. "He," "him," and "his" refer to the other kind.

2   *Singin' in the Rain*, MGM, 1952 (Technicolor; 103 min.). This didn't really merit a footnote, but editors love to publish articles filled with obscure and pretentious notes that make the authors of the articles appear far smarter than they really are.

3   Or its metric equivalent. Whatever happened to expressions like: "I wouldn't touch that with a ten-foot pole" or "Give 'em an inch and they'll take a mile" or "The whole nine yards"? Are people afraid to use them for fear of violating the *Weights and Measures Act*, R.S.C. 1990, c. W-6 (as amended)?

4   See note 3. Somehow, "7.62-centimetre gash" isn't as dramatic as "three-inch gash," is it?

ty-seven stitches to close.[5] His breathalyzer readings, taken within minutes after he was stopped, were off the chart.

Your client insisted on a trial by jury. You did not cross-examine the police officer at the trial, principally because your client was convulsing in riotous laughter during the officer's testimony and you could not hear anything the witness was saying. At your client's insistence, and against your very strong recommendation,[6] he took the witness stand. He testified under oath that, as is his invariable habit, he had had only two beers before driving that day. Unfortunately, he changed his story three times, refused to answer any questions the Crown sought to ask him and, after being directed by the trial judge to answer, made a disparaging remark about judges and juries in general and this judge and this jury in particular. He then stormed out of the courtroom and refused to participate further in the trial. The jury accepted the evidence of the police officer, completely disbelieved your client, and entered a whole bucketful of convictions against him. At the sentencing hearing, the trial judge nearly keeled over when your client's four-page criminal record for drinking-and-driving offences was introduced, and (figuratively speaking) threw the book at him.[7 & 8] Your client has instructed you to appeal. On the appeal, do you:

---

5   There is probably a way to say "twenty-seven stitches" in metric, but I haven't the heart to look it up. Will somebody please ask Measurement Canada what it is and let me know?

6   It is helpful to build a thick paper case against your client in circumstances like these. Faxing him every twenty minutes during the week before the trial, reciting the horrors that will follow if he takes the stand, will provide a useful evidentiary record when, as will invariably happen, he reports you to the Law Society for advising him that, as a matter of law, he was *obliged* to testify.

7   The operative phrase here is "figuratively speaking." All of you will remember from law school days the famous report of the proceedings in Salisbury Assizes in the summer of 1631, when Chief Justice Richardson was hearing a case involving a litigant who took exception to his conviction and who (court records were written in Law French in those days) "ject un Brickbat a le dit Justice que narrowly mist": (1631), 2 Dyer 188b. Lest anyone be tempted to re-enact this event today, please note that the Chief Justice's response was swift and terrible: the man's brick-throwing hand was cut off and the offender was then hanged in the presence of the court.

8   In fairness, not all of these incidents end so calamitously; sometimes, the judge is rather good about it. For example, the story is told about Malins, V.-C., who, when an equally unhappy litigant threw an egg at him, is said to have observed: "That must have been intended for my brother Bacon." Who says judges have no sense of humour? Those of you who think I am making this one up, please see Robert E. Megarry, *A Second Miscellany-at-Law* (London: Stevens & Sons, 1973), pp. 70–71.

(a)   express astonishment that the jury had the temerity to disbelieve your client?

(b)   attack the credibility of the police officer, of the City of Windsor police force and, for good measure, of all police officers everywhere?

(c)   argue that your client's musical rendition of "Singin' in the Rain," coupled with the fireman's hat, constituted a form of expression on his part, and that any provision of the *Criminal Code* that might tend to inhibit that expression constitutes a violation of section 2(b) of the *Canadian Charter of Rights and Freedoms*?

(d)   stress that your client has an identical twin brother and that, given the notorious frailty of identification evidence, the police officer's identification of your client as the perpetrator was laughably tenuous and that the conviction based on that evidence was unreasonable?[9]

(e)   take issue with the trial judge's instruction to the jury that your client, like any other accused person, is presumed to be guilty unless he proves his innocence beyond a reasonable doubt? or,

(f)   all of the above, except, if you are running out of time in your oral argument, concede that there is no merit in argument (e) and abandon it?

For sophisticated losing counsel, the correct answer is (f). Only a rank amateur would abandon even one of his totally untenable arguments and risk the possibility of grasping victory from the jaws of what should be certain and unmitigated disaster.

Please note that the proposition "Never discard a hopeless argument" is not limited to criminal appeals. It works nicely for civil appeals as well. Consider this example in the civil context. Your client is a distinguished professor of contract law. She gave a guarantee for a very substantial loan made by a bank to her husband for money he wanted to invest in three sure-fire stocks: Bre-X, Enron, and WorldCom. She reviewed the economic implications of the guarantee with her friend, the Governor of the Bank of Canada, and received independent legal advice from her other friend, the Chief Justice of Canada. She signed the

---

9   Before advancing this argument, it might be useful to try to think of an explanation for the fact that your client has a three-inch scar over his left eye and his twin brother doesn't.

guarantee in the lobby of the Supreme Court of Canada Building in front
of twenty-three witnesses, all of whom swore affidavits of execution
deposing to her signature. When, incomprehensibly, the sure-fire stocks
went south and her husband did the same, the bank sued her on the
guarantee.

At trial, all of your brilliant legal defences failed miserably before
the trial judge, who could barely contain herself when she rejected each
of them in giving judgment in favour of the bank. Which defences
should you pursue on the appeal that will inevitably follow?

(a)   The signature on the guarantee is a forgery?
(b)   Your client did not understand the meaning of a guarantee?
(c)   The guarantee was signed under duress, while her husband held a
      loaded gun to her head?[10]
(d)   The Governor of the Bank of Canada told her that the stock market
      only goes up, and never goes down?
(e)   The trial judge continually interrupted your client when she was
      giving evidence, and referred to her repeatedly as "a flake," "an air-
      head," and "a nutcase"? or,
(f)   All of the above, except, if you are running out of time in your oral
      argument, concede that there is no merit in argument (e) and aban-
      don it?

Again, for experienced losing counsel, this is a no-brainer: the
answer is (f).[11] Experienced losers learned long ago to ignore the advice
of those expensive continuing legal education programs that counsel
limiting your submissions to the two or three arguments that really have
some merit. If, by sheer accident, truly dedicated losing counsel stum-
ble upon a potentially winning argument, they are sure to bury it where
it will never see the light of day. Truly experienced losers know that, by
insisting on presenting all of their arguments and scrambling them all
together so that the real dogs effectively camouflage the one and only

10   For some unexplained reason, not one of the twenty-three people who swore affi-
     davits that they had seen your client sign the guarantee had any recollection of see-
     ing (a) her husband or (b) a gun, loaded or otherwise.
11   Careful readers will have noticed a pattern emerging here. Since losing counsel are
     typically not all that swift, the correct answer is *always* "(f)." No matter what the
     question is.

submission that might be said to have even a whiff of merit, the court will find the whole package so indigestible that all prospect of victory will be irretrievably lost.

There is always the possibility, however, that — despite the sheer inanity of your submissions — some undiscriminating panel will nevertheless be mildly receptive to your client's cause. If, therefore, you sense that there is a danger that your appeal may succeed, it is always a useful tactic to underline the utter hopelessness of your position by emphasizing your three most completely hopeless arguments and by underlining your client's utter lack of moral rectitude. If this doesn't do the trick, resort should be had to the loser's *coup de grace*.[12] Grasp the lectern firmly until your knuckles turn white, affect your meanest possible demeanour, and cast a withering glance at the panel that unequivocally conveys the message: "Of all the gin joints in all the towns in all the world, why did you three bozos have to walk into mine?"[13]

You are now inescapably assured of being able to add another losing appeal to your already extensive resumé.

[This article was first published in the Spring 2004 issue of *The Advocates' Society Journal*.]

---

12   This should, however, be done only once during your career. Doing it more than once will shorten your career significantly. Come to think of it, even doing it only once may shorten your career significantly, too.

13   Richard "Rick" Blaine (Humphrey Bogart), *Casablanca*, Warner Brothers, 1942 (B&W; 102 min.); used without permission. This didn't deserve a footnote either, but the editor made me do it: see note 2.

Losing Tip #14: Openers and Closers

Justice Marvin Catzman*

Judges are always reminding lawyers how important their opening and closing remarks are in the hearing of an appeal.[1] This may be news to some lawyers out there, but experienced losing counsel learned long ago that opening and closing remarks can mean the difference between defeat[2] and victory.[3] They know that an awful opener or an even awfuller[4] closer can help losing counsel stand out from the rest of the pack.

Chief Justice Gale used to tell law students that "the first three minutes are free."[5] In saying that, he meant the court will listen patiently to

---

* Mr. Justice Marvin Catzman, Court of Appeal for Ontario.

1 See, for example, the article by Moldaver J.A., "Boy, Are Your Opening and Closing Remarks Important In The Hearing of An Appeal" (2003), 22:1 *Advocates' Soc. J.* 29 (Summer 2003)

2 Which, in these articles, is a Good Thing.

3 Which, in these articles, is the Other Thing.

4 I looked for "awfuller" in the twenty-volume *Oxford English Dictionary*, 2nd ed. (Oxford: Clarendon Press, 1989), between "awe-struck" and "awkward," but it wasn't there. Although it does not appear to be a real word, it certainly should be. I used "awfuller" in draft reasons for judgment once, but the other two members of the panel refused to sign on unless I removed it, so I did. This is my way of getting even.

5 This was, of course, before time dockets were invented. Now, according to the costs grid, the first three minutes, on a substantial indemnity scale, can cost anywhere from $50 to $75.

counsel for the first three minutes, no matter how inane the argument, and the hammer will not start to fall until the fourth minute. The principle is still true, but the time limit has become a lot shorter. This is why it is so important to demonstrate to the court what a rotten case you have by the sheer inanity of your opener. Or by finishing with a terrible closer. Or, if possible, both.

Under no circumstances should the opening sentence on the argument of your appeal disclose a brief statement of the nature of your appeal and the basis on which you propose to argue it. Only a rank amateur would open by saying: "This is an appeal by the defendant from a judgment in favour of the plaintiff for $50,000 damages for wrongful dismissal." In addition to being unimaginative and pedestrian, that kind of opening tells the court too much, too soon. It removes from the judges the element of surprise and discovery to which they have become accustomed as the ranks of losing counsel grow ever larger. You should aim instead to capture their interest with an electrifying opener that will instantly generate suspense and bewilderment. Electrifying openers rivet the court's attention. You can be confident that the panel's attention will be riveted on you, the judges quivering with wonder to see whether your next sentence can possibly be more unilluminating than your first.

Let us look at some examples of guaranteed losing openers.

Counsel eager for defeat will frequently introduce their appeals by saying something Biblical. Counsel acting for the wife in a hotly-contested matrimonial proceeding should consider opening with these words:

> "This is the worst case of spousal and child abuse since Abraham banished Hagar and Ishmael into the wilderness of Beersheba."[6]

Or Shakespeare. Shakespeare is very frequently quoted in counsel's opening. But even counsel certified by the Law Society as a Specialist in Losing Appeals should take care to use some originality in the Shakespeare they quote. The minutes of a recent meeting of the judges of the Court of Appeal record a resolution that the next lawyer who begins his

---

6   Genesis 21: 9–14. Those of you with a strong memory for trivia will immediately recognize that I used this same line in "Losing Tip #8" (2002), 21:1 *Advocates' Soc. J.* 1 at 308 (Summer 2002). That is what happens when you get writer's block. Having stolen much of your material from others, you end up stealing material from yourself. But I digress.

appeal with "The quality of mercy is not strain'd"[7] will be found in contempt and strangled on the spot.

Another useful losing tactic in opening the argument of your appeal is by employing maxims and expressions that are almost, but not quite, right. In recent months, we have heard such aggravating openers as:

- "The appeal is a good example of the adage *res ipsa licorice*";
- "The husband in this appeal was found by his wife *in flagrante delicious*";
- "The appellant in this case found himself in a terrible predicament, trapped between that whirlpool thing and Charybdis";[8] and
- "This appeal turns on the application of the Hague Convention, the well-known annual meeting of Dutch tulip growers."

Any one of these dynamite openers should have the desired effect of signalling to the court that counsel's appeal is about as weak as the maxim or expression upon which he[9] relies.

If, however, as the argument proceeds, your repeated efforts to disguise the merits of your appeal appear doomed to failure, do not give up hope. You can still blow it all in your closing remarks. But under no circumstances should you close by saying something as prosaic and shopworn as the old: "That concludes my submissions. I see that I have used only half of my time, and I will be happy to deal with any questions that the court may have." That way disaster lies.[10]

Instead, consider employing a crummy closer. A crummy closer can do just as much damage as a crummy opener. Along this line, effective closers include:

---

7   *The Merchant of Venice*, Act IV, Scene 1.

8   I am confident that all of you will have gotten this one. "That whirlpool thing" *was* Charybdis, remember? And Scylla was the six-headed monster that resided on the other side of the Strait of Messina. Their chief source of recreation was bumping off sailors who tried to pass between them. Cruises were a lot more exciting in the old days.

9   I have a feeling that we have gone through this before. According to the National Standards for Gender-Neutral Writing, all good lawyers, good clients, and good judges are feminine. All of the other kind are masculine.

10   "Disaster," in this context, means "victory." Actually, this sentence is pretty meaningless, but I have always wanted to write a sentence in this format, and I promise never to do it again.

"My time is up? My time is up??? Do you want to know why my time is up? It's up because I've been interrupted every two minutes to answer one silly question after another. How can anybody keep to their allotted time around this place if they're constantly hounded like that?"

Or:

"My friend raises a lot of interesting issues in her factum. To be perfectly candid, I didn't read all of them. I read the first three and didn't understand any of them, so I quit. But you wouldn't penalize my client for that, would you? I mean, even a worthless, thieving scoundrel is entitled to competent counsel, isn't he, and in this case my client just didn't get one."

Or:

"In closing, I'd like to advise the court that I gave my instructing solicitor a written opinion that this appeal was a sure-fire[11] winner. Please don't disappoint me."

As always, chronically unsuccessful counsel would be well-advised to have some source of income other than his[12] professional earnings or, even better, a hobby to which he[13] can devote the spare time that will inevitably follow a string of losses. But any good losing counsel[14] will tell you, when it comes to choosing a hobby, for heaven's sake, don't make it golf. Too many judges play golf, and the last thing you want is to bump into one of them (or, worse yet, four of them) on the first tee. So try to find a hobby that is largely unpopulated by judges. Two good examples of such a hobby are underwater shipwreck exploration and bungee-jumping.[15]

[This article was first published in the Autumn 2004 issue of *The Advocates' Society Journal*.]

---

11   This kills me. "Sure-fire" *is* in the *Oxford English Dictionary*, 2nd ed., Vol. 17 at page 282. How "sure-fire" rates an entry while "awfuller" is excluded (see footnote 4, above) is beyond me.

12   See footnote 9.

13   Ditto.

14   There are those who argue that the expression "good losing counsel" is oxymoronic. Ignore them. They are just showing off what big words they can use.

15   Underwater shipwreck exploration and bungee-jumping should not be undertaken without prior consultation with your doctor, your insurance agent, and your loved ones. They all may have something to say on the subject.